New Longman Literature

Doctor Faustus

A-text (1604)

Christopher Marlowe

Series and Volume Editor: John O'Connor

PEARSON
Longman

Pearson Education Limited
Edinburgh Gate
Harlow
Essex
CM20 2JE
England and Associated Companies throughout the World

ISBN 978-0582-81780-7

First published 2003
Second impression 2007
Fourth impression 2008

15 14 13 12 11

Text Editor: Monica Kendall
Printed in Great Britain by Henry Ling Limited, at the Dorset Press,
Dorchester, DT1 1HD
SWTC/04

Acknowledgements

In some instances we have been unable to trace the owners of
copyright material and we would appreciate any information
that would enable us to do so.

We are grateful to the following for permission to reproduce
photographs:

Fotomas Index page 130; Ronald Grant Archive page 104;
Robbie Jack Photography pages 36, 38, 88; Museum of
London/C Walter Hodges pages vi, 132; Photostage/Donald
Cooper pages 22, 26, 31, 34, 46, 52, 56, 58, 61, 68, 75, 113, 115,
191; Shakespeare's Globe/Donald Cooper page 133.

Front cover: Robbie Jack Photography
*Jude Law as Doctor Faustus in the 2002 production at the
Young Vic*

Contents

Introduction

This book in the *New Longman Literature* series has been designed to meet the varied and complex needs of students who are making the transition from GCSE to AS level and then on to A level itself. Each feature – the *notes, commentaries, activities, critical extracts* and *background information* – will help you to meet the new **Assessment Objectives** at both AS and A2 Levels.

The textual notes

These in-depth notes, freshly written with the new-style examinations in mind, provide understandable explanations which are easily located on the page:
- **notes** are placed opposite the text with clear line references
- **explanations** of more complex words are given in context and help is provided with key imagery and historical references
- a **critical commentary**, which accompanies the textual notes, raises important critical and performance issues.

The activities

At the end of each Act – and also at the end of the book – there are activities which require AS and A2 style responses. These help you to meet the Assessment Objectives by asking for:
- **close study of particular extracts**, *focusing on dramatic technique, language, themes, structure and audience response*
- **responses to the play as a whole**
- **comments on staging and performance**.

Critical context

In your exam you will be required to express your own opinions, taking into account other readers' interpretations. This mini **critical anthology** provides you with extracts from the key critical works on the play in question, from the earliest essays to the most recent studies. There is also a suggested **Further reading** list with brief explanations of what each title is about.

Background

There are detailed sections which help you to understand the relationships between this play and others, as well as the cultural and historical contexts in which it was written. You will find sections on:
- the **date** of the play, its **sources**, and where it was first performed
- Marlowe's life and career
- the **Renaissance** (or early modern period) and key dates
- **playhouses**, **players** and **publishing**
- other **playwrights** from the period
- the **social and historical background** *to this particular play*.

Characters and language

Focusing on the play itself there are comprehensive sections on:
* the **characters** – *with all the key references*
* the **language**, **structure** and **imagery**.

Performance

This feature of the book describes the **performance history** of the play and also provides details of productions currently available on video.

Studying and writing about the play

To give you further support as you prepare for the examinations, there are sections on:
* **Marlowe's verse** *with examples from this particular play*
* **Study skills**: *titles and quotations*.

Note

This edition of *Doctor Faustus* is of the A-text (1604), following the edition by David Bevington and Eric Rasmussen (The Revels Plays, Manchester University Press, 1993). However, a number of significant B-text variants have been commented upon in the notes and the whole of B-text's Act 5 scene 3 (a scene not in the A-text, in which the three scholars discover Faustus's remains) can be found on page 117.

Date and first performances

The most likely date for the composition of *Doctor Faustus* is generally considered to be 1588, given that plays by other dramatists, thought to have been written shortly afterwards, seem to borrow from it. But there is no certainty about this date, and some critics place the play as late as 1592, influenced by the fact that the first-known edition of Marlowe's chief source, an English translation of the German *Faustbuch* (see page 137), was not published until that year. It may, however, not have been the first edition.

The first recorded performance of the play took place on 30 September 1594 at the Rose playhouse by the Admiral's Men, but it was clearly not a new play. William Prynne (writing much later, in 1633) recalls the 'visible apparition of the devil' in a performance of *Faustus* at the Bel Savage inn (just west of St Paul's Cathedral), which again suggests a likely composition date of 1588, given our (limited) knowledge of the Bel Savage's use as a playhouse at that time.

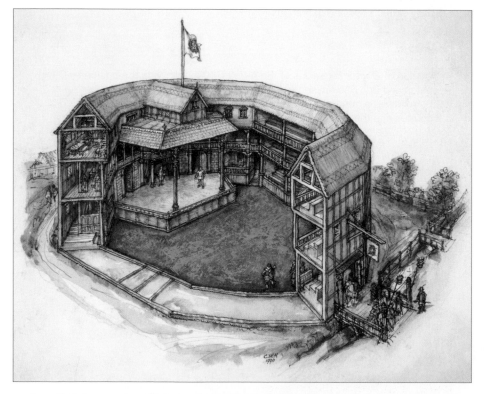

An artist's impression of what archaeologists think the Rose playhouse looked like in 1592–1603 (© C Walter Hodges)

Characters in the play

The CHORUS

DOCTOR JOHN FAUSTUS
WAGNER, *his servant*
VALDES ⎱ *friends of Faustus*
CORNELIUS ⎰
Three SCHOLARS, *Faustus's students*

ROBIN, *called the Clown; an ostler or stableman*
RAFE, *a stableman*
a VINTNER
a HORSE-COURSER

an OLD MAN

MEPHISTOPHELES
GOOD ANGEL
EVIL ANGEL
LUCIFER
BEELZEBUB

PRIDE
COVETOUSNESS
WRATH
ENVY   *the Seven Deadly Sins*
GLUTTONY
SLOTH
LECHERY

the POPE
the CARDINAL OF LORRAINE
FRIARS, *attending the Pope*
the EMPEROR, *Charles V*
a KNIGHT
the DUKE OF VANHOLT
the DUCHESS OF VANHOLT

ALEXANDER THE GREAT
his PARAMOUR   *spirits*
HELEN OF TROY

devils, attendants to the Emperor

The Prologue introduces the figure of Faustus, describing how, from humble beginnings, he became a great scholar but brought about his own destruction after practising necromancy

s.d. **Enter CHORUS** *an actor outside the drama who supplies background information and comments on the action. There are Choruses in Shakespeare's* Henry V *and* Romeo and Juliet. *Marlowe's* Tamburlaine the Great *and* Jew of Malta *also have prologues.*

1–6 **Not...verse** *The subject does not appear until line 6:* Our poet does not intend to march... *i.e. this is not going to be a story about war and conquest, like* Tamburlaine, *nor about love and politics, like* Dido Queen of Carthage.

1 **fields of Trasimene** *battlefield near Lake Trasimeno in Italy, where the Carthaginians (from North Africa) defeated the Romans in 217 BC*

2 **Mars** *the Roman god of war*

did mate the Carthaginians allied himself with the Carthaginians *(the enemies of Rome)*

3 **sporting in the dalliance** enjoying the amorous pleasures

4 **state** the government

6 **muse** poet *(or the imagined goddess who inspires the poet)*

daunt *this might mean either* control *or* exhaust; *the B-text has* vaunt *(show off)*

7–8 **perform The form** act out a representation; portray *(note wordplay)*

9 **appeal our plaud** appeal for applause *(there is legal wordplay in* **judgements** *and* **appeal**)

11 **base of stock** of low social rank

12 **Rhode** *modern Stadtroda*

13 **Wittenberg** *the famous university town in eastern Germany, founded in 1502*

14 **Whereas** where

brought him up supported him

15–16 **So soon...graced** he makes so much progress in theology (**divinity**), and enhanced the great abundance of scholarship

17 **graced with doctor's name** awarded a doctorate *(with a pun on the official 'grace' which permitted a candidate to be awarded a degree at Cambridge)*

20 **cunning of a self-conceit** intellectual pride engendered by arrogance

21–22 **waxen...overthrow** *reference to the myth of Icarus (see page 138)*

24 **glutted** overfull

25 **surfeits upon** eats too much of

necromancy black magic; conjuring the spirits of the dead

27 **prefers...bliss** regards as more important than his hopes of supreme joy in heaven (i.e. his salvation)

Performance

In many productions these lines are spoken by Wagner.

28 On Marlowe's stage, the Chorus might here have drawn a curtain to reveal Faustus reading.

Ideas and interpretations

The Prologue Chorus is fundamentally opposed to Faustus's philosophies and actions: 'Marlowe is expressing here...one of the fundamental issues of his times: man's new faith in his own intellectual resources against a deeply rooted Christian concept of the vanity of human endeavour alone' (Hilary Gatti).

Prologue

Enter CHORUS.

CHORUS   Not marching now in fields of Trasimene
Where Mars did mate the Carthaginians,
Nor sporting in the dalliance of love
In courts of kings where state is overturned,
Nor in the pomp of proud audacious deeds,   5
Intends our muse to daunt his heavenly verse.
Only this, gentlemen: we must perform
The form of Faustus' fortunes, good or bad.
To patient judgements we appeal our plaud,
And speak for Faustus in his infancy.   10
Now is he born, his parents base of stock,
In Germany, within a town called Rhode.
Of riper years to Wittenberg he went,
Whereas his kinsmen chiefly brought him up.
So soon he profits in divinity,   15
The fruitful plot of scholarism graced,
That shortly he was graced with doctor's name,
Excelling all whose sweet delight disputes
In heavenly matters of theology;
Till, swoll'n with cunning of a self-conceit,   20
His waxen wings did mount above his reach,
And melting heavens conspired his overthrow.
For, falling to a devilish exercise,
And glutted more with learning's golden gifts,
He surfeits upon cursèd necromancy;   25
Nothing so sweet as magic is to him,
Which he prefers before his chiefest bliss.
And this the man that in his study sits.

Exit.

1.1 *Alone in his study, Faustus contemplates how best to extend his already considerable learning*

1 **Settle thy studies** *possibly:* make your mind up about what it is you want to study

2 **sound...profess** study deeply whatever you intend to be an expert in

3–4 **Having commenced...art** now that you have been awarded a degree, be a theologian in appearance only, while aiming to reach the utmost limit of every discipline of learning

5–6 **Aristotle...*Analytics*** *Aristotle (384–322 BC) was a Greek philosopher and teacher of logic, whose writings, including the* Analytics, *dominated the university curriculum in the sixteenth century*

6 **ravished** enthralled; possessed

7 ***Bene disserere...logices*** 'the main purpose of logic is to be able to argue well' *(in fact, this was said by a sixteenth-century Frenchman, Petrus Ramus)*

8 **dispute** carry on a 'disputation'

12 ***On kai me on*** Greek: 'being and not being'; 'to be or not to be' *(a quotation here representing the whole discipline of philosophy)*

Galen *Claudius Galenus, second-century Greek physician and a leading authority on medicine*

13 ***ubi desinit...medicus*** 'where the philosopher ends, the physician begins' *(a much quoted Latin translation of a sentence by Aristotle)*

15 **eternised** immortalised; made famous for ever *(but the word is ominous in view of what is to happen)*

16 ***Summum...sanitas*** 'health is the greatest good that medicine can do' *(also Aristotle)*

17 **end of physic** purpose of medicine

19 **Is not...aphorisms?** Haven't your commonplace statements become reliable medical precepts?

20 **thy bills...monuments** your prescriptions been displayed as enduring examples of medical science

22 **desp'rate maladies** hopeless individual cases of sickness

eased cured *(the B-text has* cured *here)*

24 **Wouldst thou** do you wish to

26 **were to be esteemed** would be highly respected

27 **Justinian** *Roman Emperor (AD 527–65), famous for his codification of Roman law in the* Institutes

28–29 ***Si una eademque...rei*** 'If one particular thing is left as a legacy to two people, one of them shall have the thing itself and the other the value of the thing'

31 ***Exhaereditare...nisi –*** 'A father may not disinherit his son unless –' *(Justinian)*

32 **Institute** the *Institutes* of Justinian

33 **universal body of the Church** *Church law used Justinian's* Institutes; *the B-text has* law *instead of* **Church**

34 **mercenary drudge** someone willing to do menial jobs for money

35 **external trash** superficial and worthless possessions

36 **servile and illiberal** low-level and not befitting someone educated in the liberal arts *(the liberal arts included subjects such as geometry, astronomy, grammar and logic)*

38 **Jerome's Bible** the Vulgate (Bible) *(the Latin translation of the Bible most widely used in the West, which was largely the work of St Jerome, c. AD 342–420)*

39 ***Stipendium...est*** 'the wages of sin is death' *(Romans 6.23)*

Act 1

Scene 1

Enter FAUSTUS in his study.

FAUSTUS   Settle thy studies, Faustus, and begin
To sound the depth of that thou wilt profess.
Having commenced, be a divine in show,
Yet level at the end of every art,
And live and die in Aristotle's works.   5
Sweet *Analytics*, 'tis thou hast ravished me!
(*He reads*) *Bene disserere est finis logices.*
Is to dispute well logic's chiefest end?
Affords this art no greater miracle?
Then read no more; thou hast attained the end.   10
A greater subject fitteth Faustus' wit.
Bid *On kai me on* farewell. Galen, come!
Seeing *ubi desinit philosophus, ibi incipit medicus,*
Be a physician, Faustus. Heap up gold,
And be eternised for some wondrous cure.   15
(*He reads*) *Summum bonum medicinae sanitas:*
The end of physic is our body's health.
Why Faustus, hast thou not attained that end?
Is not thy common talk sound aphorisms?
Are not thy bills hung up as monuments,   20
Whereby whole cities have escaped the plague
And thousand desp'rate maladies been eased?
Yet art thou still but Faustus, and a man.
Wouldst thou make man to live eternally?
Or, being dead, raise them to life again?   25
Then this profession were to be esteemed.
Physic, farewell! Where is Justinian?
(*He reads*) *Si una eademque res legatur duobus,*
Alter rem, alter valorem rei, etc.
A pretty case of paltry legacies!   30
(*He reads*) *Exhaereditare filium non potest pater nisi* –
Such is the subject of the Institute
And universal body of the Church.
His study fits a mercenary drudge
Who aims at nothing but external trash –   35
Too servile and illiberal for me.
When all is done, divinity is best.
Jerome's Bible, Faustus, view it well.
(*He reads*) *Stipendium peccati mors est.* Ha!

1.1   *Faustus rejects the disciplines in which he has so far excelled –*
philosophy, medicine, law and theology – declaring them all unrewarding
compared with necromancy and the potential power it offers

42–43 ***Si peccasse...veritas*** *Faustus himself*
translates this line from 1 John 1.8.

46 **belike** it looks as though; it appears that

47 **And...die** *'The whole soliloquy has been*
driving towards this moment when
Faustus experiences the ultimate
frustration of all earthly ambitions'
(Roma Gill).

49 ***Che serà, serà*** *an Italian proverb (he*
translates it himself)

51 **metaphysics** *here:* magical sciences *(a*
meaning possibly only used by Marlowe)

52 **necromantic** to do with black magic
(see Prologue, line 25)

53 **Lines...characters** *Magicians engaged*
in conjuring would draw **lines** *and*
circles *around themselves for protection*
against evil spirits; **letters** *were used in*
magical combinations (see 1.3.9), as
were **characters** *(signs and symbols).*

57 **artisan** someone skilled in a craft *(here,*
in magic)

58 **quiet poles** motionless extremities of
the axis on which the universe revolves

60 **Are but...provinces** are obeyed only in
the particular provinces over which they
reign

62 **But his...this** but the territory of
someone who excels in magic

64 **sound** expert

65 **try...deity** (1) use; experiment with…
(2) exhaust yourselves, my brains, to
help me acquire the god-like powers of
a magician *(the B-text has* tire *instead of*
try*)*

70 **Their conference** a discussion with
them

71 **plod...fast** however fast I might labour
myself

Faustus

39–47 It has often been observed that Faustus is very selective in his quotations; here, he
neglects (intentionally or not?) to complete both of these sentences from the Bible in which
God's promises to those who truly repent are made clear. The first *(The reward...)* goes on to
say: 'but the gift of God is eternal life through Jesus Christ our Lord.' The second *(If we say*
that...) is followed by: 'If we confess our sins, he is faithful and just to forgive us our sins, and
to cleanse us from all unrighteousness.' These omissions lead some commentators to say
that 'Faustus's impatience is bred as much by arrogance and misunderstanding of the
traditional disciplines as by an eagerness to go beyond their bounds' (David Bevington and
Eric Rasmussen) and that 'this is an illustration of Faustus's foolishness, in spite of his
supposed great learning' (Stevie Simkin).

Language and structure: Faustus's opening soliloquy

1–4 'Faustus's diction in reviewing his orthodox studies abounds in finite images: *Settle thy*
studies...sound the depth...level at the end...; indeed, the very word *end* itself (carrying of
course another doom-laden sense in this play) occurs five times between lines 4 and 18'
(William Tydeman).

52 Faustus's description of necromantic books as *heavenly* introduces an ironic application of
religious language which will continue throughout the play (see further examples below, at
64, 122, 138 and 151, and also 1.3.28 and 2.1.74).

Stipendium, etc.   40
The reward of sin is death. That's hard.
(*He reads*) *Si peccasse negamus, fallimur*
Et nulla est in nobis veritas.
If we say that we have no sin,
We deceive ourselves, and there's no truth in us.   45
Why then belike we must sin,
And so consequently die.
Ay, we must die an everlasting death.
What doctrine call you this, *Che serà, serà,*
What will be, shall be? Divinity, adieu!   50
      (*He picks up a book of magic*)
These metaphysics of magicians
And necromantic books are heavenly,
Lines, circles, signs, letters, and characters –
Ay, these are those that Faustus most desires.
O, what a world of profit and delight,   55
Of power, of honour, of omnipotence,
Is promised to the studious artisan!
All things that move between the quiet poles
Shall be at my command. Emperors and kings
Are but obeyed in their several provinces,   60
Nor can they raise the wind or rend the clouds;
But his dominion that exceeds in this
Stretcheth as far as doth the mind of man.
A sound magician is a mighty god.
Here, Faustus, try thy brains to gain a deity.   65
Wagner!

Enter WAGNER.

                  Commend me to my dearest friends,
The German Valdes and Cornelius.
Request them earnestly to visit me.

WAGNER   I will, sir.

                                                                              Exit.

FAUSTUS   Their conference will be a greater help to me   70
                  Than all my labours, plod I ne'er so fast.

Enter the GOOD ANGEL and the EVIL ANGEL.

1.1 *Despite warnings from the Good Angel that he is courting damnation, Faustus listens to the Evil Angel's temptations and enthusiastically daydreams about the powers that magic will give him*

75 **That** that book of magic

78 **Jove** *the Evil Angel is referring to God, but uses the name of the king of the Roman gods*

79 **elements** *earth and air (sky) have already been referred to in the previous line; the other two are fire and water*

80 **glutted with…this** filled with a greedy desire by the thought of this power

82 **Resolve…ambiguities** answer all my questions

84 **India** *either the East or West Indies*

85 **orient pearl** a precious pearl from the Indian seas

86 **new-found world** America

87 **delicates** delicacies

90 **wall…with brass** *This idea is repeated in a play by Marlowe's contemporary, Robert Greene,* Friar Bacon and Friar Bungay *(see also below, line 156).*

91 **Rhine** *Wittenberg is on the Elbe.*

92 **public schools** universities

93 **bravely** splendidly

94 **I'll levy…bring** I'll enlist soldiers with the money the spirits provide

95 **Prince of Parma** *The Duke of Parma was the Spanish governor general of the Netherlands. In 1588 he was poised with his army to invade England, but the defeat of the Armada, under the command of Admiral Lord Howard (patron of the Admiral's Men, see page 127), deprived him of the support of the Spanish navy and he abandoned the attempt.*

97–99 **Yea, stranger…invent** yes, I'll make the spirits which are subject to me invent more amazing devices for attack in war than the fire-ship used to destroy the bridge at the siege of Antwerp *(in 1585)*

101 **sage conference** wise conversation

103 **won** persuaded

104 **concealèd** occult

105 **fantasy** imagination; perception of the world

106 **receive no object** (1) allow no objections; (2) think about nothing else

107 **But…skill** does nothing but thinks deeply about the craft of black magic

---

The Good and Evil Angels

In the B-text the Evil Angel is called the Bad Angel, and in the stage direction for their first entrance the Bad Angel is called 'Spirit'.

Language

82 '"Resolve" and "resolute" are key words in the play; but Faustus increasingly comes to occupy a world where to be resolved is to disintegrate or dissolve' (T McAlindon).

Faustus

It is interesting to consider whether Faustus's ambitions here are altruistic or mischievous. For example, dressing students in silk (92) would defy the university dress codes which obliged students to be clothed in plain materials in 'black, puke [bluish-black], London brown or other sad colour' (Decree of 1578). G I Duthie claims that Faustus's aim here is 'not commendable but subversive, not admirable but insolent, and ridiculous as well'.

GOOD ANGEL　O Faustus, lay that damnèd book aside
　　　　　　　And gaze not on it, lest it tempt thy soul
　　　　　　　And heap God's heavy wrath upon thy head!
　　　　　　　Read, read the Scriptures. That is blasphemy.　　75

EVIL ANGEL　　Go forward, Faustus, in that famous art
　　　　　　　Wherein all nature's treasury is contained.
　　　　　　　Be thou on earth as Jove is in the sky,
　　　　　　　Lord and commander of these elements.

　　　　　　　　　　　　　　　　　　　　Exeunt ANGELS.

FAUSTUS　　　How am I glutted with conceit of this!　　　80
　　　　　　　Shall I make spirits fetch me what I please,
　　　　　　　Resolve me of all ambiguities,
　　　　　　　Perform what desperate enterprise I will?
　　　　　　　I'll have them fly to India for gold,
　　　　　　　Ransack the ocean for orient pearl,　　　　85
　　　　　　　And search all corners of the new-found world
　　　　　　　For pleasant fruits and princely delicates.
　　　　　　　I'll have them read me strange philosophy
　　　　　　　And tell the secrets of all foreign kings.
　　　　　　　I'll have them wall all Germany with brass　　90
　　　　　　　And make swift Rhine circle fair Wittenberg.
　　　　　　　I'll have them fill the public schools with silk,
　　　　　　　Wherewith the students shall be bravely clad.
　　　　　　　I'll levy soldiers with the coin they bring
　　　　　　　And chase the Prince of Parma from our land,　95
　　　　　　　And reign sole king of all our provinces;
　　　　　　　Yea, stranger engines for the brunt of war
　　　　　　　Than was the fiery keel at Antwerp's bridge
　　　　　　　I'll make my servile spirits to invent.
　　　　　　　Come, German Valdes and Cornelius,　　　100
　　　　　　　And make me blest with your sage conference!

　　　Enter VALDES and CORNELIUS.

　　　　　　　Valdes, sweet Valdes, and Cornelius,
　　　　　　　Know that your words have won me at the last
　　　　　　　To practise magic and concealèd arts.
　　　　　　　Yet not your words only, but mine own fantasy,　105
　　　　　　　That will receive no object, for my head
　　　　　　　But ruminates on necromantic skill.
　　　　　　　Philosophy is odious and obscure;

109 **petty wits** lesser intellects

110 **basest of the three** even baser than the other three

113 **gentle** (1) well-born and honourable; (2) kind

114 **concise syllogisms** brief, well-phrased arguments based on logic

115 **Gravelled** 'floored'; defeated in argument; amazed

117 **infernal** from hell

118 **Musaeus** a poet who appears in the epic Latin poem *The Aeneid* by the Roman poet Virgil

119 **cunning** skilful *(Agrippa was said to be able to summon spirits of the dead: see page 139.)*

121 **wit** intellect

122 **canonise us** treat us like celebrities; *literally:* make us saints *(ironic inversion: see note to line 52 above)*

123 **Indian Moors** native Americans

125 **serviceable to** ready to serve

127 **Like Almaine...staves** like German cavalrymen with their lances

128 **Lapland** *a region famous for its mysterious inhabitants*

130 **Shadowing** giving an impression of

airy heavenly

131 **Queen of Love** the Roman goddess Venus

132 **argosies** rich merchant ships

133 **golden fleece** *here:* golden treasure

134 **Philip** *King Philip II of Spain (ruled 1556–98), whose treasury was annually filled by gold from the Americas*

137 **object it not** *either* you don't have to promise me riches to make me determined to go ahead; *or* don't accuse me of irresolution

138 **miracles** *ironic inversion; see note to line 52 above*

140 **grounded** given a good education

141 **Enriched with tongues** learned in the classical languages *(Greek, Hebrew and Latin; the last one important for communicating with spirits)*

well seen in minerals knowledgeable about the properties of minerals

142 **principles** essential skills and knowledge

143 **doubt not...renowned** do not doubt that you will be famous

144 **frequented** visited and consulted

mystery skill

145 **Than heretofore...oracle** than the oracle at Delphi once was

Language

135 The word *resolute* is a key one: some commentators feel that Faustus seems to be making a virtue out of sheer wilfulness.

138 'The word *perform* also carries the theatrical meaning (perform on stage; play tricks) which aptly describes the way in which Faustus's power will actually be used' (T McAlindon).

Ideas and interpretations

132–134 'These fantasies, together with Faustus's earlier desire to defeat the Prince of Parma, reveal the kind of anti-Spanish prejudices that were commonplace on the Elizabethan stage' (Roger Sales).

	Both law and physic are for petty wits;	
	Divinity is basest of the three,	110
	Unpleasant, harsh, contemptible, and vile.	
	'Tis magic, magic that hath ravished me.	
	Then, gentle friends, aid me in this attempt,	
	And I, that have with concise syllogisms	
	Gravelled the pastors of the German Church	115
	And made the flow'ring pride of Wittenberg	
	Swarm to my problems as the infernal spirits	
	On sweet Musaeus when he came to hell,	
	Will be as cunning as Agrippa was,	
	Whose shadows made all Europe honour him.	120
VALDES	Faustus, these books, thy wit, and our experience	
	Shall make all nations to canonise us.	
	As Indian Moors obey their Spanish lords,	
	So shall the subjects of every element	
	Be always serviceable to us three.	125
	Like lions shall they guard us when we please,	
	Like Almaine rutters with their horsemen's staves,	
	Or Lapland giants, trotting by our sides;	
	Sometimes like women, or unwedded maids,	
	Shadowing more beauty in their airy brows	130
	Than in the white breasts of the Queen of Love.	
	From Venice shall they drag huge argosies,	
	And from America the golden fleece	
	That yearly stuffs old Philip's treasury,	
	If learnèd Faustus will be resolute.	135
FAUSTUS	Valdes, as resolute am I in this	
	As thou to live. Therefore object it not.	
CORNELIUS	The miracles that magic will perform	
	Will make thee vow to study nothing else.	
	He that is grounded in astrology,	140
	Enriched with tongues, well seen in minerals,	
	Hath all the principles magic doth require.	
	Then doubt not, Faustus, but to be renowned	
	And more frequented for this mystery	
	Than heretofore the Delphian oracle.	145
	The spirits tell me they can dry the sea	
	And fetch the treasure of all foreign wrecks –	
	Ay, all the wealth that our forefathers hid	

1.2 *Valdes and Cornelius offer to give Faustus some basic instruction in the black art. Meanwhile some of Faustus's fellow-scholars have noted his absence*

149 **massy entrails** massive interior

150 **want** lack *(Cornelius's* **we three** *suggests an expectation that he and Valdes will also profit from Faustus's conjuring)*

151 **this cheers my soul!** *ironic inversion; see note to line 52 above*

153 **conjure** call up the spirits of the dead

lusty pleasant

156 **Bacon's and Albanus'** *Roger Bacon (a Franciscan friar at Oxford, died c. 1292) and the Italian Pietro d'Abano (died 1316) were philosophers and scientists; both had a reputation for being magicians and sorcerers.*

157 **The Hebrew...Testament** *The Psalms and the opening verses of St John's Gospel were used in conjuring spirits.*

158–159 **whatsoever else...cease** we will tell you what other things you need before we finish our discussion

160 **words of art** words needed to call up spirits

162 **cunning** skill

165 **meat** food (dinner)

166 **canvass...thereof** examine the business in detail

167 **ere** before

168 **therefore** for doing it

1–2 **was wont to** used to

2 **schools** universities

sic probo I have proved it in this way *(a Latin phrase used in academic arguments)*

3 **boy** servant

4 **sirrah** *a common term of address for servants or inferiors ('you there')*

Valdes and Cornelius

'Cornelius leaves us in no doubt of their intention to use Faustus as a cat's paw rather than run into danger themselves [see 160–162]...The precious pair...serve their purpose in giving a dramatic turn to the scene of his temptation, and except for a passing mention by the students, we hear no more of them' (W W Greg).

| | Within the massy entrails of the earth. | |
| | Then tell me, Faustus, what shall we three want? | 150 |

FAUSTUS Nothing, Cornelius. O, this cheers my soul!
Come, show me some demonstrations magical,
That I may conjure in some lusty grove
And have these joys in full possession.

VALDES Then haste thee to some solitary grove, 155
And bear wise Bacon's and Albanus' works,
The Hebrew Psalter, and New Testament;
And whatsoever else is requisite
We will inform thee ere our conference cease.

CORNELIUS Valdes, first let him know the words of art, 160
And then, all other ceremonies learned,
Faustus may try his cunning by himself.

VALDES First I'll instruct thee in the rudiments,
And then wilt thou be perfecter than I.

FAUSTUS Then come and dine with me, and after meat 165
We'll canvass every quiddity thereof,
For ere I sleep I'll try what I can do.
This night I'll conjure, though I die therefore.

Exeunt.

Scene 2

Enter two SCHOLARS.

FIRST   I wonder what's become of Faustus, that was
SCHOLAR wont to make our schools ring with *'sic probo'*.

SECOND   That shall we know, for see, here comes his boy.
SCHOLAR

Enter WAGNER, carrying wine.

FIRST   How now, sirrah, where's thy master?
SCHOLAR

WAGNER   God in heaven knows.   5

When Wagner informs the scholars that Faustus is dining with the infamous Valdes and Cornelius, they are immediately alarmed for the safety of his soul

10 **follows not necessary** does not necessarily follow logically *(Latin: non sequitur)*

11 **licentiate** 'licensed' as scholars to take a higher degree

stand upon't depend upon it; count on it

14 **witness on't** *i.e. to prove that he said he knew where Faustus was*

16 **Ask…thief** *a proverbial expression: i.e. the First Scholar's word is worthless, as he is as much a liar as his friend*

18 **dunces** (1) idiots; (2) subtle reasoners *(the name comes from the Scottish medieval scholar Duns Scotus)*

20 ***corpus naturale…mobile*** a natural body…capable of movement *(Latin terms from Aristotle)*

21–22 **But that…phlegmatic** if it weren't for the fact that I am by nature calm and unemotional

22 **slow to wrath** even-tempered

23 **prone to** *wordplay:* (1) inclined to; (2) lying down for

it were not it would not be advisable

24–25 **place of execution** (1) the room where Faustus and the others are 'executing' their food; (2) the gallows *(there was a proverbial saying about never coming within forty feet of the gallows)*

26 **sessions** law sessions of justices of the peace

27 **countenance** face; expression

precisian someone 'precise' in their religious observance: a Puritan *(Puritans were hard-line Protestants who wanted to rid Church ceremonies of the last vestiges of Catholic ritual; because they also advocated closing the playhouses, claiming that they were dens of sin, they were frequently mocked on the stage. Here Wagner goes on to mimic their modes of address:* **my dear brethren…** *etc.)*

30 **this wine** the wine he is carrying

Language

Wagner's language is a parody of academic discourse and debate. Line 5 normally means 'I've no idea', but Wagner plays on the expression's literal meaning – and, just because God does know where Faustus is, that doesn't mean that Wagner does not know, as he explains in 7. Later (20) Wagner ridiculously employs terms from Aristotle simply to point out that, as Faustus is an ordinary human, he is capable of movement and therefore able to be wherever he chooses.

Structure

Act 1 scene 2 introduces an important feature of the play's structure: an engagement in dramatic parallelism, in which Faustus's actions (essentially tragic in import) are in some senses replayed on a lower level by servants. 'The scene holds up a comic mirror to Faustus's dispute about forms of knowledge. The two Scholars may have been dressed in gowns and ruffs as badges of their superior status and yet they are unable to make a simple deduction…The exchange offers a comic version of a university dispute in which Wagner turns the swords of the Scholars against them' (Roger Sales).

SECOND SCHOLAR	Why, dost not thou know?
WAGNER	Yes, I know; but that follows not.
FIRST SCHOLAR	Go to, sirrah! Leave your jesting, and tell us where he is.
WAGNER	That follows not necessary by force of argument 10 that you, being licentiate, should stand upon't. Therefore, acknowledge your error, and be attentive.
SECOND SCHOLAR	Why, didst thou not say thou knew'st?
WAGNER	Have you any witness on't?
FIRST SCHOLAR	Yes, sirrah, I heard you. 15
WAGNER	Ask my fellow if I be a thief.
SECOND SCHOLAR	Well, you will not tell us.
WAGNER	Yes, sir, I will tell you. Yet if you were not dunces, you would never ask me such a question. For is not he *corpus naturale*? And is not that *mobile*? Then, 20 wherefore should you ask me such a question? But that I am by nature phlegmatic, slow to wrath, and prone to lechery – to love, I would say – it were not for you to come within forty foot of the place of execution, although I do not doubt to see you both 25 hanged the next sessions. Thus, having triumphed over you, I will set my countenance like a precisian and begin to speak thus: Truly, my dear brethren, my master is within at dinner with Valdes and Cornelius, as this wine, if it could speak, it would 30 inform your worships. And so the Lord bless you, preserve you, and keep you, my dear brethren, my dear brethren.

Exit.

FIRST SCHOLAR	Nay, then, I fear he is fall'n into that damned art for which they two are infamous through the world. 35

36 **Were he** even if he were

not allied to me not an associate of mine

38 **Rector** head of the university

grave counsel serious and wise advice

1 **gloomy shadow** *This reflects the belief that night was caused by the shadow of the Earth cast by the sun on the heavens; this shadow would appear to advance from the poles (see line 3).*

2 **Orion's drizzling look** *Orion, high in the winter sky, was associated with rain.*

4 **welkin** sky; heavens

pitchy black

5 **incantations** magical chants

6 **hest** command

8 **this circle** *A circle drawn on the ground 'both forced the spirits to appear and protected the conjurer from them' (David Bevington and Eric Rasmussen).*

Jehovah God; the Hebrew Jahweh

9 **anagrammatised** made into anagrams *(Sir Walter Ralegh's friends in the infamous 'School of Night' – a secret philosophical society – were alleged to*

have spelled the name of God backwards)

10 **breviated** abbreviated

11–12 **Figures…erring stars** charts of all the stars fixed in the firmament, and the symbols of the constellations of the Zodiac and the planets

16–20 ***Sint mihi…et surgat Mephistopheles!*** May the gods of Acheron *(the underworld)* be favourable to me! Let the threefold name of Jehovah be strong! Hail, spirits of fire, air, water and earth! Lucifer, prince of the east, Beelzebub, monarch of burning hell, and Demogorgon, we ask your favour that Mephistopheles may appear and rise!

20 ***surgat Mephistopheles!*** *At this point in the B-text, a stage direction has a dragon appearing. The Admiral's Men's list of properties in March 1598 at the Rose playhouse included 'i dragon in fostes' (1 dragon in* Faustus).

20–23 ***Quid tu…dicatus Mephistopheles!*** Why do you delay? By Jehovah, Gehennah (the hell of the Jews) and the holy water which I now sprinkle, by the sign of the cross which I now make, and by our prayers, may Mephistopheles himself now arise, compelled to obey us!

Performance

s.d. *Enter FAUSTUS…* Valdes has advised Faustus to conjure in *some solitary grove*, but there is nothing in the text of 1.3 which suggests a particular location for the events that follow. Perhaps the action took place downstage while Faustus's study was curtained off.

16–23 In the 1989 Royal Shakespeare Company production, Faustus's incantation was almost drowned out by the groans and cries of devils suffering in hell, forcing him to deliver it in a determined, almost violent manner.

Language

15 The diction of the play 'characteristically embodies duality of meaning' (T McAlindon). Here, 'the word *perform* ambivalently suggests both active accomplishment and illusory fabrication of dramatic spectacles' (David Bevington and Eric Rasmussen).

| SECOND SCHOLAR | Were he a stranger, and not allied to me, yet should I grieve for him. But come, let us go and inform the Rector, and see if he, by his grave counsel, can reclaim him. |

| FIRST SCHOLAR | O, but I fear me nothing can reclaim him. 40 |

| SECOND SCHOLAR | Yet let us try what we can do. |

Exeunt.

Scene 3

Enter FAUSTUS to conjure, holding a book.

FAUSTUS	Now that the gloomy shadow of the earth,
	Longing to view Orion's drizzling look,
	Leaps from th'Antarctic world unto the sky
	And dims the welkin with her pitchy breath,
	Faustus, begin thine incantations, 5
	And try if devils will obey thy hest,
	Seeing thou hast prayed and sacrificed to them.
	(*He draws a circle*)
	Within this circle is Jehovah's name,
	Forward and backward anagrammatised,
	The breviated names of holy saints, 10
	Figures of every adjunct to the heavens,
	And characters of signs and erring stars,
	By which the spirits are enforced to rise.
	Then fear not, Faustus, but be resolute,
	And try the uttermost magic can perform. 15
	Sint mihi dei Acherontis propitii! Valeat numen triplex
	Jehovae! Ignei, aerii, aquatici, terreni, spiritus, salvete!
	Orientis princeps Lucifer, Beelzebub, inferni ardentis
	monarcha, et Demogorgon, propitiamus vos, ut appareat
	et surgat Mephistopheles! Quid tu moraris? Per Jehovam, 20
	Gehennam, et consecratam aquam quam nunc spargo,
	signumque crucis quod nunc facio, et per vota nostra,
	ipse nunc surgat nobis dicatus Mephistopheles!

FAUSTUS sprinkles holy water and makes a sign of the cross.

1.3 *Faustus succeeds in raising a devil, Mephistopheles, one of Lucifer's ministers, who informs him that he came because he heard someone abjuring the scriptures, as devils always do in the hope of securing a man's soul*

24 **charge** order

26 **Franciscan** *a member of the Grey Friars, founded by St Francis of Assisi in 1209; in line 27 Marlowe takes the opportunity to make an anti-Catholic jibe at the alleged corruption of friars*

28 **virtue** power *(but Faustus is to discover that it isn't the words themselves which have summoned the devil; see lines 48–50 below)*

heavenly words scriptural phrases *(ironic inversion; see note to 1.1.52 above)*

30 **pliant** obedient

33 **conjurer laureate** *i.e. the greatest conjurer of spirits in the land*

35 ***Quin redis...imagine!*** Why don't you return, Mephistopheles, in the likeness of a friar!

39 **Be it** even if I ask you

sphere *This refers to the belief that the universe was made up of a set of concentric spheres, rotating around the Earth; the sun, each planet and the moon were fixed in their own revolving spheres.*

40 **overwhelm** submerge

41 **Lucifer** *the Angel of Light, expelled from heaven after his rebellion against God*

42 **leave** permission

49 **Abjure** swear to reject

Performance

25 Faustus describes the form that Mephistopheles first takes as *too ugly*. In the 1967 film he first appeared as a skeleton, full of writhing maggots; in the 1989 RSC production, as the figure of the wounded and suffering Christ.

Ideas and interpretations

47–52 The Latin phrase *per accidens* means that Mephistopheles did not come in answer to Faustus's magic incantations, but simply because he heard someone abuse (*rack* 48) the name of God. As he says, *I came now hither of mine own accord* (45). Mephistopheles's explanation is very important, because it shows unambiguously that the mere act of conjuring is not enough in itself to damn Faustus; at this point he is only in *danger* of damnation (52).

Enter a Devil (MEPHISTOPHELES).

> I charge thee to return and change thy shape.
> Thou art too ugly to attend on me.   25
> Go, and return an old Franciscan friar;
> That holy shape becomes a devil best.

Exit Devil (MEPHISTOPHELES).

> I see there's virtue in my heavenly words.
> Who would not be proficient in this art?
> How pliant is this Mephistopheles,   30
> Full of obedience and humility!
> Such is the force of magic and my spells.
> Now, Faustus, thou art conjurer laureate,
> That canst command great Mephistopheles.
> *Quin redis, Mephistopheles, fratris imagine!*   35

Enter MEPHISTOPHELES disguised as a friar.

MEPHISTOPHELES   Now, Faustus, what wouldst thou have me
do?

FAUSTUS   I charge thee wait upon me whilst I live,
To do whatever Faustus shall command,
Be it to make the moon drop from her sphere
Or the ocean to overwhelm the world.   40

MEPHISTOPHELES   I am a servant to great Lucifer
And may not follow thee without his leave.
No more than he commands must we perform.

FAUSTUS   Did not he charge thee to appear to me?

MEPHISTOPHELES   No, I came now hither of mine own accord. 45

FAUSTUS   Did not my conjuring speeches raise thee? Speak.

MEPHISTOPHELES   That was the cause, but yet *per accidens*.
For when we hear one rack the name of God,
Abjure the Scriptures and his Saviour Christ,
We fly in hope to get his glorious soul,   50
Nor will we come unless he use such means
Whereby he is in danger to be damned.
Therefore, the shortest cut for conjuring

1.3 *In answer to Faustus's questions, Mephistopheles explains that he is one of the rebellious spirits forever damned with Lucifer, and he entreats Faustus not to ask 'frivolous' questions*

54 **stoutly** (1) bravely; (2) arrogantly

57 **holds this principle** believes firmly in this fundamental truth

58 **Beelzebub** another of Lucifer's agents, his name in Hebrew means 'lord of the flies'

61 **confounds hell in Elysium** cannot see any distinction between the Christian hell and the classical (pagan) heaven

62 **His ghost…philosophers!** in spirit he is one of the old Greek philosophers

(because, like them, he does not believe in the Christian concept of eternal punishment in hell – or so he asserts here)

63 **vain trifles** pointless irrelevancies

65 **Arch-regent** chief ruler

83 **demands** questions

85 **passionate** emotional; swayed by strong feeling

Language

65–74 Mephistopheles's replies are 'dignified, courteous, terse: two single lines, then a couplet, then a triplet' (William Tydeman).

Lucifer and hell

69–70 The story of Lucifer's rebellion is told most fully in John Milton's seventeenth-century epic poem *Paradise Lost*. The Bible does not relate it in detail, though there are references in 2 Peter 2.4, Jude 6 and Isaiah 14.12–15.

78 *Why, this is hell*…: see also 2.1.126–128. Milton's Satan expresses a very similar view of hell: 'Which way I fly is hell; myself am hell' (*Paradise Lost*, Book IV, line 75). For Mephistopheles, hell is the absence of God (see 82).

Mephistopheles

In the 1967 film, Andreas Teuber's Mephistopheles weeps as he utters *Why, this is hell…* (78) and seems totally sincere in his attempt to dissuade Faustus from a course of action that will damn him (83–84). In this speech, claims J P Brockbank, 'Mephistopheles promptly displaces Faustus as the intellectual centre of the play. His eloquence sticks to the facts and sheds the airy and fiery qualities which continue to characterise the fantasies of Faustus…Yet, unlike Valdes and Cornelius, he is not a tempter' (but see the note to 2.1.73 and 82).

Ideas and interpretations

'Ideologically this scene's significance lies in its demonstration that Faustus is in full possession of all the facts: he has been cautioned about the consequences that will ensue if he persists in his chosen action, and urged by Mephistopheles…to restrain his folly. He can now make no appeal on grounds of ignorance' (Roma Gill).

Is stoutly to abjure the Trinity
And pray devoutly to the prince of hell.   55

FAUSTUS   So Faustus hath
Already done, and holds this principle:
There is no chief but only Beelzebub,
To whom Faustus doth dedicate himself.
This word 'damnation' terrifies not him,   60
For he confounds hell in Elysium.
His ghost be with the old philosophers!
But leaving these vain trifles of men's souls,
Tell me what is that Lucifer thy lord?

MEPHISTOPHELES   Arch-regent and commander of all spirits.   65

FAUSTUS   Was not that Lucifer an angel once?

MEPHISTOPHELES   Yes, Faustus, and most dearly loved of God.

FAUSTUS   How comes it then that he is prince of devils?

MEPHISTOPHELES   O, by aspiring pride and insolence,
For which God threw him from the face of heaven.   70

FAUSTUS   And what are you that live with Lucifer?

MEPHISTOPHELES   Unhappy spirits that fell with Lucifer,
Conspired against our God with Lucifer,
And are for ever damned with Lucifer.

FAUSTUS   Where are you damned?   75

MEPHISTOPHELES   In hell.

FAUSTUS   How comes it then that thou art out of hell?

MEPHISTOPHELES   Why, this is hell, nor am I out of it.
Think'st thou that I, who saw the face of God
And tasted the eternal joys of heaven,   80
Am not tormented with ten thousand hells
In being deprived of everlasting bliss?
O Faustus, leave these frivolous demands,
Which strike a terror to my fainting soul!

FAUSTUS   What, is great Mephistopheles so passionate   85
For being deprivèd of the joys of heaven?

Laughing off the devil's warnings, Faustus offers to surrender his soul to Lucifer in return for twenty-four years of pleasure and power

91 **Jove's deity** the divine nature of God *(see note to 1.1.78)*

93 **So** on condition that

94 **...voluptuousness** a life dedicated to satisfying the senses

102 **resolve me...mind** tell me what your master thinks (of my offer)

108 **pass** cross

109–110 **I'll join...Spain** *i.e. create a land bridge across the Straits of Gibraltar*

111 **contributory...crown** under my rule, paying tribute to me

112 **but by my leave** except with my permission

113 **potentate** powerful ruler

115 **speculation** deep study

s.d. **Enter...ROBIN the Clown** *'Clown' signified a type of actor in the company.*

1 **Sirrah boy** *both words are terms of address to inferiors – which is why Robin objects and throws the name back in Wagner's face (lines 2–3)*

David Bradley as Mephistopheles, in the figure of a Franciscan friar (Royal Shakespeare Company, 1989)

Faustus

87 *manly*: 'By using this word, Faustus expresses the sense of human self-sufficiency which he enjoys at this stage in his career. For the reader or listener there is irony in his arrogant recommendation of manliness to a supernatural being' (J D Jump). 'The unhappy devil speaks with a bleak infinity of misery and experience to the uncomprehending doctor who is exuberant, overconfident, and so ignorant that he can offer to instruct his mentor: *Learn thou of Faustus* (87)' (Roma Gill).

Learn thou of Faustus manly fortitude,
And scorn those joys thou never shalt possess.
Go bear these tidings to great Lucifer:
Seeing Faustus hath incurred eternal death   90
By desp'rate thoughts against Jove's deity,
Say he surrenders up to him his soul,
So he will spare him four-and-twenty years,
Letting him live in all voluptuousness,
Having thee ever to attend on me,   95
To give me whatsoever I shall ask,
To tell me whatsoever I demand,
To slay mine enemies and aid my friends,
And always be obedient to my will.
Go and return to mighty Lucifer,   100
And meet me in my study at midnight,
And then resolve me of thy master's mind.

MEPHISTOPHELES   I will, Faustus.

                                                    Exit.

FAUSTUS   Had I as many souls as there be stars,
I'd give them all for Mephistopheles.   105
By him I'll be great emperor of the world
And make a bridge through the moving air
To pass the ocean with a band of men;
I'll join the hills that bind the Afric shore
And make that land continent to Spain,   110
And both contributory to my crown.
The Emp'ror shall not live but by my leave,
Nor any potentate of Germany.
Now that I have obtained what I desire,
I'll live in speculation of this art   115
Till Mephistopheles return again.

                                                    Exit.

Scene 4

Enter WAGNER and ROBIN the Clown.

WAGNER   Sirrah boy, come hither.

1.4 *Faustus's servant Wagner threatens Robin with painful torments unless he agrees to bind himself to him in servitude for seven years*

2 **'Swounds** By God's wounds! *(a powerful oath)*

3 **pickedevants** short, pointed beards

4 **quotha** *literally:* he said *(i.e. 'I'll give him "Boy"!')*

5 **comings in** income

6 **goings out** (1) expenditure; (2) parts of his body showing through his threadbare clothes

7–8 **see how...nakedness!** Look at poverty making a joke about its own nakedness!

8 **out of service** unemployed

17 ***Qui mihi discipulus*** You who are my pupil *(the opening words of a Latin poem often used in Elizabethan schools)*

19 **beaten** embroidered *(with a punning secondary meaning that he will thrash Robin)*

stavesacre seeds of the delphinium plant used for killing body lice *(also*

continuing the 'beaten' pun: Robin will have the 'ache' produced by a 'stave'. Wagner alleges that Robin is infested with vermin and needs a treatment of flea-powder.)

20–23 **knave's acre...living** *Playing on the word* **stavesacre***, Robin jokes that Wagner inherited no more than a* **knave's acre** *(= nothing) of land from his father, which he now depends on for his* **living***.*

25 **belike** probably

28–29 **bind...me** swear immediately to be my servant/become my apprentice

30 **familiars** devils (often in the form of animals) who wait on people

32–35 **They are...drink** *Punning on* **familiar***, Robin jokes grimly that his fleas are taking as many liberties with him, feeding off his blood and flesh, as they would if they were customers who had paid for food and drink.*

Structure

There are clear echoes of the main plot here. Firstly, Robin's reply that he would only accept a well-roasted shoulder of mutton in return for his soul, is a parody of the bargain that Faustus is about to make and highlights its foolishness. Secondly, Wagner engages Robin as his servant for seven years (29), just as Faustus will enlist Mephistopheles for twenty-four: neither will be getting much value out of the agreement. Finally, Wagner's threat that Robin's lice will be turned into devils and tear him in pieces, backed up by the entrance of Balioll and Belcher, foreshadows the more serious threats of the Evil Angel, supported by Lucifer's appearance at 2.3.85; in both cases, the devils' purposes are to convince and terrify a subject who is attempting to repent.

ROBIN	How, 'boy'? 'Swounds, 'boy'! I hope you have seen many boys with such pickedevants as I have. 'Boy', quotha?
WAGNER	Tell me, sirrah, hast thou any comings in? 5
ROBIN	Ay, and goings out too, you may see else.
WAGNER	Alas, poor slave, see how poverty jesteth in his nakedness! The villain is bare and out of service, and so hungry that I know he would give his soul to the devil for a shoulder of mutton, though it 10 were blood raw.
ROBIN	How? My soul to the devil for a shoulder of mutton, though 'twere blood raw? Not so, good friend. By'r Lady, I had need have it well roasted, and good sauce to it, if I pay so dear. 15
WAGNER	Well, wilt thou serve me, and I'll make thee go like *Qui mihi discipulus?*
ROBIN	How, in verse?
WAGNER	No, sirrah, in beaten silk and stavesacre.
ROBIN	How, how, knave's acre? (*Aside*) Aye, I thought that 20 was all the land his father left him. (*To* WAGNER) Do ye hear? I would be sorry to rob you of your living.
WAGNER	Sirrah, I say in stavesacre.
ROBIN	Oho, oho, 'stavesacre'! Why then, belike, if I were 25 your man, I should be full of vermin.
WAGNER	So thou shalt, whether thou beest with me or no. But sirrah, leave your jesting, and bind yourself presently unto me for seven years, or I'll turn all the lice about thee into familiars, and they shall tear 30 thee in pieces.
ROBIN	Do you hear, sir? You may save that labour. They are too familiar with me already. 'Swounds, they are as bold with my flesh as if they had paid for my meat and drink. 35

36   **guilders** Dutch coins *(in payment for his service; Wagner calls them* **French crowns** *at line 38)*

37   **Gridirons** *Robin's misinterpretation of* **guilders**; *gridirons were used to support pots over a cook's fire, but also as instruments of torture by fire*

39   **Mass** By the holy mass! *(a mild oath)*

39–40   **but for…counters** if they didn't have such an impressive-sounding French name, a man might just as well have as many English counting tokens *(which are worthless)*

45   **again** back *(Robin immediately repents of the bargain)*

51   **Balioll and Belcher!** *Balioll might have been pronounced like belly-o, giving both devils names which reflect Wagner's obsession with food.*

53   **knock** beat

55   **tall** brave

56   **round slop** baggy breeches

62   **clefts** (1) cloven hoofs; (2) vulvas

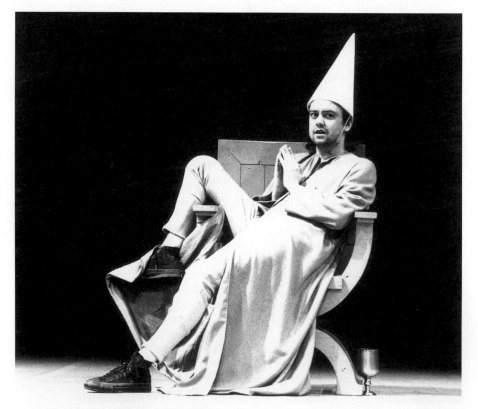

Richard McCabe as Wagner (RSC, 1989)

WAGNER	Well, do you hear, sirrah? Hold, take these guilders. (*Offering money*)
ROBIN	Gridirons? What be they?
WAGNER	Why, French crowns.
ROBIN	Mass, but for the name of French crowns a man were as good have as many English counters. And what should I do with these? 40
WAGNER	Why now, sirrah, thou art at an hour's warning whensoever or wheresoever the devil shall fetch thee.
ROBIN	No, no, here, take your gridirons again. (*He attempts to return the money*) 45
WAGNER	Truly, I'll none of them.
ROBIN	Truly, but you shall.
WAGNER	(*To the audience*) Bear witness I gave them him.
ROBIN	Bear witness I give them you again.
WAGNER	Well, I will cause two devils presently to fetch thee away. – Balioll and Belcher! 50
ROBIN	Let your Balio and your Belcher come here and I'll knock them. They were never so knocked since they were devils. Say I should kill one of them, what would folks say? 'Do ye see yonder tall fellow in the round slop? He has killed the devil.' So I should be called 'Kill devil' all the parish over. 55

Enter two DEVILS, and ROBIN the Clown runs up and down crying.

WAGNER	Balioll and Belcher! Spirits, away!

Exeunt DEVILS.

ROBIN	What, are they gone? A vengeance on them! They have vile long nails. There was a he devil and a she devil. I'll tell you how you shall know them: all he devils has horns, and all she devils has clefts and cloven feet. 60

27

1.4 *Impressed by the appearance of the devils, Robin agrees to serve Wagner*

73 **plackets** vaginas *(originally, a slit in a skirt; then, by extension, the vagina)*

80 **diametarily** *Wagner uses an astrological term based on 'diameter' in order to sound impressive.*

80–81 *quasi...insistere Latin:* as though treading in our footsteps

82 **Dutch fustian** gibberish *(compare double Dutch)*

83 **serve him** (1) be his servant; (2) give him what's coming to him

that's flat that's for sure

WAGNER	Well, sirrah, follow me.
ROBIN	But do you hear? If I should serve you, would you 65 teach me to raise up Banios and Belcheos?
WAGNER	I will teach thee to turn thyself to anything, to a dog, or a cat, or a mouse, or a rat, or anything.
ROBIN	How? A Christian fellow to a dog or a cat, a mouse or a rat? No, no, sir. If you turn me into anything, 70 let it be in the likeness of a little, pretty, frisking flea, that I may be here and there and everywhere. O, I'll tickle the pretty wenches' plackets! I'll be amongst them, i'faith!
WAGNER	Well, sirrah, come. 75
ROBIN	But do you hear, Wagner?
WAGNER	How? – Balioll and Belcher!
ROBIN	O Lord, I pray sir, let Banio and Belcher go sleep.
WAGNER	Villain, call me Master Wagner, and let thy left eye be diametarily fixed upon my right heel, with *quasi* 80 *vestigiis nostris insistere*.

Exit.

ROBIN	God forgive me, he speaks Dutch fustian. Well, I'll follow him, I'll serve him, that's flat.

Exit.

Exam practice

Extracts

1. Reread the Prologue and 1.1.1–65 ('…gain a deity'). How far does the opening of the play support L C Knights's observation that Marlowe is presenting 'the perverse and infantile desire for enormous power and immediate gratifications'? In your answer you should:
   - comment on the Prologue's view of Faustus's ambitions
   - describe the ways in which Faustus's soliloquy expresses ambitions for 'enormous power and immediate gratifications'
   - show in detail how the language of the Prologue and Faustus's soliloquy suggests that Faustus's desires are 'perverse and infantile'
   - demonstrate an understanding of the texts to which Faustus refers and their significance in the context of his soliloquy.

2. Reread 1.3.1–103 ('Now that…I will, Faustus'). In what ways does this scene introduce the concepts of hell which are to be explored throughout the play? In your answer you should:
   - describe and comment upon Faustus's conjuring and Mephistopheles's statements concerning his reasons for appearing to Faustus
   - discuss the concept of hell expressed by Mephistopheles
   - show an understanding of the biblical accounts which underlie Mephistopheles's references to Lucifer and God.

3. Reread 1.2 and 1.4. What are the purposes of these scenes, in your opinion? In your answer you should:
   - consider in detail what takes place in the scenes
   - show how Wagner's language in 1.2 parodies academic discourse and debate
   - comment on the role of the Scholars in 1.2 in contributing to the atmosphere of tension and foreboding
   - explain how the events of 1.4 create a perspective from which to view Faustus's actions in 1.1 and 1.3
   - show an awareness of the morality play traditions of knockabout comedy and comment on the functions of comedy in Act 1.

Extended writing

4. By a close examination of Act 1, describe and comment upon the ways in which Marlowe establishes a background of academic scholarship for the story of Faustus's past and present life, and discuss the importance of this context in view of Faustus's deliberations and decisions.

Performance

5. When Mephistopheles first appears (at 1.3.23), Faustus dismisses him as 'too ugly'. Henslowe's 'Diary' (see page 126) suggests that he might have appeared as a dragon; in the 1989 RSC production, he entered as a tortured Christ with crown of thorns. If you were directing the play, how would you deal with this moment? What effect would you want to achieve and how could it be accomplished? (It might help first to evaluate the two possibilities described above.)

6. In a number of productions of the play, 1.4 has not been played for comedy (in one version, the dialogue was accompanied by the constant wailing of tormented souls in hell). In groups, rehearse the scene in two very different ways: firstly, seriously – perhaps trying the background wailing; secondly, as comically as you can manage. Discuss and evaluate the benefits of the two approaches, paying attention to the relationship of 1.4 to the scenes which come before and after.

Mephistopheles as he first appears to Faustus (RSC, 1989)

2.1 *At midnight in his study Faustus wavers irresolutely between God and Lucifer as the Good and Evil Angels contend for his soul*

s.d. **in his study** *Presumably Faustus is again revealed by the drawing back of a curtain.*

1 **must thou needs** you must *(i.e. there is no avoiding it)*

3 **What boots it then** what good will it do

4 **vain fancies** pointless thoughts

5 **Beelzebub** *Why does Faustus name Beelzebub here, rather than Lucifer? Both names fit the metre.*

8 **Abjure** swear to reject

11 **appetite** desires

s.d. **Enter GOOD ANGEL...** *see the note below*

15 **execrable** accursed

16 **Contrition...repentance** *feelings of regret for sins that have been committed*

what of them? are they any use?

23 **seigniory of Emden** governorship of Emden *(a rich German trading port)*

26 **Cast** (1) give birth to; (2) consider

27 **glad tidings** *'The ironic echo of the angelic announcement of Christ's birth, "I bring you good tidings of great joy" (Luke 2.10), is related to other passages in which Faustus blasphemously compares himself to Christ (as at 1.1.24 and 2.1.74)' (David Bevington and Eric Rasmussen).*

29 **Veni...** *Latin:* Come, come, Mephistopheles! *(another parody of Christian celebration, this time of the hymn 'O come, O come, Emmanuel!' See also 2.1.74.)*

Ideas and interpretations

1 'Even before he abjures God, Faustus expresses a sense of being isolated and trapped' (Jonathan Dollimore).

2 In the actual A-text this line ends with a question mark (omitted by David Bevington and Eric Rasmussen as they believe it was meant as an exclamation mark); in the B-text both this line and line 1 end with question marks: 'the B-text...offers a ray of hope that the A-text shuts out' (Stevie Simkin).

Performance

These figures from the morality plays (see page 139) seem to appear especially when Faustus is wavering. In the 1967 film, the voice of the Good Angel came from a religious statue, that of the Evil Angel from a skull on Faustus's desk. In the 1974 production at Stratford, Ian McKellen's Faustus operated the Angels himself, as glove puppets. While these characters appear to us to be allegorical representations of good and evil, or conscience and temptation, 'many members of Marlowe's original audience would have understood the spiritual realm as equally real as, or more real than, the physical, material realm' (Stevie Simkin).

Structure

'The Good and Bad Angels...speak only after the soliloquy has done its work, and their function is to keep the audience's moral perspective clear. The Good offers the moral view of the Prologue, and the Bad the heroic and hubristic one of the soliloquy' (J P Brockbank; hubristic = to do with the overweening pride that leads to a tragic fall).

Act 2

Scene 1

Enter FAUSTUS in his study.

FAUSTUS   Now, Faustus, must thou needs be damned,
And canst thou not be saved.
What boots it then to think of God or heaven?
Away with such vain fancies and despair!
Despair in God and trust in Beelzebub.   5
Now go not backward. No, Faustus, be resolute.
Why waverest thou? O, something soundeth in
     mine ears:
'Abjure this magic, turn to God again!'
Ay, and Faustus will turn to God again.
To God? He loves thee not.   10
The god thou servest is thine own appetite,
Wherein is fixed the love of Beelzebub.
To him I'll build an altar and a church,
And offer lukewarm blood of new-born babes.

Enter GOOD ANGEL and EVIL ANGEL.

GOOD ANGEL   Sweet Faustus, leave that execrable art.   15

FAUSTUS   Contrition, prayer, repentance – what of them?

GOOD ANGEL   O, they are means to bring thee unto heaven.

EVIL ANGEL   Rather illusions, fruits of lunacy,
That makes men foolish that do trust them most.

GOOD ANGEL   Sweet Faustus, think of heaven and heavenly things. 20

EVIL ANGEL   No, Faustus; think of honour and wealth.

Exeunt ANGELS.

FAUSTUS   Of wealth?
Why, the seigniory of Emden shall be mine.
When Mephistopheles shall stand by me,
What god can hurt thee, Faustus? Thou art safe;   25
Cast no more doubts. Come, Mephistopheles,
And bring glad tidings from great Lucifer.
Is't not midnight? Come, Mephistopheles!
Veni, veni, Mephistophile!

Swayed by the temptations of wealth and power, Faustus calls up Mephistopheles who informs him that, in order to secure the bargain, he will be required to sign a deed in his own blood

32 **So** on condition that

33 **hazarded that** risked his soul

36 **that security...Lucifer** Lucifer demands that as a written guarantee

42 ***Solamen...doloris*** *a Latin proverb:* It is a comfort to the wretched to have companions in misery.

43 **Have you...others?** Do you, who torture other people, suffer pain yourselves?

47 **wit** intellect

50 **bind** enter into a bond concerning

52 **as great** *both in the positive sense:* as powerful *and the negative sense:* as arrogant, and therefore in the same plight

54 **proper** own

55 **Assure** legally pledge; convey by deed

56 **regent** ruler

58 **propitious** favourable

59–60 **in manner...gift** in the form of a legal contract transferring a possession from one person to another

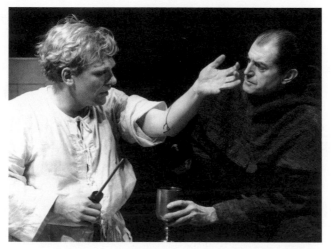

Faustus draws blood, watched by Mephistopheles (Gerard Murphy and David Bradley) (RSC, 1989)

Mephistopheles

'As before, none of the devil's answers are reassuring. Faustus's soul will merely "enlarge the kingdom" of Lucifer, and man is tempted only because misery loves company' (J P Brockbank).

Performance

57 In the 1989 RSC production, Mephistopheles held a chalice under Faustus's arm at this point to catch the drops of blood (see photograph above).

Act 2 Scene 1

Enter MEPHISTOPHELES.

Now tell, what says Lucifer thy lord? 30

MEPHISTOPHELES   That I shall wait on Faustus whilst he lives,
So he will buy my service with his soul.

FAUSTUS   Already Faustus hath hazarded that for thee.

MEPHISTOPHELES   But, Faustus, thou must bequeath it solemnly
And write a deed of gift with thine own blood, 35
For that security craves great Lucifer.
If thou deny it, I will back to hell.

FAUSTUS   Stay, Mephistopheles, and tell me, what good will
my soul do thy lord?

MEPHISTOPHELES   Enlarge his kingdom. 40

FAUSTUS   Is that the reason he tempts us thus?

MEPHISTOPHELES   *Solamen miseris socios habuisse doloris.*

FAUSTUS   Have you any pain, that tortures other?

MEPHISTOPHELES   As great as have the human souls of men.
But tell me, Faustus, shall I have thy soul? 45
And I will be thy slave, and wait on thee,
And give thee more than thou hast wit to ask.

FAUSTUS   Ay, Mephistopheles, I give it thee.

MEPHISTOPHELES   Then stab thine arm courageously,
And bind thy soul that at some certain day 50
Great Lucifer may claim it as his own,
And then be thou as great as Lucifer.

FAUSTUS   (*Cutting his arm*) Lo, Mephistopheles, for love of thee
I cut mine arm, and with my proper blood
Assure my soul to be great Lucifer's, 55
Chief lord and regent of perpetual night.
View here the blood that trickles from mine arm,
And let it be propitious for my wish.

MEPHISTOPHELES   But Faustus, thou must write it in manner of
a deed of gift. 60

2.1 As Faustus attempts to sign the deed, his blood congeals and has to be liquefied by hot coals. Faustus seals the bargain and, as words appear on his arm warning him to flee, Mephistopheles conjures devils to distract him

63 **dissolve** turn to liquid

straight immediately

64 **staying** stopping; drying up

portend signify; mean

65 **bill** contract; deed

s.d. *chafer* portable grate

70 **set it on** place the container of blood over the fire

72 **make an end** finish writing the contract

74 ***Consummatum est*** *Latin:* It is finished *(the last words of Christ on the cross – see St John's Gospel 19.30 – but here given a sinister interpretation)*

77 ***Homo, fuge!*** *Latin:* Fly, O man! *(from the Bible: 1 Timothy 6.11)*

82 **somewhat** something

83 **show** theatrical presentation; pageant

Mephistopheles (Richard McCabe) provides fire for Faustus (Jude Law) (Young Vic, 2002)

Structure

63 Mephistopheles's exit to fetch fire in order to dissolve Faustus's blood 'is a simple yet brilliant moment of dramatic suspense, one which invites us to dwell on the full extent of the violation about to be enacted' (Jonathan Dollimore).

Mephistopheles

73 and 82 Mephistopheles's asides (brief comments made to the audience which, by convention, cannot be heard by other onstage characters) suddenly create a new actor–audience relationship, turning Mephistopheles into a cunning plotter, who shares his devilish plans with us, as he often is in the old morality plays. The asides seem to reveal his motives clearly, but they are at variance with 1.3.83–84.

Language

74 Faustus's *Consummatum est* is typical of a play which deals in irony, inversion and parody (see note to 1.1.52). Earlier Valdes assures Faustus that the world will *canonise* those who practise magic (1.1.122: a term normally applied to saints); Faustus boasts of the *virtue* of his *heavenly words* (1.3.28); and Mephistopheles urges Faustus to *pray devoutly* to the prince of hell (1.3.55). As Jonathan Dollimore observes, 'Faustus is not liberating himself, he is ending himself: "it is finished".'

77 and 81 Commenting on *Homo, fuge!*, J P Brockbank observes, 'The admonitory words…fade and return like an hallucination of conscience.'

FAUSTUS　　Ay, so I will. (*He writes*) But Mephistopheles,
　　　　　　My blood congeals, and I can write no more.

MEPHISTOPHELES　　I'll fetch thee fire to dissolve it straight.

Exit.

FAUSTUS　　What might the staying of my blood portend?
　　　　　　Is it unwilling I should write this bill?　　　　　65
　　　　　　Why streams it not, that I may write afresh?
　　　　　　'Faustus gives to thee his soul' – ah, there it stayed!
　　　　　　Why shouldst thou not? Is not thy soul thine own?
　　　　　　Then write again: 'Faustus gives to thee his soul.'

　　　Enter MEPHISTOPHELES with a chafer of coals.

MEPHISTOPHELES　　Here's fire. Come Faustus, set it on.　　　70

FAUSTUS　　So; now the blood begins to clear again,
　　　　　　Now will I make an end immediately. (*He writes*)

MEPHISTOPHELES　　(*Aside*) O, what will not I do to obtain his
　　　　　　soul?

FAUSTUS　　*Consummatum est.* This bill is ended,
　　　　　　And Faustus hath bequeathed his soul to Lucifer.　　75
　　　　　　But what is this inscription on mine arm?
　　　　　　'*Homo, fuge!*' Whither should I fly?
　　　　　　If unto God, he'll throw thee down to hell. –
　　　　　　My senses are deceived; here's nothing writ. –
　　　　　　I see it plain. Here in this place is writ　　　　　80
　　　　　　'*Homo, fuge!*' Yet shall not Faustus fly.

MEPHISTOPHELES　　(*Aside*) I'll fetch him somewhat to delight
　　　　　　his mind.

Exit.

　　　Enter MEPHISTOPHELES with DEVILS, giving crowns and rich apparel to
　　　FAUSTUS, and dance and then depart.

FAUSTUS　　Speak, Mephistopheles. What means this show?

MEPHISTOPHELES　　Nothing, Faustus, but to delight thy mind
　　　　　　withal
　　　　　　And to show thee what magic can perform.　　　85

The deed specifies that Faustus may be a spirit and that Mephistopheles will be at his command. In return, Lucifer is allowed to carry Faustus off, body and soul, at the end of twenty-four years

91 **conditionally** on condition

92 **articles prescribed** special terms agreed

94 **effect** fulfil

102 **whatsoever** whatever he asks for

107–108 **by these presents** by the terms of this contract

109 **Prince of the East** *Lucifer (= 'light-bearer') was associated with the morning star, Venus, which rises in the east.*

111–112 **the articles...inviolate** on condition that the above terms have not been infringed

114 **their habitation wheresoever** wherever they live

116 **deliver** formally hand over

117 **deed** *not only 'contract', but 'that which is done, acted, or performed by an intelligent or responsible agent' (quoted from the Oxford English Dictionary by Roma Gill)*

118–119 **the devil...on't** *This was a common oath, but there is dramatic irony in its literal meaning here.*

121 **question with thee** ask you questions

Faustus (Jude Law) signs the deed (Young Vic, 2002)

Ideas and interpretations

97 Some commentators maintain that Faustus's transformation into a spirit implies that he is damned from this point – given that 'spirit' in this play invariably means 'devil'. For example, in the B-text, the first entry of the Good and Evil Angels has the stage direction: '*Enter the Angel and Spirit.*' Others maintain that, despite the spirit clause, Faustus remains capable of salvation.

110–111 The point is often made that Faustus strikes a poor bargain, getting very little in return for his soul, but Christopher Ricks has observed that, at a time when the plague was rife, Faustus's request for twenty-four years of guaranteed life 'is the greatest and most fundamental thing he buys'.

FAUSTUS   But may I raise up spirits when I please?

MEPHISTOPHELES   Ay, Faustus, and do greater things than these.

FAUSTUS   Then there's enough for a thousand souls.
               Here, Mephistopheles, receive this scroll,
               A deed of gift of body and of soul –   90
               But yet conditionally that thou perform
               All articles prescribed between us both.

MEPHISTOPHELES   Faustus, I swear by hell and Lucifer
               To effect all promises between us made.

FAUSTUS   Then hear me read them.   95
               'On these conditions following:
               First, that Faustus may be a spirit in form and
               substance.
               Secondly, that Mephistopheles shall be his servant,
               and at his command.   100
               Thirdly, that Mephistopheles shall do for him and
               bring him whatsoever.
               Fourthly, that he shall be in his chamber or house
               invisible.
               Lastly, that he shall appear to the said John Faustus 105
               at all times in what form or shape soever he please.
               I, John Faustus of Wittenberg, Doctor, by these
               presents, do give both body and soul to Lucifer,
               Prince of the East, and his minister Mephistopheles;
               and furthermore grant unto them that four-and-   110
               twenty years being expired, the articles above
               written inviolate, full power to fetch or carry the
               said John Faustus, body and soul, flesh, blood, or
               goods, into their habitation wheresoever.
                                        By me, John Faustus.' 115

MEPHISTOPHELES   Speak, Faustus. Do you deliver this as your
               deed?

FAUSTUS   (*Giving the deed*) Ay. Take it, and the devil give thee
               good on't.

MEPHISTOPHELES   Now, Faustus, ask what thou wilt.   120

FAUSTUS   First will I question with thee about hell.
               Tell me, where is the place that men call hell?

2.1 *Faustus asks Mephistopheles a series of questions about hell, scoffing at the concept of eternal torment*

124 **these elements** *the four elements that make up all that exists beneath the moon: earth, air, fire and water*

126–127 **circumscribed...place** confined to one and the same place

127–128 **for where we are...be** *see 1.3.78*

129 **dissolves** *i.e. at Doomsday, the Day of Judgement, when everything is purified by fire*

132 **fable** myth

133 **think so still** continue to believe that

138 **fond** foolish

140 **trifles...tales** trivial, meaningless stories

141 **instance** example

143 **an** if

144 **disputing** engaging in debate

146 **wanton and lascivious** sexually active and lustful

Ideas and interpretations

132 Paul Kocher believes that this line has 'the same note of bravado that we hear in the Baines note and the Kyd letters' (see page 120). Thomas Healy believes that it demonstrates 'a type of adolescent refusal [in Faustus] to recognise the powers he has invoked'. For W W Greg, 'After the bond is signed, the discussion is renewed, but while the devil loses nothing in dignity of serious discourse, we can already detect a change in Faustus; his sceptical levity takes on a more truculent and jeering tone.'

Performance

In a 1980 production, Patrick McGee's Mephistopheles 'became a passive and helpless spectator of Faustus's ruin, an almost fatherly figure hopelessly watching his son slide down the slippery slope as he had once slid himself' (William Tydeman).

Mephistopheles

148–149 Mephistopheles refuses to provide Faustus with a wife because marriage is an institution ordained by God.

MEPHISTOPHELES   Under the heavens.

FAUSTUS   Ay, but whereabout?

MEPHISTOPHELES   Within the bowels of these elements,
                  Where we are tortured and remain for ever.   125
                  Hell hath no limits, nor is circumscribed
                  In one self place, for where we are is hell,
                  And where hell is must we ever be.
                  And, to conclude, when all the world dissolves,
                  And every creature shall be purified,   130
                  All places shall be hell that is not heaven.

FAUSTUS   Come, I think hell's a fable.

MEPHISTOPHELES   Ay, think so still, till experience change thy
                  mind.

FAUSTUS   Why, think'st thou then that Faustus shall be
           damned?

MEPHISTOPHELES   Ay, of necessity, for here's the scroll   135
                  Wherein thou hast given thy soul to Lucifer.

FAUSTUS   Ay, and body too. But what of that?
           Think'st thou that Faustus is so fond
           To imagine that after this life there is any pain?
           Tush, these are trifles and mere old wives' tales.   140

MEPHISTOPHELES   But, Faustus, I am an instance to prove the
                  contrary,
                  For I am damned and am now in hell.

FAUSTUS   How? Now in hell? Nay, an this be hell, I'll willingly
           be damned here. What? Walking, disputing, etc.?
           But leaving off this, let me have a wife, the fairest   145
           maid in Germany, for I am wanton and lascivious
           and cannot live without a wife.

MEPHISTOPHELES   How, a wife? I prithee, Faustus, talk not of a
                  wife.

FAUSTUS   Nay, sweet Mephistopheles, fetch me one, for I will   150
           have one.

2.1

Mephistopheles provides Faustus with a 'wife' in the form of a devil dressed like a woman, alive with fireworks, and gives him books of necromantic spells and astronomy

156   **but** nothing more than

156–157   **ceremonial toy** pointless ceremony

158   **cull thee out** select for you

      courtesans high-class prostitutes

161   **Penelope** *the faithful wife of Odysseus in Homer's ancient Greek epic* The Odyssey; *she refused numerous suitors when he was away for twenty years, hoping that one day he would return*

162   **Saba** *the Queen of Sheba who taxed the wise King Solomon with her difficult questions (see the Bible: 1 Kings 10)*

164   **Peruse** read

165   **iterating** repetition (*or* writing more than once)

lines *possibly occult symbols*

166   **framing** drawing

171   **fain would I have** I would love to have

s.d.   ***There turn to them*** *Mephistopheles turns to the appropriate pages in the book to show Faustus what he has asked for.*

176   **would I have** I want

177   **characters** symbols

178   **dispositions** situations of the planets in a horoscope

179   ***Turn to them*** *either Mephistopheles shows him different pages in the same book, or pages in another book*

Performance

s.d. The stage direction makes it clear that Faustus's *wife* is actually a devil, but *dressed like a woman, with fireworks*. In the 1989 production, Faustus seemed to receive an electric shock every time he attempted to touch 'her'. The fireworks might well represent venereal disease.

Language

162–163 Interestingly, when Mephistopheles looks for an example of great beauty, he chooses a man, Lucifer. (See also 5.1.106–109.)

MEPHISTOPHELES   Well, thou wilt have one. Sit there till I come.
                   I'll fetch thee a wife, in the devil's name.

Exit.

Enter MEPHISTOPHELES with a DEVIL dressed like a woman, with fireworks.

MEPHISTOPHELES   Tell, Faustus, how dost thou like thy wife?

FAUSTUS   A plague on her for a hot whore!   155

MEPHISTOPHELES   Tut, Faustus, marriage is but a ceremonial
                   toy. If thou lovest me, think no more of it.

Exit DEVIL.

           I'll cull thee out the fairest courtesans
           And bring them ev'ry morning to thy bed.
           She whom thine eye shall like, thy heart shall have, 160
           Be she as chaste as was Penelope,
           As wise as Saba, or as beautiful
           As was bright Lucifer before his fall.
               (*Presenting a book*)
           Hold, take this book. Peruse it thoroughly.
           The iterating of these lines brings gold;   165
           The framing of this circle on the ground
           Brings whirlwinds, tempests, thunder, and lightning.
           Pronounce this thrice devoutly to thyself,
           And men in armour shall appear to thee,
           Ready to execute what thou desir'st.   170

FAUSTUS   Thanks, Mephistopheles. Yet fain would I have a
            book wherein I might behold all spells and
            incantations, that I might raise up spirits when
            I please.

MEPHISTOPHELES   Here they are in this book. (*There turn to*   175
                   them)

FAUSTUS   Now would I have a book where I might see all
            characters and planets of the heavens, that I might
            know their motions and dispositions.

MEPHISTOPHELES   Here they are too. (*Turn to them*)

2.2 *Robin has stolen one of Faustus's books of magic and tells Rafe the stableboy what delights he will be able to accomplish*

3   **some circles** *i.e. magic circles (see 1.3.8; 'circle' is also a common term for the vulva – see* Romeo and Juliet *2.1.23–27)*

s.d.   ***Enter RAFE*** *a version of Ralph – the spelling represents the traditional pronunciation; we learn later (at 3.2.3) that Rafe is another stableman*

9   **his things** *his saddle, harness etc; but with the possibility of a sexual connotation*

9–10   **he keeps...chafing** *(1) he keeps going on about it; (2) he keeps rubbing (following the sexual connotation of line 9)*

14   **roaring** *noisy and riotous*

18   **for his forehead** *by being made a cuckold (an example of the numerous references in the drama of this period to the idea that a man whose wife was unfaithful – a cuckold – would sprout horns on his forehead)*

19   **bear with me** *(1) put up with me; (2) carry my weight during sexual intercourse; (3) have my children*

Faustus

184 Why does Faustus say this? Perhaps he is expressing doubt that the book or books contain all that Mephistopheles promises; this would certainly account for the devil's impatient *Tut* and reassuring *I warrant* [assure] *thee*.

Performance

Where is 2.2 set? From the dialogue, and the description of Robin as the *ostler* (a stableman), it appears that he has got a job looking after customers' horses in an inn.

Structure

In the A-text this scene is printed later in the play, but some modern editors place it here, especially as the dramatic and thematic parallels are very clear: 'Wagner tries to imitate Faustus and the pattern repeats itself when Robin tries to imitate Wagner' (Roger Sales).

Language

8–19 The dialogue is full of sexual innuendo: the gentleman who *would have his things rubbed* and keeps *chafing* his mistress; the possibility of being *blown up* and *dismembered*; the reference to cuckolding and the woman's *private* parts (18) and the sexual act (19).

FAUSTUS Nay, let me have one book more – and then I have   180
done – wherein I might see all plants, herbs, and
trees that grow upon the earth.

MEPHISTOPHELES   Here they be. (*Turn to them*)

FAUSTUS O, thou art deceived.

MEPHISTOPHELES   Tut. I warrant thee.   185

Exeunt.

Scene 2

Enter ROBIN the ostler with a book in his hand.

ROBIN O, this is admirable! Here I ha' stol'n one of Doctor
Faustus' conjuring books, and, i'faith, I mean to
search some circles for my own use. Now will I
make all the maidens in our parish dance at my
pleasure stark naked before me, and so by that   5
means I shall see more than e'er I felt or saw yet.

Enter RAFE, calling ROBIN.

RAFE Robin, prithee, come away. There's a gentleman
tarries to have his horse, and he would have his
things rubbed and made clean; he keeps such a
chafing with my mistress about it, and she has sent   10
me to look thee out. Prithee, come away.

ROBIN Keep out, keep out, or else you are blown up, you
are dismembered, Rafe! Keep out, for I am about a
roaring piece of work.

RAFE Come, what dost thou with that same book? Thou   15
canst not read.

ROBIN Yes, my master and mistress shall find that I can
read – he for his forehead, she for her private study.
She's born to bear with me, or else my art fails.

RAFE Why, Robin, what book is that?   20

2.3 *Wondering at the stars, Faustus curses Lucifer for having deprived him of the joys of heaven*

21 **intolerable** *perhaps a malapropism for* incomparable

22 **brimstone** sulphur *(suggesting the fires of hell)*

26 **hippocras** spiced wine

31 **turn...wind** *both common terms for the sexual act (presumably Nan Spit is as easily 'turned' as a cooking-spit)*

33 **midnight** *i.e. 'the witching hour'*

34 **brave** wonderful

36 **horse-bread** feed made of beans and bran

39 **in the devil's name** *a common oath, but here with an additional literal meaning*

Gerard Murphy as Faustus and David Bradley as Mephistopheles (RSC, 1989)

Structure

25–33 In declaring that he can obtain wine *for nothing* and Nan Spit for Rafe whenever he wants, Robin might remind us of Faustus, who proposes to indulge himself in sensual and intellectual pleasures while seemingly dismissing the fact that a reckoning will have to be made.

Robin and Rafe

The clowns embody a number of the features of carnival: the upsetting of the normal social order (Robin presumes to conjure, an activity which ought to be the province of scholars); the preoccupation with sex; and the engagement in a great deal of activity centring on food, drink and other bodily needs.

Language

1 'Marlowe has throughout the play used the words *heaven* and *heavenly* in a tantalisingly double sense. Heavenly refers to the structure of the cosmos as seen from the earth, but it also has associations with the divine – the sphere from which Faustus has cut himself off' (Cleanth Brooks).

ROBIN   What book? Why the most intolerable book for
conjuring that e'er was invented by any brimstone
devil.

RAFE   Can'st thou conjure with it?

ROBIN   I can do all these things easily with it: first, I can   25
make thee drunk with hippocras at any tavern in
Europe for nothing. That's one of my conjuring
works.

RAFE   Our Master Parson says that's nothing.

ROBIN   True, Rafe; and more, Rafe, if thou hast any mind to 30
Nan Spit, our kitchen maid, then turn her and wind
her to thy own use as often as thou wilt, and at
midnight.

RAFE   O brave, Robin! Shall I have Nan Spit, and to mine
own use? On that condition I'll feed thy devil with 35
horse-bread as long as he lives, of free cost.

ROBIN   No more, sweet Rafe. Let's go and make clean our
boots, which lie foul upon our hands, and then to
our conjuring, in the devil's name.

Exeunt.

Scene 3

Enter FAUSTUS in his study and MEPHISTOPHELES.

FAUSTUS   When I behold the heavens, then I repent
And curse thee, wicked Mephistopheles,
Because thou hast deprived me of those joys.

MEPHISTOPHELES   Why Faustus,
Think'st thou heaven is such a glorious thing?   5
I tell thee, 'tis not half so fair as thou
Or any man that breathes on earth.

FAUSTUS   How provest thou that?

MEPHISTOPHELES   It was made for man; therefore is man more
excellent.   10

2.3 *Listening to the promptings of the Good and Evil Angels, Faustus is unable to repent. He consoles himself with reminders of the pleasures he has experienced thanks to his new-won powers*

s.d. **Enter GOOD ANGEL...** *another example of the angels appearing when Faustus wavers (see 1.1.72–79)*

13 **yet** even at this stage; while there is time *(i.e. it's not too late)*

14 **spirit** devil *(see note to 2.1.97)*

15 **buzzeth** mutters

20 **name** speak about

23 **halters** hangman's ropes

    envenomed steel a poisoned dagger/sword

24 **dispatch** kill

25 **ere** before

27 **blind Homer** *the supposed author of the ancient Greek epics* The Iliad *and* The Odyssey, *reputedly blind*

28 **Alexander...Oenone** *Alexander is Homer's usual name for Paris (see note to 5.1.12). In later stories Paris abandons the nymph Oenone for Helen, and when he is fatally wounded in the war, Oenone refuses to cure him and later kills herself in remorse. (Oenone is here pronounced with two syllables like 'E-known'.)*

29–30 **he that built...harp** *Amphion, ruler of Thebes, was such a great harpist that his playing caused the stones to build themselves into a wall around the city.*

34 **dispute** engage in scholarly debate

35 **argue of...astrology** discuss astronomy

36 **are there...moon?** *see page 136*

37–38 **Are all...earth?** Do the heavenly spheres form a single globe, like the Earth at its centre?

39–42 **As are the elements...pole** The universe is arranged in spheres, just like the elements (Earth at the centre enclosed by a sphere of water; then a sphere of air; then fire), and as you move outward, each sphere encloses the next, from the sphere of the moon to the outermost sphere; and they all turn on the same axis, the end (**terminine**) of which is called the pole.

43–44 **Nor are...stars** And it is not wrong to give Saturn, Mars and Jupiter individual names, because each one is a planet revolving in its own sphere.

Ideas and interpretations

16 *Be I a devil* can mean either 'Even if I were a devil' or 'It doesn't matter that I am a devil'. The meaning depends on whether we believe that Faustus is already a spirit or not. See note to 2.1.97.

19 'Faustus is beginning to lose his confidence in the heroic consolations of evil and his moral distress is becoming genuine' (J P Brockbank).

Structure

22–25 As part of the chiastic structure (see pages 149–150), this threatened suicide balances a later one at 5.1.50–52.

Faustus

31 Faustus's apparently affectionate term of address here – *my Mephistopheles* – is repeated in varying forms throughout (more than once he is *sweet Mephistopheles*, for example); this leads some interpreters to see a homoerotic element in their relationship which can be made clear on stage (as it was in the 1989 RSC production). See, for example, 2.3.70, 3.1.1 and the note to 5.1.70.

FAUSTUS If it were made for man, 'twas made for me.
 I will renounce this magic and repent.

Enter GOOD ANGEL and EVIL ANGEL.

GOOD ANGEL Faustus, repent yet, God will pity thee.

EVIL ANGEL Thou art a spirit. God cannot pity thee.

FAUSTUS Who buzzeth in mine ears I am a spirit?   15
 Be I a devil, yet God may pity me;
 Ay, God will pity me if I repent.

EVIL ANGEL Ay, but Faustus never shall repent.

Exeunt ANGELS.

FAUSTUS My heart's so hardened I cannot repent.
 Scarce can I name salvation, faith, or heaven   20
 But fearful echoes thunder in mine ears:
 'Faustus, thou art damned!' Then swords and knives,
 Poison, guns, halters, and envenomed steel
 Are laid before me to dispatch myself;
 And long ere this I should have slain myself   25
 Had not sweet pleasure conquered deep despair.
 Have not I made blind Homer sing to me
 Of Alexander's love and Oenone's death?
 And hath not he that built the walls of Thebes
 With ravishing sound of his melodious harp   30
 Made music with my Mephistopheles?
 Why should I die, then, or basely despair?
 I am resolved Faustus shall ne'er repent.
 Come, Mephistopheles, let us dispute again
 And argue of divine astrology.   35
 Tell me, are there many heavens above the moon?
 Are all celestial bodies but one globe,
 As is the substance of this centric earth?

MEPHISTOPHELES As are the elements, such are the spheres,
 Mutually folded in each others' orb;   40
 And, Faustus, all jointly move upon one axletree,
 Whose terminine is termed the world's wide pole.
 Nor are the names of Saturn, Mars, or Jupiter
 Feigned, but are erring stars.

2.3   *Mephistopheles answers Faustus's questions about the universe, but refuses to tell him who made the world*

45–46   **both *situ et tempore?*** *Latin:* both in space and time? (*i.e.* Do they all revolve around the Earth in the same direction and taking the same time?)

47–49   **All…zodiac** They all revolve around the Earth from east to west in twenty-four hours (and on the Earth's axis), but each one also has a different revolution based on the axis of the universe on which the spheres revolve.

53–56   **The first…days** *These figures might have been taken from a popular Elizabethan handbook,* The Castle of Knowledge, *1556.*

57   **freshmen's suppositions** the kind of basic assumptions held by first-year students; *or* simple 'facts' that those studying logic first argue about

58   **dominion or *intelligentia*** controlling power or angel *(Latin)*

61   **firmament** the sphere containing the stars

62   **empyreal heaven** the sphere of pure fire or highest heaven

64   **conjunctions** *when two stars or planets appear close together*

oppositions *when they appear opposite each other*

aspects *the relative positions of two stars or planets seen from Earth*

64–65   **all at one time** at regular intervals

67   ***Per…totius*** *Latin:* on account of their unequal motion with respect to the whole *(i.e. each planet moves at a different speed)*

71   **Move me not** don't provoke me

73   **against our kingdom** *i.e. the monarchy of hell*

Performance

68   Faustus's *Well, I am answered* can be delivered ironically: he has not learned anything new.

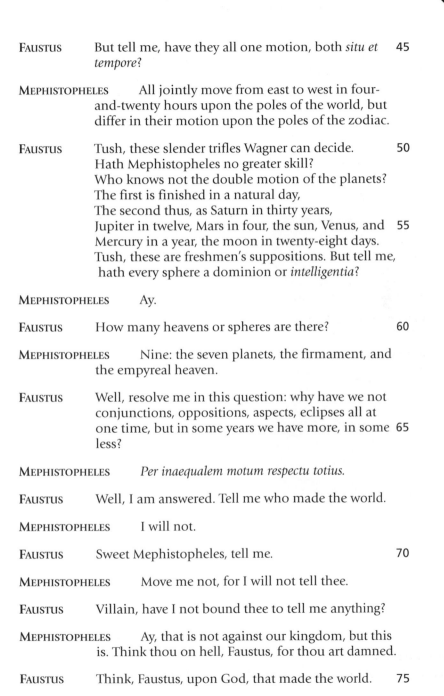

FAUSTUS   But tell me, have they all one motion, both *situ et*   45
             tempore?

MEPHISTOPHELES   All jointly move from east to west in four-
             and-twenty hours upon the poles of the world, but
             differ in their motion upon the poles of the zodiac.

FAUSTUS   Tush, these slender trifles Wagner can decide.   50
             Hath Mephistopheles no greater skill?
             Who knows not the double motion of the planets?
             The first is finished in a natural day,
             The second thus, as Saturn in thirty years,
             Jupiter in twelve, Mars in four, the sun, Venus, and   55
             Mercury in a year, the moon in twenty-eight days.
             Tush, these are freshmen's suppositions. But tell me,
             hath every sphere a dominion or *intelligentia?*

MEPHISTOPHELES   Ay.

FAUSTUS   How many heavens or spheres are there?   60

MEPHISTOPHELES   Nine: the seven planets, the firmament, and
             the empyreal heaven.

FAUSTUS   Well, resolve me in this question: why have we not
             conjunctions, oppositions, aspects, eclipses all at
             one time, but in some years we have more, in some   65
             less?

MEPHISTOPHELES   *Per inaequalem motum respectu totius.*

FAUSTUS   Well, I am answered. Tell me who made the world.

MEPHISTOPHELES   I will not.

FAUSTUS   Sweet Mephistopheles, tell me.   70

MEPHISTOPHELES   Move me not, for I will not tell thee.

FAUSTUS   Villain, have I not bound thee to tell me anything?

MEPHISTOPHELES   Ay, that is not against our kingdom, but this
             is. Think thou on hell, Faustus, for thou art damned.

FAUSTUS   Think, Faustus, upon God, that made the world.   75

Mephistopheles angrily departs when Faustus pushes him to an answer, returning with Lucifer and another of his chief ministers, Beelzebub. Lucifer reminds Faustus of his pact

76 **Remember this** *either* remember that you are damned; *or* remember later what you have said (when Lucifer calls you to account)

83 **raze** scratch

85 **Seek** *the B-text has* Help

87 **int'rest in the same** a legal right to your soul *(with also the financial idea of 'interest')*

92 **thou dost injure us** you wrong us

95 **dame** mother *or* wife *(the expression 'the devil and his dam' was a common saying about certain women – that they were even worse than the devil)*

The appearance of Lucifer and Beelzebub with Mephistopheles (RSC, 1989)

Ideas and interpretations

81 The word *can* in *can repent* is very significant. It implies that repentance is beyond Faustus's control – a hard and unforgiving view of humanity's relationship with God. The B-text has 'if Faustus *will* repent', suggesting more hopefully that, if Faustus *is willing* to repent, he will find forgiveness and salvation.

84 Faustus calls on Christ, *my Saviour*. But Christ either does not hear, or chooses not to help; instead Lucifer makes his first appearance. Max Bluestone considers God's non-appearance to be 'an inexplicable rebuff'. Robert West points out that true repentance has to withstand hell's onslaughts. David Bevington and Eric Rasmussen state that 'We are left…with the perception that God (Christ) is starkly absent from the play.'

MEPHISTOPHELES   Remember this!

Exit.

FAUSTUS   Ay, go, accursèd spirit, to ugly hell!
'Tis thou hast damned distressèd Faustus' soul.
Is't not too late?

Enter GOOD ANGEL and EVIL ANGEL.

EVIL ANGEL   Too late.   80

GOOD ANGEL   Never too late, if Faustus can repent.

EVIL ANGEL   If thou repent, devils shall tear thee in pieces.

GOOD ANGEL   Repent, and they shall never raze thy skin.

Exeunt ANGELS.

FAUSTUS   Ah, Christ, my Saviour,
Seek to save distressèd Faustus' soul!   85

Enter LUCIFER, BEELZEBUB and MEPHISTOPHELES.

LUCIFER   Christ cannot save thy soul, for he is just.
There's none but I have int'rest in the same

FAUSTUS   O, who art thou that look'st so terrible?

LUCIFER   I am Lucifer,
And this is my companion prince in hell.   90

FAUSTUS   O Faustus, they are come to fetch away thy soul.

LUCIFER   We come to tell thee thou dost injure us.
Thou talk'st of Christ, contrary to thy promise.
Thou shouldst not think of God. Think of the devil,
And of his dame, too.   95

FAUSTUS   Nor will I henceforth. Pardon me in this,
And Faustus vows never to look to heaven,
Never to name God or to pray to him,
To burn his Scriptures, slay his ministers,
And make my spirits pull his churches down.   100

2.3 *Lucifer distracts and entertains Faustus with a show of the Seven Deadly Sins*

101 **gratify** reward

103 **pastime** entertainment

103–104 **Seven Deadly Sins** *figures from the medieval morality plays (see page 139)*

104 **proper** own; particular

107–108 **mark this show** watch this pageant

109 **Come away!** Come in!

111 **dispositions** characters

113 **Pride** *the sin which caused Lucifer to fall from heaven (see 1.3.69–70) and which is behind Faustus's actions (Prologue 20)*

114 **Ovid's flea** *a reference to a poem, once thought to be by the Roman poet Ovid, in which the poet envies the flea's ability to visit his mistress's most intimate parts (see also 1.4.70–74)*

115 **periwig** wig

118 **except** unless

119 **cloth of arras** *a rich fabric from Arras in northern France, used for wall tapestries, and too luxurious to use on the floor, as Pride requires*

121 **Covetousness** *the sin of desiring other people's possessions*

begotten of fathered by

churl miser

122 **leathern bag** miser's leather money-bag *(a common detail in medieval images of covetousness)*

might I if I could

127 **Wrath** *the sin of anger*

130 **case of rapiers** pair of sharp-pointed swords

131 **withal** with

132 **look to it** watch out

shall be will prove to be

132–133 **my father** *i.e. the 'begetter' of anger*

LUCIFER	Do so, and we will highly gratify thee.
	Faustus, we are come from hell to show thee some
	pastime. Sit down, and thou shalt see all the Seven
	Deadly Sins appear in their proper shapes.

FAUSTUS	That sight will be as pleasing unto me as paradise	105
	was to Adam the first day of his creation.	

LUCIFER	Talk not of paradise nor creation, but mark this
	show. Talk of the devil, and nothing else. – (*Calling*
	offstage) Come away!

FAUSTUS sits. Enter the SEVEN DEADLY SINS.

	Now, Faustus, examine them of their several names	110
	and dispositions.	

FAUSTUS	What art thou, the first?

PRIDE	I am Pride. I disdain to have any parents. I am like	
	to Ovid's flea: I can creep into every corner of a	
	wench. Sometimes like a periwig I sit upon her	115
	brow, or like a fan of feathers I kiss her lips. Indeed	
	I do – what do I not? But fie, what a scent is here!	
	I'll not speak another word, except the ground were	
	perfumed and covered with cloth of arras.	

FAUSTUS	What art thou, the second?	120

COVETOUSNESS	I am Covetousness, begotten of an old churl	
	in an old leathern bag; and might I have my wish,	
	I would desire that this house and all the people in	
	it were turned to gold, that I might lock you up in	
	my good chest. O my sweet gold!	125

FAUSTUS	What art thou, the third?

WRATH	I am Wrath. I had neither father nor mother. I	
	leaped out of a lion's mouth when I was scarce half	
	an hour old, and ever since I have run up and down	
	the world with this case of rapiers, wounding myself	130
	when I had nobody to fight withal. I was born in	
	hell, and look to it, for some of you shall be my	
	father.	

135–136 **begotten...oyster-wife** *i.e. dirty and foul-smelling (an oyster-wife was a woman who sold oysters)*

141 **with a vengeance** with God's curse on you

143 **Gluttony** *the sin of overeating and drinking*

144 **the devil...left me** I'm damned if they've left me a penny

145 **pension** small allowance for basic board and lodging

146 **bevers** between-meals snacks, *or* drinks

to suffice nature to keep me alive *(i.e. properly nourished)*

148 **hogshead** enormous cask

150 **Martin Martlemas-beef** *cattle slaughtered at Martinmas (St Martin's day: 11 November), which provided enough preserved beef to last through the winter*

153 **March-beer** strong beer brewed in March

154 **progeny** parentage

156 **victuals** food

159 **Sloth** *the sin of laziness*

161 **injury** wrong; injustice

162 **thither** back there

Lechery *the sin of lust*

163 **king's ransom** the enormous payment needed to buy back a captured king

164 **Minx** promiscuous woman

165–166 **that loves...stockfish** 'Raw mutton *is common slang for lust or for prostitutes...*stockfish *or dried cod is a slang term of contempt suggesting...sexual insufficiency...By choosing an* inch *of one over an* ell *(a measure of 45 inches [120 cm]) of the other, Lechery expresses her preference for quality rather than inferior quantity' (David Bevington and Eric Rasmussen).*

166–167 **and the first...lechery** This joke is on the lines of: 'I won't mention his name, but it begins with Michael...'

The Seven Deadly Sins (RSC, 1989)

FAUSTUS	What art thou, the fourth?
ENVY	I am Envy, begotten of a chimney-sweeper and an 135 oyster-wife. I cannot read, and therefore wish all books were burnt. I am lean with seeing others eat. O, that there would come a famine through all the world, that all might die, and I live alone! Then thou shouldst see how fat I would be. But must 140 thou sit and I stand? Come down, with a vengeance!
FAUSTUS	Away, envious rascal! – What are thou, the fifth?
GLUTTONY	Who, I, sir? I am Gluttony. My parents are all dead, and the devil a penny they have left me but a bare pension, and that is thirty meals a day, and ten 145 bevers – a small trifle to suffice nature. O, I come of a royal parentage. My grandfather was a gammon of bacon, my grandmother a hogshead of claret wine. My godfathers were these: Peter Pickle-herring and Martin Martlemas-beef. O, but my godmother, she 150 was a jolly gentlewoman, and well beloved in every good town and city; her name was Mistress Margery March-beer. Now, Faustus, thou hast heard all my progeny, wilt thou bid me to supper?
FAUSTUS	No, I'll see thee hanged. Thou wilt eat up all my 155 victuals.
GLUTTONY	Then the devil choke thee!
FAUSTUS	Choke thyself, glutton! – What art thou, the sixth?
SLOTH	I am Sloth. I was begotten on a sunny bank, where I have lain ever since, and you have done me great 160 injury to bring me from thence. Let me be carried thither again by Gluttony and Lechery. I'll not speak another word for a king's ransom.
FAUSTUS	What are you, Mistress Minx, the seventh and last?
LECHERY	Who, I, sir? I am one that loves an inch of raw 165 mutton better than an ell of fried stockfish, and the first letter of my name begins with lechery.
LUCIFER	Away, to hell, to hell!

Exeunt the SINS.

2.3 *Faustus is delighted by the vision of the Sins and by a book given to him by Lucifer*

176 **throughly** thoroughly

179 **chary** carefully

s.d. ***Exeunt omnes...*** They all go out in different directions.

Gerard Murphy as Faustus, having been crowned by devils (RSC, 1989)

Faustus

170–173 As Faustus cries *O, this feeds my soul!* 'his exultant disgust springs from his enjoyment of sharing the privilege of Lucifer's throne (like a royal guest) and being superior to the vices that overtake mankind. He asks to visit hell and return safely, but hell has already visited him and left him contaminated' (J P Brockbank).

Now, Faustus, how dost thou like this?

FAUSTUS O, this feeds my soul!   170

LUCIFER Tut, Faustus, in hell is all manner of delight.

FAUSTUS O, might I see hell and return again, how happy were
      I then!

LUCIFER Thou shalt. I will send for thee at midnight.
      (*Presenting a book*) In meantime, take this book. 175
      Peruse it throughly, and thou shalt turn thyself into
      what shape thou wilt.

FAUSTUS (*Taking the book*) Great thanks, mighty Lucifer.
      This will I keep as chary as my life.

LUCIFER Farewell, Faustus, and think on the devil. 180

FAUSTUS Farewell, great Lucifer. Come, Mephistopheles.

               Exeunt omnes, different ways.

Exam practice

Extracts

1. Reread 2.1.30–119 ('Now tell me…good on't'). What might the thoughts and feelings of an audience be as they watch this part of the scene? In your answer you should:
   - show in detail how characterisation, atmosphere and dramatic qualities are created by Marlowe's choice of language
   - express your own thoughts and feelings about the scene at this point in the play, as well as suggesting how other audiences might respond to it
   - show an awareness of dramatic tension and the nature of the Marlovian tragic hero.

2. Reread 2.2. In what ways does this scene, and 1.4, illustrate Stevie Simkin's idea that the comic scenes display all the features of carnival, in that 'As well as preoccupations with sex, one of the fundamental features of carnival, there is dialogue and business centring around food, drink, and other bodily needs.' In your answer you should:
   - make detailed reference to dialogue and comic business centring around what Simkin calls 'bodily needs'
   - comment on the ways in which these scenes help to set Faustus's activities in perspective
   - show an awareness of the ways in which carnival elements in this comedy represent a challenge to social order (see the section on morality plays, pages 139–140, and the extract by Stevie Simkin on pages 168–169).

3. Reread 2.3.1–100 ('…his churches down'). What does this scene add to our picture of Faustus as a man undergoing a series of desperate internal conflicts? In your answer you should:
   - show how Faustus seems to veer between the extremes of regretting his pact with Lucifer and exulting in the pleasures it has brought
   - comment on his seeming inability to repent
   - show an awareness of the variety of attitudes and beliefs in Marlowe's time concerning the soul and the will (see pages 134–135).

Extended writing

4. How important is Act 2 in furthering the central debates and issues of the play and exploring its underlying concepts? In your answer you should:
   - examine the deed that Faustus signs and discuss its implications
   - discuss the roles played by the Good and Evil Angels, and Lucifer
   - show understanding of attitudes in Marlowe's time to sin, repentance and damnation (see pages 134–135).

Performance

5. In 2.1 devils appear, who crown Faustus and give him rich apparel. In a 1968 production, they were 'horrid, red-eyed and hairy as beasts'; in 1974 they were life-size puppets, operated by black-habited monks, embodying figments of Faustus's diseased imagination. If you were directing the play, how would you present them on stage? What effect would you want to achieve and how could it be accomplished?

6. The same question applies to the Seven Deadly Sins, which have taken many different forms over the years. In the 1989 RSC version, the Sins were represented by a group of black-clad actors taking up different positions and tableaux; in a 1970 production at Stratford, they had huge carnival heads; in 1968 they were weird, skeletal figures. In groups, rehearse 2.3.112–167 ('What art thou...' to 'with lechery') and then discuss what form you think the Seven Deadly Sins should take. Remember that any decisions should be made in the context of the overall interpretation that you have in mind. (For example, puppets suit an interpretation in which the Sins are representations of Faustus's own corruption; skeletal figures can be effective in embodying the death and decay lying in wait for him.)

Gerard Murphy as Faustus, surrounded by devils (RSC, 1989)

3.1 *Wagner gives an account of Faustus's travels to view the universe and informs us that he has arrived in Rome. Faustus discusses the sights he has seen with Mephistopheles*

s.d. **Enter WAGNER** *Wagner's name here is an indication that he speaks the Chorus lines throughout.*

solus *alone*

3 **Graven** *inscribed; engraved*

Jove's...firmament *God's high heaven (see 1.1.78)*

4 **Olympus** *the highest mountain in Greece, home of the Greek gods*

6 **yoky** *coupled by a yoke*

7 **prove cosmography** *test the truth of alleged facts concerning the geography of the universe*

9 **the Pope** *In Marlowe's lifetime there were eight popes; the Pope in 3.1 does not seem to be based on any particular pope.*

10 **take some part of** *take part in*

holy Peter's feast *St Peter's day (29 June)*

11 **highly solemnised** *celebrated with special ceremonies*

2 **Trier** *a very old town in western Germany, near modern-day Luxembourg*

3 **Environed round** *surrounded*

4 **intrenchèd lakes** *moats*

6 **coasting** *exploring*

7 **fall into** *join*

9 **Naples, rich Campania** *Marlowe follows his English source for the story (see page 137), which mistakenly assumes that Naples and Campania in central Italy are the same place; Naples was then the capital of the Kingdom of Naples, and Campania was a small region near the city.*

11 **straight forth** *in straight lines*

12 **Quarters** *quarter (in Elizabethan English, plural subjects were often followed by verbs with singular endings)*

equivalents *equal areas*

13 **Maro** *the Roman poet Virgil (Publius Vergilius Maro; see note to 1.1.118)*

14–15 **The way he cut** *the road that he cut (Virgil was thought at this time to have been a magician; Marlowe refers to the story that Virgil cut a mile-long tunnel through rock in a single night)*

17–18 **In midst...top** *This refers to St Mark's in Venice, though the spire he describes is the nearby bell-tower.*

19 **hitherto** *until now*

21 **erst** *a little while ago*

22 **Rome** *The props list for the Admiral's Men in 1598 (see also note to 1.3.20) includes 'the sittie of Rome', possibly a back-drop.*

Act 3

Chorus

Enter WAGNER solus.

WAGNER   Learnèd Faustus,
           To know the secrets of astronomy
           Graven in the book of Jove's high firmament,
           Did mount himself to scale Olympus' top,
           Being seated in a chariot burning bright   5
           Drawn by the strength of yoky dragons' necks.
           He now is gone to prove cosmography,
           And, as I guess, will first arrive at Rome
           To see the Pope and manner of his court
           And take some part of holy Peter's feast   10
           That to this day is highly solemnised.

                                                Exit WAGNER.

Scene 1

Enter FAUSTUS and MEPHISTOPHELES.

FAUSTUS   Having now, my good Mephistopheles,
            Passed with delight the stately town of Trier,
            Environed round with airy mountain-tops,
            With walls of flint and deep intrenchèd lakes,
            Not to be won by any conquering prince;   5
            From Paris next, coasting the realm of France,
            We saw the river Maine fall into Rhine,
            Whose banks are set with groves of fruitful vines.
            Then up to Naples, rich Campania,
            Whose buildings, fair and gorgeous to the eye,   10
            The streets straight forth and paved with finest brick,
            Quarters the town in four equivalents.
            There saw we learnèd Maro's golden tomb,
            The way he cut an English mile in length
            Thorough a rock of stone in one night's space.   15
            From thence to Venice, Padua, and the rest,
            In midst of which a sumptuous temple stands
            That threats the stars with her aspiring top.
            Thus hitherto hath Faustus spent his time.
            But tell me now, what resting place is this?   20
            Hast thou, as erst I did command,
            Conducted me within the walls of Rome?

3.1 *Mephistopheles confirms that, in accordance with Faustus's request, they are now in the Vatican where they can witness – and mischievously participate in – the celebration of 'holy Peter's feast'*

23 **because** in order that

24 **unprovided** *i.e. with comfortable lodgings and food*

24–25 **his Holiness' privy chamber** the Pope's private apartment

27 **'tis no matter** it makes no difference whether he will or not

　　be bold with take liberties with *(e.g. eat without being invited)*

29 **that** so that

32 **underprops the…same** support its foundations *(see line 12)*

33 **Tiber's stream** the waters of the River Tiber *(which runs through Rome)*

35 **lean** are built

36 **makes** make *(another singular ending to a plural verb – see **underprops** at line 32 above)*

38 **passing** extremely; surpassingly

39 **store of ordnance** quantity of artillery

40 **double cannons** *probably large-calibre cannon*

41 **match** equal

42–43 **pyramides…Africa** *actually a single obelisk, brought from Egypt by Emperor Constantius (David Bevington and Eric Rasmussen); the word is pronounced with stresses on the second and fourth syllables: pyr-**am**-i-**des***

45–46 **Styx, Acheron…Phlegethon** *three of the rivers of Hades, the Greek underworld*

48 **situation** sites

　　bright splendent brilliantly magnificent; shining brightly and resplendent

50 **you'd fain see** you would like to see

51 **of** in

52 **bald-pate** bald-headed

53 ***summum bonum*** greatest good *(normally a theological term referring to the goodness of God; here referring to the friars' chief delight – gluttony: **belly cheer**)*

54 **compass** contrive

59 **discerned** seen

MEPHISTOPHELES   Faustus, I have. And because we will not be
unprovided, I have taken up his Holiness' privy
chamber for our use.   25

FAUSTUS   I hope his Holiness will bid us welcome.

MEPHISTOPHELES   Tut, 'tis no matter, man. We'll be bold with
his good cheer.
And now, my Faustus, that thou mayst perceive
What Rome containeth to delight thee with,   30
Know that this city stands upon seven hills
That underprops the groundwork of the same.
Just through the midst runs flowing Tiber's stream,
With winding banks that cut it in two parts,
Over the which four stately bridges lean,   35
That makes safe passage to each part of Rome.
Upon the bridge called Ponte Angelo
Erected is a castle passing strong,
Within whose walls such store of ordnance are,
And double cannons, framed of carvèd brass,   40
As match the days within one complete year –
Besides the gates and high pyramides
Which Julius Caesar brought from Africa.

FAUSTUS   Now, by the kingdoms of infernal rule,
Of Styx, Acheron, and the fiery lake   45
Of ever-burning Phlegethon, I swear
That I do long to see the monuments
And situation of bright splendent Rome.
Come, therefore, let's away!

MEPHISTOPHELES   Nay, Faustus, stay. I know you'd fain see the
Pope   50
And take some part of holy Peter's feast,
Where thou shalt see a troupe of bald-pate friars
Whose *summum bonum* is in belly cheer.

FAUSTUS   Well, I am content to compass then some sport,
And by their folly make us merriment.   55
Then charm me that I may be invisible, to do what I
please unseen of any whilst I stay in Rome.

MEPHISTOPHELES   (*Placing a robe on* FAUSTUS) So, Faustus,
now do what thou wilt, thou shalt not be discerned.

3.1 *At the banquet, Faustus, who is invisible, disrupts the feast by snatching food and wine from the Pope and his guest*

s.d. **sennet** *a set of notes on a trumpet to signal a ceremonial entrance*

Enter...CARDINAL OF LORRAINE *Charles de Guise, Cardinal of Lorraine, was a member of the powerful Guise family and uncle of Mary Queen of Scots. He is also a character in Marlowe's* The Massacre at Paris, *in which he is murdered.*

61 **Fall to** start eating

an you spare if you hold back/show restraint

63 **like** please

64 **was sent me** which was sent to me

70 **ha't** have it

72 **pledge** drink to the health of

74 **purgatory...pardon** *According to Catholic doctrine, souls not ready for heaven would spend time purifying themselves in purgatory; their sentence could be shortened if they had bought a pardon from the Church.*

75 **dirge** lament or prayers for the dead; funeral chant

lay allay; reduce

79 **Aware** beware; watch out for

s.d. **hits him a box of the ear** *boxes his ears; hits him round the ear*

Performance

60–100 Productions have often made the most of the possibilities for slapstick in this scene. In the 1968 RSC production magical effects included grape pips that exploded when Mephistopheles spat them out, a turban that belched smoke and a hand that suddenly emerged from a plate of food. The 1970 RSC production even included the custard-pie gag.

Performance and structure

This scene is as carnivalesque as anything in the Robin and Rafe plot (compare 2.2 and 3.2), embodying as it does an explicit challenge to – and disruption of – social ritual, order and hierarchy, with everything reduced to slapstick games with food and drink. A 1961 production changed the order of the central comic scenes, so that they culminated in Faustus's antics with the Pope. They were genuinely funny and showed that 'Faustus was using farce to distract himself from his own approaching fate...Faustus laughed, but at the end of the scene his laughter became hysterical' (Lois Potter).

Ideas and interpretations

60–100 'The depiction of the Pope and his bishops indulging themselves with rich food and drink is fairly blatant, and predictable, anti-Catholic propaganda' (Stevie Simkin). (In this scene in the B-text there are two cardinals and an archbishop.) In line with the recurrent gluttony imagery (see pages 150–151), this feasting is a visual representation of what was seen as the Church's inner corruption.

Sound a sennet. Enter the POPE and the CARDINAL OF LORRAINE to the
banquet, with FRIARS attending.

POPE	My lord of Lorraine, will't please you draw near?	60
FAUSTUS	Fall to, and the devil choke you an you spare.	
POPE	How now, who's that which spake? Friars, look about.	
FRIAR	Here's nobody, if it like your Holiness.	
POPE	My lord, here is a dainty dish was sent me from the Bishop of Milan. (*He presents a dish*)	65
FAUSTUS	I thank you, sir. (*Snatch it*)	
POPE	How now, who's that which snatched the meat from me? Will no man look? – My lord, this dish was sent me from the Cardinal of Florence.	
FAUSTUS	(*Snatching the dish*) You say true, I'll ha't.	70
POPE	What again? – My lord, I'll drink to your Grace.	
FAUSTUS	(*Snatching the cup*) I'll pledge your Grace.	
LORRAINE	My lord, it may be some ghost, newly crept out of purgatory, come to beg a pardon of your Holiness.	
POPE	It may be so. Friars, prepare a dirge to lay the fury of this ghost. Once again, my lord, fall to. (*The POPE crosseth himself*)	75
FAUSTUS	What, are you crossing of yourself? Well, use that trick no more, I would advise you.	

The POPE crosses himself again.

> Well, there's a second time. Aware the third, I give
> you fair warning.   80

The POPE crosses himself again and FAUSTUS hits him a box of the ear, and
they all run away.

> Come on, Mephistopheles. What shall we do?

3.2 *Believing that they are being haunted by a ghost from purgatory, the friars ineffectually attempt an exorcism/excommunication and flee when Faustus and Mephistopheles throw fireworks among them*

82–83 **cursed with...candle** *This refers to the ceremony of excommunication (i.e. officially excluding a person from the Church). The ceremony ended with a bell being tolled, a book (Bible) closed and a candle extinguished. David Bevington and Eric Rasmussen think it was confused by Marlowe and his source for the ceremony of exorcism.*

86 **Anon** straightaway

91 ***Maledicat Dominus!*** *Latin:* May the Lord curse him!

94 **took** gave

100 ***Et omnes sancti*** *Latin:* And all the saints *(may they also curse him)*

1 **made** 'set up'; financially secure

2 ***Ecce signum!*** *Latin:* Behold the sign! *(this phrase echoes the language of the Catholic Mass)*

2–3 **Here's...horse-keepers** This isn't a bad day's work for a couple of stableboys.

4 **eat no hay** *i.e. eat very well*

Faustus (centre) disrupting the Pope's feast (RSC, 1989)

Ideas and interpretations

Queen Elizabeth I had herself been excommunicated by the Pope in 1570. 'Faustus and Mephistopheles are therefore, disconcertingly, allowed to speak for England when they ridicule the Pope's curses' (Roger Sales).

MEPHISTOPHELES   Nay, I know not. We shall be cursed with
          bell, book, and candle.

FAUSTUS   How? Bell, book, and candle, candle, book, and bell,
          Forward and backward, to curse Faustus to hell.   85
          Anon you shall hear a hog grunt, a calf bleat, and
            an ass bray,
          Because it is Saint Peter's holy day.

Enter all the FRIARS to sing the dirge.

FRIAR   Come, brethren, let's about our business with good
          devotion.

The FRIARS sing this:

          Cursèd be he that stole away his Holiness' meat
            from the table.   90
            Maledicat Dominus!
          Cursèd be he that struck his Holiness a blow on the
            face.
            Maledicat Dominus!
          Cursèd be he that took Friar Sandelo a blow on the
            pate.
            Maledicat Dominus!   95
          Cursèd be he that disturbeth our holy dirge.
            Maledicat Dominus!
          Cursèd be he that took away his Holiness' wine.
            Maledicat Dominus!
          Et omnes sancti. Amen.   100

*FAUSTUS and MEPHISTOPHELES beat the FRIARS, and fling fireworks
among them, and so exeunt.*

Scene 2

Enter ROBIN with a conjuring book and RAFE with a silver goblet.

ROBIN   Come, Rafe, did not I tell thee we were for ever made
          by this Doctor Faustus' book? *Ecce signum!* Here's a
          simple purchase for horse-keepers. Our horses shall
          eat no hay as long as this lasts.

3.2 *Robin, accompanied by Rafe, has stolen a cup from a tavern and attempts to outwit the furious vintner by sleight of hand and then by conjuring*

s.d. **VINTNER** innkeeper who sells wine; wine-merchant

6 **gull** cheat

Drawer barman *(someone who 'draws' beer – therefore of lower status than a vintner)*

8 **Soft** wait a minute

10–11 **you are but a etc.** *'etc.' possibly indicates that the actor is expected to improvise some insults, though it might simply be a euphemism ('you're a so-and-so')*

12 **favour** permission

14 **somewhat** something

20 **afore me** in front of me

21 **impeach** accuse

scour punish

26–29 **Sanctobulorum...etc.** *gibberish made to sound like Latin and Greek*

27 **tickle** beat

Look to keep an eye on; look after

Performance

15–28 *He gives the goblet...*: It seems likely that some kind of juggling act might have been intended here, with the cup cleverly switched from one character to the other. By 20, the goblet has been produced.

Structure

Roger Sales notes a further possible parallel with the Faustus plot here. Comparing the scene with Faustus's custard-pie antics in 3.1, he observes: 'The clown who created the part of Robin seems to have been an experienced juggler. Perhaps that is all that Faustus becomes as a result of his contract with Lucifer.'

Act 3 Scene 2

Enter the VINTNER.

RAFE	But Robin, here comes the Vintner. 5
ROBIN	Hush, I'll gull him supernaturally. – Drawer, I hope all is paid. God be with you. Come, Rafe. (*They start to go*)
VINTNER	(*To ROBIN*) Soft, sir, a word with you. I must yet have a goblet paid from you ere you go.
ROBIN	I, a goblet? Rafe, I, a goblet? I scorn you, and you 10 are but a etc. I, a goblet? Search me.
VINTNER	I mean so, sir, with your favour. (*The VINTNER searches ROBIN*)
ROBIN	How say you now?
VINTNER	I must say somewhat to your fellow – you, sir.
RAFE	Me, sir? Me, sir? Search your fill. (*He gives the goblet* 15 *to ROBIN; then the VINTNER searches RAFE*) Now, sir, you may be ashamed to burden honest men with a matter of truth.
VINTNER	Well, t'one of you hath this goblet about you.
ROBIN	You lie, drawer, 'tis afore me. Sirrah, you, I'll teach 20 ye to impeach honest men. Stand by. I'll scour you for a goblet. Stand aside, you had best, I charge you in the name of Beelzebub. (*Tossing the goblet to RAFE*) Look to the goblet, Rafe.
VINTNER	What mean you, sirrah? 25
ROBIN	I'll tell you what I mean. (*He reads*) *Sanctobulorum Periphrasticon!* Nay, I'll tickle you, Vintner. Look to the goblet, Rafe. *Polypragmos Belseborams framanto pacostiphos tostu Mephistopheles!* etc.

Enter to them MEPHISTOPHELES.

Exit the VINTNER, running.

3.2 *Robin's incantations succeed in raising Mephistopheles, who angrily turns Robin into an ape and Rafe into a dog*

31   **awful** terrible; awe-inspiring

34   **Constantinople** modern Istanbul, then capital of the Ottoman Empire

42   **brave** wonderful

45   **pottage** porridge

Mephistopheles

30–37 Mephistopheles's expression of annoyance at being summoned against his will seems at variance with his earlier comment that he does not come at command but only when he chooses (see 1.3.45). (In the 1989 production, his short-tempered outburst and Robin's observation that he had *had a great journey* raised laughs.)

Structure

42–45 Robin and Rafe are absurdly pleased with their transformations into ape and dog, which helps us to appreciate just how deluded Faustus is to be satisfied with his transformation into a spirit (see 2.1.97).

MEPHISTOPHELES	Monarch of hell, under whose black survey 30
	Great potentates do kneel with awful fear,
	Upon whose altars thousand souls do lie,
	How am I vexèd with these villains' charms!
	From Constantinople am I hither come
	Only for pleasure of these damnèd slaves. 35
ROBIN	How, from Constantinople? You have had a great journey. Will you take sixpence in your purse to pay for your supper and be gone?
MEPHISTOPHELES	Well, villains, for your presumption I transform thee (*To* ROBIN) into an ape and thee 40 (*To* RAFE) into a dog. And so, begone!

Exit.

ROBIN	How, into an ape? That's brave. I'll have fine sport with the boys; I'll get nuts and apples enough.
RAFE	And I must be a dog.
ROBIN	I'faith, thy head will never be out of the pottage pot. 45

Exeunt.

Exam practice

Extracts

1. Reread the Act 3 Chorus and 3.1.1–48 ('…bright splendent Rome'). What does this part of the play reveal about the Renaissance world out of which *Doctor Faustus* arose? In your answer you should:
    *   consider the importance of the classical world in early modern drama (see Chorus 2–3, 3.1.13–15 and 42–48, and the section on pages 154–156)
    *   show in detail how the language describing the places visited in Faustus's travels creates a sense of exoticism and wonder
    *   discuss the effects that this Renaissance context – the world of *Doctor Faustus* – had upon Marlowe's retelling of the Faust legend.

2. Reread 3.1, from line 60 ('My lord of Lorraine…'), and 3.2. How far would you agree that these scenes are remarkable for their wide variety of comic effects? In your answer you should comment upon:
    *   satire (on Roman Catholic Church luxury and excess)
    *   parody (of Church rituals)
    *   slapstick and farce
    *   verbal humour (in Robin's speeches, for example)
    *   any other comic forms that you notice.

3. Reread 3.2. What are the purposes of this scene, in your opinion? In your answer you should:
    *   comment upon the way in which the humour serves as a respite from the high emotions of the first two Acts, and a break from continuous focus upon Faustus himself
    *   discuss the ways in which the Clowns' actions help to provide a new perspective on Faustus's pact with Lucifer, and on his actions in 3.1
    *   show an awareness of the place of 'low' comedy in the morality play tradition.

Extended writing

4. Roger Sales believes that the scene showing Faustus with the Pope (3.1) places audiences in an ambiguous position: 'They are asked to condemn Faustus for his pact with Lucifer at the same time as they are encouraged to applaud him for playing practical jokes on a national enemy.' Give your own responses to this scene, using Sales's statement as a basis for your comments. Do you find yourself condemning Faustus here, given that the powers he is using have been bought at the cost of his soul, or cheering him on in his sportive anarchy?

Performance

5. The only available film of *Doctor Faustus* was shot wholly in a studio (see page 175); a modern version would almost certainly shoot a number of scenes on location, and exploit a range of sophisticated technical effects to show Faustus's travels and magic exploits. In groups, discuss how much of the reported material in Act 3 ought to be shown as part of the action. (You might consider the Chorus's accounts of Faustus viewing the universe and Faustus's report of his travels at the opening of 3.1.) How would you show the invisible pranks against the Pope and the transformation of Robin and Rafe into an ape and a dog? In what ways would location filming and special effects enhance the performance of Marlowe's play, and what might be lost, in your opinion?

6. In groups, discuss the opportunities that exist for physical comedy in Act 3. Plan some stage business for one of the scenes, rehearse it, and evaluate its effect: what would it add to a performance of *Doctor Faustus* as a whole?

The aftermath of the Pope's feast (RSC, 1989)

The Chorus reports that Faustus, having completed his travels, has returned to Germany where he is welcomed by admiring friends. Faustus is now a famous man and has been invited to court by the Emperor, Charles the Fifth

2   **rarest** most amazing

3   **stayed his course** ceased his journey

4   **such as bear...grief** people who were only saddened by his travels

6   **gratulate** celebrate; welcome; express joy at

7   **conference** talk

      befell happened

8   **Touching** concerning

9   **of astrology** about the stars

11   **As** that

      wit intellect

14   **Carolus the Fifth** King Charles V of Spain, who was also Holy Roman Emperor from 1519 to 1556

16–17   **What there...performed** You will see acted out whatever I fail to relate concerning what he did there in experimenting with his skills.

1   **strange** amazing

4   **rare** remarkable

5   **familiar** *i.e. in attendance to perform Faustus's commands*

6   **list** like

12   **prejudiced or endamaged** *he will not be prosecuted for engaging in the forbidden art of black magic*

13   **he looks...conjurer** *an ironic comment:* presumably Faustus does not look like a conjurer at all

Act 4

Chorus

Enter CHORUS.

CHORUS   When Faustus had with pleasure ta'en the view
           Of rarest things and royal courts of kings,
           He stayed his course and so returnèd home,
           Where such as bear his absence but with grief –
           I mean his friends and nearest companions –   5
           Did gratulate his safety with kind words.
           And in their conference of what befell,
           Touching his journey through the world and air,
           They put forth questions of astrology,
           Which Faustus answered with such learnèd skill   10
           As they admired and wondered at his wit.
           Now is his fame spread forth in every land.
           Amongst the rest the Emperor is one,
           Carolus the Fifth, at whose palace now
           Faustus is feasted 'mongst his noblemen.   15
           What there he did in trial of his art
           I leave untold, your eyes shall see performed.

                                                           Exit.

Scene 1

Enter EMPEROR, FAUSTUS, MEPHISTOPHELES and a KNIGHT,
with ATTENDANTS.

EMPEROR   Master Doctor Faustus, I have heard strange report
           of thy knowledge in the black art – how that none
           in my empire, nor in the whole world, can compare
           with thee for the rare effects of magic. They say
           thou hast a familiar spirit by whom thou canst   5
           accomplish what thou list. This, therefore, is my
           request: that thou let me see some proof of thy skill,
           that mine eyes may be witnesses to confirm what
           mine ears have heard reported. And here I swear to
           thee, by the honour of mine imperial crown, that   10
           whatever thou dost, thou shalt be no ways
           prejudiced or endamaged.

KNIGHT   (*Aside*) I'faith, he looks much like a conjurer.

At court, the Emperor asks Faustus to conjure the shapes of Alexander and his paramour, which he agrees to do

16	**nothing answerable to** in no way fitting	31	**Chief…pre-eminence** the most remarkable of all the men who have been pre-eminent in the world's history
17	**for that** because		
18	**thereunto** to it *(i.e. to the Emperor's honour)*	34–35	**As…soul** to such an extent that, I only have to hear a mention of him, for it to grieve my soul
21	**sometime solitary set** seated alone recently	39	**paramour** mistress *(her name was Thais)*
22	**closet** study; private room		
	sundry various		

Performance

40–41 The Emperor's specific request to see Alexander and his paramour exactly as they were in their lifetime is seen by some people as evidence that characters on the Elizabethan stage sometimes wore costumes which reflected the historical period of the plays.

4.1

FAUSTUS   My gracious sovereign, though I must confess
          myself far inferior to the report men have published, 15
          and nothing answerable to the honour of your
          Imperial Majesty, yet, for that love and duty binds
          me thereunto, I am content to do whatsoever your
          Majesty shall command me.

EMPEROR   Then, Doctor Faustus, mark what I shall say.   20
          As I was sometime solitary set
          Within my closet, sundry thoughts arose
          About the honour of mine ancestors –
          How they had won by prowess such exploits,
          Got such riches, subdued so many kingdoms   25
          As we that do succeed or they that shall
          Hereafter possess our throne shall,
          I fear me, never attain to that degree
          Of high renown and great authority.
          Amongst which kings is Alexander the Great,   30
          Chief spectacle of the world's pre-eminence,
          The bright shining of whose glorious acts
          Lightens the world with his reflecting beams –
          As when I hear but motion made of him,
          It grieves my soul I never saw the man.   35
          If, therefore, thou by cunning of thine art
          Canst raise this man from hollow vaults below
          Where lies entombed this famous conqueror,
          And bring with him his beauteous paramour,
          Both in their right shapes, gesture, and attire   40
          They used to wear during their time of life,
          Thou shalt both satisfy my just desire
          And give me cause to praise thee whilst I live.

FAUSTUS   My gracious lord, I am ready to accomplish your
          request, so far forth as by art and power of my spirit 45
          I am able to perform.

KNIGHT   (*Aside*) I'faith, that's just nothing at all.

FAUSTUS   But if it like your Grace, it is not in my ability to
          present before your eyes the true substantial bodies
          of those two deceased princes, which long since are 50
          consumed to dust.

4.1 *Alexander and his paramour appear, much to the Emperor's amazement and admiration, but Faustus is irritated by the sceptical interruptions of one of the Emperor's knights*

52 **marry** By the Virgin Mary *(a mild oath)*

56–57 **in their most flourishing estate** in the prime of life

59 **presently** at once

60 **You bring** are you telling me you're going to bring

63–64 **Diana...Actaeon** *This refers to the fate of Actaeon, a huntsman in classical mythology, who saw the goddess Diana (Artemis) while she was bathing; he was punished by being turned into a stag and torn to pieces by his own hounds. The tale is told in Ovid's Metamorphoses.*

67 **an** if

68 **meet with** get even with

Ideas and interpretations

J P Brockbank comments: 'The scenes [in Acts 3 and 4] remind us that great magicians...are at best reputable court entertainers and not masters of empire' and he goes on to observe that the Emperor's desire to see the wart on the neck of Alexander's paramour is the sole example of Marlowe's scepticism (concerning the exercise of Faustus's powers) turning into 'calculated dramatic bathos' – deliberate anticlimax.

KNIGHT   (*Aside*) Ay, marry, Master Doctor, now there's a sign
          of grace in you, when you will confess the truth.

FAUSTUS   But such spirits as can lively resemble Alexander and
          his paramour shall appear before your Grace in that 55
          manner that they best lived in, in their most
          flourishing estate – which I doubt not shall
          sufficiently content your Imperial Majesty.

EMPEROR   Go to, Master Doctor. Let me see them presently.

KNIGHT   Do you hear, Master Doctor? You bring Alexander   60
          and his paramour before the Emperor?

FAUSTUS   How then, sir?

KNIGHT   I'faith, that's as true as Diana turned me to a stag.

FAUSTUS   No, sir, but when Actaeon died, he left the horns for
          you. (*Aside to* MEPHISTOPHELES) Mephistopheles,   65
          begone!

                                        Exit MEPHISTOPHELES.

KNIGHT   Nay, an you go to conjuring, I'll be gone.

                                             Exit KNIGHT.

FAUSTUS   (*Aside*) I'll meet with you anon for interrupting me
          so. – Here they are, my gracious lord.

          Enter MEPHISTOPHELES with ALEXANDER and his PARAMOUR.

EMPEROR   Master Doctor, I heard this lady while she lived had 70
          a wart or mole in her neck. How shall I know
          whether it be so or no?

FAUSTUS   Your Highness may boldly go and see.

          *The EMPEROR makes an inspection, and then exeunt ALEXANDER and his
          PARAMOUR.*

EMPEROR   Sure these are no spirits, but the true substantial
          bodies of those two deceased princes.   75

4.1 *Angered by the Knight's continued insults, Faustus punishes him by causing horns to sprout from his head. The Emperor promises to reward Faustus for the demonstration of his art*

77 **pleasant** facetious

80 **a bachelor** (1) a trainee knight; (2) an unmarried man *(the joke is that, if he was unmarried, he could not have a wife who would make him a cuckold – see also 2.2.18)*

84 **concave** hollow

87 **There's no...good** *a proverb:* Not so hasty!

89–90 **met with you** got even with you

91 **release him** *i.e. from the spell that has given him horns*

92 **done penance** suffered punishment for his sin

93 **injury** wrong; insult

95 **requited** paid back; taken revenge on

96 **injurious** insulting

100 **straight** at once

Structure

There might be a link between the Knight's fate and Faustus's. The critic Nigel Alexander points out that the fate of Actaeon (64), commonly interpreted in Marlowe's time as a punishment for desiring forbidden things, reflects on that of Faustus. In this sense it can be seen as 'a low-life variant of the tragedy's fable' (Roy T Eriksen).

FAUSTUS Will't please your Highness now to send for the
knight that was so pleasant with me here of late?

EMPEROR One of you call him forth.

An ATTENDANT goes to summon the KNIGHT.

Enter the KNIGHT with a pair of horns on his head.

How now, sir knight? Why, I had thought thou
hadst been a bachelor, but now I see thou hast a   80
wife, that not only gives thee horns but makes thee
wear them. Feel on thy head.

KNIGHT (*To* FAUSTUS) Thou damnèd wretch and execrable
    dog,
Bred in the concave of some monstrous rock,
How dar'st thou thus abuse a gentleman?   85
Villain, I say, undo what thou hast done.

FAUSTUS O, not so fast, sir. There's no haste but good.
Are you remembered how you crossed me in my
conference with the Emperor? I think I have met
with you for it.   90

EMPEROR Good Master Doctor, at my entreaty release him.
He hath done penance sufficient.

FAUSTUS My gracious lord, not so much for the injury he
offered me here in your presence as to delight you
with some mirth hath Faustus worthily requited   95
this injurious knight; which being all I desire, I am
content to release him of his horns. – And, sir
knight, hereafter speak well of scholars. (*Aside to*
MEPHISTOPHELES) Mephistopheles, transform
him straight. (*The horns are removed*) Now, my good   100
lord, having done my duty, I humbly take my leave.

EMPEROR Farewell, Master Doctor. Yet, ere you go,
Expect from me a bounteous reward.

Exeunt EMPEROR, KNIGHT and ATTENDANTS.

FAUSTUS Now, Mephistopheles, the restless course
That time doth run with calm and silent foot,   105

Pestered by a horse-courser, Faustus agrees to sell his horse for forty dollars, but warns the man not to ride the animal through water

106   **thread** *The Three Fates were said to spin out the thread of a person's life, measure it out, and cut it off at the allotted span.*

s.d.   ***Enter a HORSE-COURSER*** *'A horse-dealer had a ready-made reputation for dishonesty' (J D Jump) – rather like the used-car salesman today; the audience would be hoping to see him cheated.*

113   **Fustian** *the Horse-courser's version of Faustus's name; fitting, because 'fustian' was the name given to overblown bragging speech, the kind of thing Faustus has been guilty of in his overweening ambitions*

114   **Mass** By the holy Mass *(a mild oath)*

117   **dollars** silver coins

123   **a great charge** heavy responsibilities *(Mephistopheles's joke – the Horse-courser has no family to maintain)*

128   **at any hand** whatever you do

129   **drink of all waters** *a proverbial expression:* do anything; be infinitely adaptable

133   **Now am I...ever** I'm set up for life *(see 3.2.1)*

133–134   **I'll...for forty** I wouldn't sell my horse at any price.

135   **hey, ding...ding** *a popular song refrain with sexual connotations; he hopes that the horse is virile so that he can put him to stud (both a* **slick buttock** *and the* **eel** *are associated with sex)*

Short'ning my days and thread of vital life,
Calls for the payment of my latest years.
Therefore, sweet Mephistopheles, let us make haste
To Wittenberg.

MEPHISTOPHELES   What, will you go on horseback or on foot? 110

FAUSTUS   Nay, till I am past this fair and pleasant green,
I'll walk on foot.

Enter a HORSE-COURSER.

HORSE-   I have been all this day seeking one Master Fustian.
COURSER   Mass, see where he is – God save you, Master Doctor.

FAUSTUS   What, Horse-courser! You are well met.   115

HORSE-   (*Offering money*) Do you hear, sir? I have brought
COURSER   you forty dollars for your horse.

FAUSTUS   I cannot sell him so. If thou lik'st him for fifty, take
him.

HORSE-   Alas, sir, I have no more. (*To MEPHISTOPHELES*)   120
COURSER   I pray you, speak for me.

MEPHISTOPHELES   (*To FAUSTUS*) I pray you, let him have him.
He is an honest fellow, and he has a great charge,
neither wife nor child.

FAUSTUS   Well, come, give me your money. (*He takes the*   125
money) My boy will deliver him to you. But I must
tell you one thing before you have him: ride him
not into the water, at any hand.

HORSE-   Why, sir, will he not drink of all waters?
COURSER

FAUSTUS   O, yes, he will drink of all waters, but ride him not   130
into the water. Ride him over hedge, or ditch, or
where thou wilt, but not into the water.

HORSE-   Well, sir. (*Aside*) Now am I made man for ever. I'll
COURSER   not leave my horse for forty. If he had but the
quality of hey, ding, ding, hey, ding, ding, I'd make   135

4.1 *Faustus descends into a fit of despair, which he tries to allay with sleep. The horse-courser returns, complaining bitterly that, having ridden the horse into water, it had dematerialised beneath him*

136 **brave** excellent

slick smooth

139 **water** urine *(used to diagnose illness)*

144 **fatal time** period of time allotted by fate

146 **Confound** defeat

passions agitating emotions

147 **Tush!** *an exclamation of impatience suggesting 'What does it matter?' or 'Don't be stupid!'*

Christ...cross *see St Luke's Gospel 23.39–43, where Christ promises salvation to one of the thieves crucified alongside him*

148 **in conceit** in your thoughts

149 **quotha!** he said *(i.e. Claimed to be a doctor, did he?)*

149–150 **Doctor Lopus** *Dr Roderigo Lopez, a Portuguese Jew, was physician to Queen Elizabeth from 1586; he was hanged, drawn and quartered at Tyburn in 1594 having allegedly planned to poison her.*

150–151 **a purgation** an emetic *(i.e. He has cleaned me out!)*

156 **known of** aware of

159 **bottle** bundle

161 **again** back

162 **dearest** *because he will exact revenge*

162–163 **snipper-snapper** *the term implies a servant 'too big for his boots'; compare 'whipper-snapper'*

163 **hey-pass** *a term used by conjurers (compare 'hey presto')*

Faustus

145 Is his *distrust* a distrust of God (the sin of despair), or of Lucifer?

a brave living on him; he has a buttock as slick as an
eel. (*To* FAUSTUS) Well, goodbye, sir. Your boy will
deliver him me? But hark ye, sir: if my horse be sick
or ill at ease, if I bring his water to you, you'll tell
me what it is?   140

FAUSTUS   Away, you villain! What, dost think I am a horse-
doctor?

Exit HORSE-COURSER.

What art thou, Faustus, but a man condemned to
    die?
Thy fatal time doth draw to final end.
Despair doth drive distrust unto my thoughts.   145
Confound these passions with a quiet sleep.
Tush! Christ did call the thief upon the cross;
Then rest thee, Faustus, quiet in conceit.

Sleep in his chair.

Enter HORSE-COURSER all wet, crying.

HORSE-   Alas, alas! 'Doctor' Fustian, quotha! Mass, Doctor
COURSER   Lopus was never such a doctor. H'as given me a   150
purgation, h'as purged me of forty dollars. I shall
never see them more. But yet, like an ass as I was, I
would not be ruled by him, for he bade me I should
ride him into no water. Now I, thinking my horse
had had some rare quality that he would not have   155
had me known of, I, like a venturous youth, rid him
into the deep pond at the town's end. I was no
sooner in the middle of the pond but my horse
vanished away and I sat upon a bottle of hay, never
so near drowning in my life. But I'll seek out my   160
doctor and have my forty dollars again, or I'll make
it the dearest horse! O, yonder is his snipper-
snapper. – Do you hear? You, hey-pass, where's
your master?

MEPHISTOPHELES   Why, sir, what would you? You cannot speak 165
with him.

HORSE-   But I will speak with him.
COURSER

Attempting to rouse Faustus, the horse-courser pulls at his leg – which immediately comes off. The terrified man readily agrees to pay Faustus another forty dollars

169–170 **glass windows** spectacles

171 **this eight nights** for a week

179 **So-ho** *a call used by huntsmen*

181 **undone** ruined; done for

189 **hostry** inn; hostelry

Jude Law as Faustus (Young Vic, 2002)

Performance

192–193 *Faustus has his leg again*: After hopping around in feigned pursuit of the Horse-courser, Faustus's real leg pops back down into view.

Ideas and interpretations

'This bizarre episode…in which the horse-courser pulls off Faustus's leg, is comic and grotesque…Rooted in medieval dramatic tradition, the comical dismemberment serves to prefigure Faustus's eventual fate' (Stevie Simkin).

4.1

MEPHISTOPHELES	Why, he's fast asleep. Come some other time.
HORSE-COURSER	I'll speak with him now, or I'll break his glass windows about his ears. 170
MEPHISTOPHELES	I tell thee he has not slept this eight nights.
HORSE-COURSER	An he have not slept this eight weeks, I'll speak with him.
MEPHISTOPHELES	See where he is, fast asleep.
HORSE-COURSER	Ay, this is he. – God save ye, Master Doctor. Master 175 Doctor, Master Doctor Fustian! Forty dollars, forty dollars for a bottle of hay!
MEPHISTOPHELES	Why, thou seest he hears thee not.
HORSE-COURSER	(*Holler in his ear*) So-ho, ho! So-ho, ho! No, will you not wake? I'll make you wake ere I go. 180

Pull him by the leg, and pull it away.

Alas, I am undone! What shall I do?

FAUSTUS	O my leg, my leg! Help, Mephistopheles! Call the officers! My leg, my leg!
MEPHISTOPHELES	(*Seizing the* HORSE-COURSER) Come, villain, to the constable. 185
HORSE-COURSER	O Lord, sir, let me go, and I'll give you forty dollars more.
MEPHISTOPHELES	Where be they?
HORSE-COURSER	I have none about me. Come to my hostry, and I'll give them you. 190
MEPHISTOPHELES	Begone, quickly.

HORSE-COURSER runs away.

FAUSTUS	What, is he gone? Farewell, he! Faustus has his leg again, and the Horse-courser, I take it, a bottle of hay for his labour. Well, this trick shall cost him forty dollars more. 195

4.2 *Wagner informs Faustus that the Duke of Vanholt has asked to see him. At the Duke's court, Faustus instructs Mephistopheles to fetch grapes to satisfy the longing of the pregnant Duchess*

197 **earnestly entreat** strongly request

200 **must be no...cunning** must not be mean in withholding my magical skill

5 **great-bellied** *not an offensive expression here; it simply means:* pregnant

6 **dainties** delicacies

8 **for** because

12 **meat** food

16 **so...content** if it would please

Performance

It is most unusual on the Elizabethan stage for characters to re-enter immediately after exiting, as Faustus and Mephistopheles do here. It has led some editors to assume that there must be a lost scene which would have come between the existing 4.1 and 4.2. On the modern stage, music can play between these scenes to indicate a change in time and place.

15 Mephistopheles is possibly 'invisible' in this scene.

Ideas and interpretations

Have the Duke and Duchess of Vanholt colluded in Faustus's use of demonic powers? 'They are on-stage spectators who are able to enjoy the Theatre of Hell without being made to suffer for it' (Roger Sales).

Enter WAGNER.

How now, Wagner, what's the news with thee?

WAGNER   Sir, the Duke of Vanholt doth earnestly entreat your
company.

FAUSTUS   The Duke of Vanholt! An honourable gentleman, to
whom I must be no niggard of my cunning. Come, 200
Mephistopheles, let's away to him.

Exeunt.

Scene 2

*Enter FAUSTUS with MEPHISTOPHELES. Enter to them the
DUKE OF VANHOLT and the pregnant DUCHESS. The DUKE
speaks.*

DUKE   Believe me, Master Doctor, this merriment hath
much pleased me.

FAUSTUS   My gracious lord, I am glad it contents you so well.
– But it may be, madam, you take no delight in this.
I have heard that great-bellied women do long for   5
some dainties or other. What is it, madam? Tell me,
and you shall have it.

DUCHESS   Thanks, good Master Doctor. And, for I see your
courteous intent to pleasure me, I will not hide
from you the thing my heart desires. And were it   10
now summer, as it is January and the dead time of
the winter, I would desire no better meat than a
dish of ripe grapes.

FAUSTUS   Alas, madam, that's nothing. (*Aside to
MEPHISTOPHELES*) Mephistopheles, begone!   15

Exit MEPHISTOPHELES.

Were it a greater thing than this, so it would content you,
you should have it.

Enter MEPHISTOPHELES with the grapes.

4.2 *The Duchess is delighted by the grapes and Faustus explains that they have been brought from a part of the world where the season is summer*

24 **circles** hemispheres

25 **in the contrary circle** in the other hemisphere *(Some editors take the view that Marlowe mistakenly assumes the hemispheres to be east and west. In the B-text, there is no confusion, as Faustus appears to be making two points: the first about the hemispheres;* the second about climates that 'have [bear] fruit twice a year' (a line not in the A-text), such as India and Saba – Sheba, a region in the Arabian peninsula.)

33 **let us in** let us go in

37 **Rest beholding** remain in his debt

Here they be, madam. Will't please you taste on them?

The DUCHESS tastes the grapes.

DUKE	Believe me, Master Doctor, this makes me wonder above the rest, that, being in the dead time of winter 20 and in the month of January, how you should come by these grapes.
FAUSTUS	If it like your Grace, the year is divided into two circles over the whole world, that when it is here winter with us, in the contrary circle it is summer 25 with them, as in India, Saba, and farther countries in the East; and by means of a swift spirit that I have, I had them brought hither, as ye see. – How do you like them, madam? Be they good?
DUCHESS	Believe me, Master Doctor, they be the best grapes 30 that e'er I tasted in my life before.
FAUSTUS	I am glad they content you so, madam.
DUKE	Come, madam, let us in, Where you must well reward this learnèd man For the great kindness he hath showed to you. 35
DUCHESS	And so I will, my lord, and whilst I live Rest beholding for this courtesy.
FAUSTUS	I humbly thank your Grace.
DUKE	Come, Master Doctor, follow us and receive your reward. 40

Exeunt.

Exam practice

Extracts

1   Reread 4.1. What part does Mephistopheles play in this scene? Why is he
    there at all? In your answer you should:
    - comment on the terms of the pact that Faustus has made with Lucifer (see
      2.1.96–115)
    - discuss the value of having Mephistopheles observing Faustus's actions
      and the use Faustus is making of the powers allotted him
    - show an understanding of staging and the dramatic effectiveness of
      Mephistopheles's presence.

2. Reread the comic scenes in Acts 3 and 4. What importance do they have in
    terms of the overall structure of *Doctor Faustus*? In your answer you should
    discuss and evaluate the following arguments; that the comic scenes:
    - provide a respite from the intense emotions of Acts 1, 2 and 5
    - form a transitional phase in the action of the play – in particular, moving the
      action out of the study
    - illustrate the contrast between the apparently insignificant achievements of
      Faustus, and what he might have hoped to attain
    - allow Marlowe to represent the passage of twenty-four years between the
      signing of the pact and his final hours
    - carry grim reminders and forebodings of Faustus's eventual fate
    - reflect a pattern of low comedy amidst high seriousness, familiar to
      Marlowe's audience from the morality plays and easily understood as a way
      of conveying themes and meanings.

3. Reread the sections in 3.1 and 4.1 which involve the Pope, the Knight and the
    Horse-courser. Discuss how far you would agree with William Tydeman's
    assertion that 'All the incidents demonstrate a streak of spitefulness [in
    Faustus], an urge to humiliate and score off others, very much in keeping with
    the cruelty displayed by the demonic fraternity towards him.' In your answer
    you should:
    - describe and comment upon the ways in which Faustus treats these
      characters
    - offer your own opinion about whether or not his actions seem to be spiteful
      and designed to humiliate
    - discuss the possibility that his treatment of others reflects the cruelty
      inflicted upon him by Lucifer and the devils
    - show an awareness of attitudes towards punishment and cruelty in
      Marlowe's time (see pages 136–137).

Extended writing

4. Here are three examples of critics who have observed that Faustus does not
    seem to accomplish much with the powers he acquires through his pact with
    Lucifer:
    *   Faustus's 'shows do not change the world, but merely allow himself and
        others to pass the time within it' (Roger Sales).
    *   'After the ambitions voiced earlier in the play, Faustus's exercise of the
        privilege of power is disappointing. It is, of course, appropriate that it should
        be' (J P Brockbank).
    *   'Faustus is the man who is all dressed up with no place to go. His plight is
        that he cannot find anything really worthy of the supernatural powers that
        he has come to possess. Faustus never carries out in practice his dreams of
        great accomplishments' (Cleanth Brooks).
    How far would you agree with these opinions? Compare Faustus's ambitions,
    as expressed in the opening Acts, with his actual accomplishments, described
    in Acts 3 and 4, and address the points made by the three critics quoted
    above.

Performance

5. Writing about the comic scenes, Michael Hattaway has pointed out that what
    seems flat and trivial on the page may come to life in performance. What
    opportunities are there in performance for visual effects in Acts 3 and 4?

6. Act 4 scene 1 poses some interesting questions concerning performance.
    Write director's notes in response to the following:
    *   In the Rose playhouse, how does the Knight enter '*with a pair of horns on
        his head*' (s.d. after line 78)? What are the possibilities bearing in mind the
        nature of the stage? (See the photographs and drawings on pages vi, 132
        and 133.)
    *   How should the Horse-courser be acted? Should we have any sympathy for
        him, for example?
    *   What exactly happens when the Horse-courser pulls Faustus's leg off (s.d.
        after line 180)?
    *   What does Faustus do at the end of the scene?
    *   What is Mephistopheles's reaction throughout?

5.1

Nearing the end of his twenty-four years, Faustus has made a will, bequeathing his possessions to Wagner, and is now sharing a last supper with his fellow-scholars. The scholars ask Faustus to let them see Helen of Troy, the most beautiful woman who has ever lived

4 **carouse and swill** *both terms for drinking heavily*

5 **even now** at this very moment

6 **belly-cheer** hearty consumption of good food

8 **Belike** probably

9 **conference** conversation

11 **determined with ourselves** come to an agreement

12 **Helen of Greece** *These days more commonly known as Helen of Troy, she was the wife of the Spartan king Menelaus and reputedly the most beautiful woman in the world; in* The Iliad *Homer describes how her abduction by the Trojan prince Paris led to the ten-year siege of Troy and its ultimate destruction by the Greek army.*

14 **peerless** without equal

dame lady

16 **much beholding unto you** greatly in your debt

18 **For that** because

unfeigned real *(i.e. not put on to flatter him)*

22 **No otherways for** no different in

pomp splendour; magnificence

23 **Sir Paris** *Sir 'assimilates Paris to the hero of a medieval romance' (J D Jump)*

24 **spoils** booty *(Helen)*

Dardania Troy

25 **Be silent…words** *It was dangerous to speak during conjuring.*

s.d. **passeth over the stage** *She enters from one of the upstage doors and exits through the other.*

26 **Too simple…praise** I am not eloquent enough to give her the praise she deserves

Wagner/Chorus

1–8 Wagner's speech is similar in many respects to the earlier choruses, but, as it describes events which are in progress in the next room, it has the effect of being part of the action, spoken by Wagner 'in character'.

Performance and structure

4–8 Faustus's final banquet can be seen as a blasphemous parody of Christ's Last Supper with his disciples. This develops the parallelism throughout, in which Faustus's magic accomplishments, for example, are a debased version of Christ's miracles. Stage productions have sometimes brought out this parallelism visually.

Performance

In the 1967 film, Helen was played by Elizabeth Taylor, who also personified all Faustus's earlier visions of female beauty and lust (including Alexander's paramour); in the 1989 RSC production, Helen was played by a male actor (it was an all-male cast), and this intensified a homoerotic strand which had been present throughout. In 1974 Helen was simply a marionette in a blond wig, mask and nightdress, carried in by Mephistopheles, symbolising 'the illusory nature of Faustus's pleasure' (Michael Billington).

Act 5

Scene 1

Enter WAGNER solus.

WAGNER   I think my master means to die shortly,
For he hath given to me all his goods.
And yet methinks if that death were near
He would not banquet and carouse and swill
Amongst the students, as even now he doth,   5
Who are at supper with such belly-cheer
As Wagner ne'er beheld in all his life.
See where they come. Belike the feast is ended.

Exit.

Enter FAUSTUS with two or three SCHOLARS and MEPHISTOPHELES.

FIRST SCHOLAR   Master Doctor Faustus, since our conference
about fair ladies – which was the beautifull'st in all 10
the world – we have determined with ourselves that
Helen of Greece was the admirablest lady that ever
lived. Therefore, Master Doctor, if you will do us
that favour as to let us see that peerless dame of
Greece, whom all the world admires for majesty, we 15
should think ourselves much beholding unto you.

FAUSTUS   Gentlemen,
For that I know your friendship is unfeigned,
And Faustus' custom is not to deny
The just requests of those that wish him well,   20
You shall behold that peerless dame of Greece
No otherways for pomp and majesty
Than when Sir Paris crossed the seas with her
And brought the spoils to rich Dardania.
Be silent then, for danger is in words.   25

MEPHISTOPHELES goes to the door.

Music sounds. MEPHISTOPHELES returns, and HELEN passeth over the stage.

SECOND SCHOLAR   Too simple is my wit to tell her praise,
Whom all the world admires for majesty.

5.1

*Amazed by the vision of Helen, the scholars depart. An Old Man appears
and begs Faustus to give up necromancy and repent. Faustus despairs,
and the Old Man prevents him from ending his life with the dagger
offered by Mephistopheles*

28 **No marvel** no wonder

   pursued sought to avenge

29 **ten years' war** *the siege of Troy; see
   the note to line 12 above*

   rape forceful abduction

30 **passeth all compare** is beyond all
   comparison

32 **only paragon of excellence** standard
   of beauty which can never be matched

36 **prevail** succeed

41 **heaviness** misery

44 **flagitious** wicked

45 **As** that

   commiseration expression of pity

50 **Hell calls for right** *Lucifer claims what
   is owed to him – Faustus's soul.*

52 **do thee right** pay you what is due

53 **stay** stop

   desperate caused by the sin of despair
   (see note to s.d. below)

55 **vial** vessel for containing liquids

   grace the power to accept God's love
   (and therefore resist temptation)

Language

30 The heavily ironic use of *heavenly* sometimes goes unnoticed in performance. It is
underlined by the Scholar's wish that Faustus might be *Happy and blest…evermore* (34).

Performance

The Old Man, like the Good and Evil Angels, is a figure from the morality plays (see pages
139–140) and in performance it is difficult to know how he ought to be presented. In the 1967
film, he is simply a well-dressed old gentleman; the 1989 stage version had him carried in on
the shoulders of several actors, all of whom joined in his exhortation to Faustus, rather like a
chorus in a Greek tragedy.

Ideas and interpretations

s.d. By offering a dagger, Mephistopheles hopes that Faustus will commit suicide, thus
committing the ultimate sin of despair – a refusal to believe God's word that any soul can be
saved – the sin against the Holy Ghost: 'I say unto you, All manner of sin and blasphemy shall
be forgiven unto men: but the blasphemy against the Holy Ghost shall not be forgiven unto
men' (Matthew 12.31). See also lines 57 and 64 below.

Structure

50–52 As part of the chiastic structure (see pages 149–150), this urged suicide balances the
earlier threatened one at 2.3.22–26.

THIRD SCHOLAR	No marvel though the angry Greeks pursued
	With ten years' war the rape of such a queen,
	Whose heavenly beauty passeth all compare. 30

FIRST SCHOLAR	Since we have seen the pride of nature's works
	And only paragon of excellence,

Enter an OLD MAN.

Let us depart; and for this glorious deed
Happy and blest be Faustus evermore.

FAUSTUS   Gentlemen, farewell. The same I wish to you.   35

Exeunt SCHOLARS.

OLD MAN	Ah, Doctor Faustus, that I might prevail
	To guide thy steps unto the way of life,
	By which sweet path thou mayst attain the goal
	That shall conduct thee to celestial rest!
	Break heart, drop blood, and mingle it with tears – 40
	Tears falling from repentant heaviness
	Of thy most vile and loathsome filthiness,
	The stench whereof corrupts the inward soul
	With such flagitious crimes of heinous sins
	As no commiseration may expel 45
	But mercy, Faustus, of thy Saviour sweet,
	Whose blood alone must wash away thy guilt

FAUSTUS	Where art thou, Faustus? Wretch, what hast thou done?
	Damned art thou, Faustus, damned! Despair and die!
	Hell calls for right, and with a roaring voice 50
	Says, 'Faustus, come! Thine hour is come.'

MEPHISTOPHELES gives him a dagger.

And Faustus will come to do thee right.

FAUSTUS prepares to stab himself.

OLD MAN	Ah, stay, good Faustus, stay thy desperate steps!
	I see an angel hovers o'er thy head,
	And with a vial full of precious grace 55

5.1

Faustus is now torn between repentance and despair, but at Mephistopheles's threats, promises to reaffirm the pact made with Lucifer, and asks the devil to torment the Old Man. Faustus asks Mephistopheles to raise Helen again

66 **shun** determinedly avoid

69 **Revolt** return to your allegiance to Lucifer

in piecemeal into tiny pieces

71 **presumption** *i.e. in daring to consider breaking his word to Lucifer*

74 **unfeignèd** open; honest

75 **thy drift** the direction you are taking

76 **age** the Old Man

83 **glut** fully satisfy

84 **unto my paramour** as my lover *(sexual partner)*

86 **clean** wholly

Ideas and interpretations

63–66 'Is it that Faustus cannot repent because he is without grace, and cannot have grace because he will not repent?' (J P Brockbank). This concept of good and evil striving within the human soul was a key Manichaean belief (see pages 134–135).

Faustus

70 His form of address for his devilish companion – ***Sweet*** *Mephistopheles* – is consistent with the terms of endearment he uses earlier (see 2.3.31, 2.3.70 and 3.1.1, for example).

76–78 'Faustus…shows himself now, perhaps for the first time, to be truly a lost soul' (Cleanth Brooks).

78 It is significant that, in confirming his allegiance, he now talks of *our* hell.

82–88 'Sexual desire and sycophancy combine to shut out the truth Faustus cannot face. It is precisely this love of "vain pleasure", this need for constant stimulation and the avoidance of boredom, this inconsistent attitude to life's immense possibilities which connect the aspiring but easily distracted scholar with the boisterous prankster of the central scenes' (William Tydeman).

Performance

s.d. after 75 Does Faustus cut his arm and sign the bond again at this point? The text implies that he does, but on stage such a piece of stage business might cause the scene to lose some momentum.

	Offers to pour the same into thy soul. Then call for mercy and avoid despair.	
FAUSTUS	Ah, my sweet friend, I feel thy words To comfort my distressèd soul. Leave me a while to ponder on my sins.	60
OLD MAN	I go, sweet Faustus, but with heavy cheer, Fearing the ruin of thy hopeless soul.	

Exit.

FAUSTUS	Accursèd Faustus, where is mercy now? I do repent, and yet I do despair. Hell strives with grace for conquest in my breast. What shall I do to shun the snares of death?	65
MEPHISTOPHELES	Thou traitor, Faustus, I arrest thy soul For disobedience to my sovereign lord. Revolt, or I'll in piecemeal tear thy flesh.	
FAUSTUS	Sweet Mephistopheles, entreat thy lord To pardon my unjust presumption, And with my blood again I will confirm My former vow I made to Lucifer.	70
MEPHISTOPHELES	Do it then quickly, with unfeignèd heart, Lest greater danger do attend thy drift.	75

FAUSTUS cuts his arm and writes with his blood.

FAUSTUS	Torment, sweet friend, that base and crooked age That durst dissuade me from thy Lucifer, With greatest torments that our hell affords.	
MEPHISTOPHELES	His faith is great. I cannot touch his soul. But what I may afflict his body with I will attempt, which is but little worth.	80
FAUSTUS	One thing, good servant, let me crave of thee To glut the longing of my heart's desire: That I might have unto my paramour That heavenly Helen which I saw of late, Whose sweet embracings may extinguish clean These thoughts that do dissuade me from my vow, And keep mine oath I made to Lucifer.	85

When Helen appears, Faustus is enthralled by her beauty and, to the dismay of the Old Man, takes Helen as his lover

91 **launched…ships** It was Helen's flight with Paris which caused the vast Greek fleet to set sail in pursuit.

92 **topless** immeasurably high *('The topless towers are recurrent symbols [in Marlowe's plays] for illimitable aspiration, and Marlowe habitually juxtaposes them to the all-consuming element of fire' (Harry Levin).)*

Ilium Troy

94 **sucks** suck *(see 3.1.12 etc)*

95 **again** back

97 **dross** worthless rubbish *(literally: the impurities left over when smelting metal)*

99 **sacked** destroyed and plundered

100 **weak Menelaus** *Helen's husband*

101 **colours** *a glove or scarf worn by a medieval knight as a sign that a particular lady favours him*

plumèd crest helmet topped with a plume of feathers

102 **Achilles…heel** *In some versions of the Troy myth, Paris fires an arrow which fatally strikes the Greek hero Achilles in the heel – the only part of his body which is not invulnerable.*

106–107 **flaming…Semele** *Semele was one of Jupiter's lovers, unfortunate* **(hapless)** *in that she foolishly asked to see the king of the gods in his full brilliance (instead of his customary mortal disguise) and was consumed by his fire and lightning; this, of course, is to be Faustus's fate.*

109 **wanton** sexually playful

Arethusa *The nymph Arethusa awakened the lust of the river god Alpheus and was transformed by Artemis/Diana into a fountain (though line 108 suggests that Jupiter or the sun god was her lover).*

azured made blue

113 **fliest** flees from

tribunal judgement

114 **sift** *literally:* strain through a sieve to separate the coarse from the fine; examine closely (*i.e.* try to select me as one of his; make a trial of me)

115 **in this furnace…faith** *God is putting the Old Man's faith to the severest of tests. In the Bible, Shadrach, Meshach and Abednego are thrown into a fiery furnace for refusing to worship a golden image, but they are joined by an angel and come out safe – see Daniel 3.*

Ideas and interpretations

93–95 'Even at the brink of damnation, Faustus looks to mortal love, or satisfaction of his lusts, for salvation' (Stevie Simkin). W W Greg argues that it is Faustus's sexual relationship with a devil in Helen's shape (the sin of demoniality) that irrevocably damns him. If that is so, there is added irony in the thought that Helen's kiss could make Faustus *immortal* and a chilling literalness in the fact that her lips *sucks forth* his soul (94), never to be returned, despite his plea (95). Against Greg's viewpoint, T W Craik points out that Faustus does not intend to commit demoniality and therefore cannot be damned for sinning inadvertently, while Nicolas Kiessling makes the point that demoniality was not necessarily unforgivable anyway.

Language

94 This line 'mingles ecstasy and despair, the heavy stresses in the middle of the line rendering a powerful impression of regret and a yearning to linger in that inevitably fleeting moment' (Stevie Simkin).

MEPHISTOPHELES   Faustus, this, or what else thou shalt desire,
         Shall be performed in twinkling of an eye.   90

Enter HELEN, brought in by MEPHISTOPHELES.

FAUSTUS   Was this the face that launched a thousand ships
         And burnt the topless towers of Ilium?
         Sweet Helen, make me immortal with a kiss.

They kiss.

         Her lips sucks forth my soul. See where it flies!
         Come, Helen, come, give me my soul again.   95

They kiss again.

         Here will I dwell, for heaven be in these lips,
         And all is dross that is not Helena.

Enter OLD MAN.

         I will be Paris, and for love of thee
         Instead of Troy shall Wittenberg be sacked,
         And I will combat with weak Menelaus,   100
         And wear thy colours on my plumèd crest.
         Yea, I will wound Achilles in the heel
         And then return to Helen for a kiss.
         O, thou art fairer than the evening air,
         Clad in the beauty of a thousand stars.   105
         Brighter art thou than flaming Jupiter
         When he appeared to hapless Semele,
         More lovely than the monarch of the sky
         In wanton Arethusa's azured arms;
         And none but thou shalt be my paramour.   110

Exeunt FAUSTUS and HELEN.

OLD MAN   Accursèd Faustus, miserable man,
         That from thy soul exclud'st the grace of heaven
         And fliest the throne of His tribunal seat!

Enter the DEVILS. They menace the OLD MAN.

         Satan begins to sift me with his pride.
         As in this furnace God shall try my faith,   115

117 **smiles** smile *(see line 94)*

118 **your repulse** the way you have been fought off

laughs your state to scorn defeats your power by mockery

3 **chamber-fellow** room-mate *(e.g. at university)*

Had I if I had

5 **Comes he not?** *Is Faustus imagining the approach of Lucifer?*

10 **surfeit** sickness caused by overeating or heavy drinking

16 **serpent...Eve** *in the Bible, the serpent tempted Eve, the first woman, to eat the forbidden fruit in the Garden of Eden (Genesis 3)*

Richard Burton as Faustus and Elizabeth Taylor as Helen in the 1967 film

---

Ideas and interpretations

How impressive is the Old Man as a force for good in this scene? 'One of the problems for spectators…is that Faustus has the most memorable lines. The Old Man might have the kind of choric [like a Chorus] authority that was granted to characters like Good Counsel in earlier drama and yet, rhetorically, he is eminently forgettable' (Roger Sales).

My faith, vile hell, shall triumph over thee.
Ambitious fiends, see how the heavens smiles
At your repulse and laughs your state to scorn!
Hence, hell! For hence I fly unto my God.

Exeunt different ways.

Scene 2

Enter FAUSTUS with the SCHOLARS.

FAUSTUS	Ah, gentlemen!
FIRST SCHOLAR	What ails Faustus?
FAUSTUS	Ah, my sweet chamber-fellow! Had I lived with thee, then had I lived still, but now I die eternally. Look, comes he not? Comes he not? 5
SECOND SCHOLAR	What means Faustus?
THIRD SCHOLAR	Belike he is grown into some sickness by being over-solitary.
FIRST SCHOLAR	If it be so, we'll have physicians to cure him. (*To FAUSTUS*) 'Tis but a surfeit. Never fear, man. 10
FAUSTUS	A surfeit of deadly sin that hath damned both body and soul.
SECOND SCHOLAR	Yet, Faustus, look up to heaven. Remember God's mercies are infinite.
FAUSTUS	But Faustus' offence can ne'er be pardoned. The 15 serpent that tempted Eve may be saved, but not Faustus. Ah, gentlemen, hear me with patience, and tremble not at my speeches. Though my heart pants and quivers to remember that I have been a student here these thirty years, O, would I had never seen 20 Wittenberg, never read book! And what wonders I have done, all Germany can witness, yea, all the world, for which Faustus hath lost both Germany

5.2 *Faustus tells the appalled scholars of his bargain with Lucifer and they promise to stay in an adjoining room until morning and pray for him*

30 **abjured** sworn an oath to renounce

34 **stays** stops

38 **cunning** skill; knowledge

39–40 **God forbid!…indeed** *The Scholars' exclamation is a mild oath meaning 'Pray God it isn't so!', but Faustus plays bitterly on its literal meaning.*

41 **vain** empty; pointless

42 **felicity** happiness

bill deed; contract

46 **divines** priests

47–48 **the devil…God** *see 2.3.83 and 5.1.69; 'Unlike the Old Man [of 5.1], Faustus is a physical coward' (William Tydeman)*

49 **gave ear** listened

Performance

34–35 In many productions, the devils physically hold down Faustus's arms here, an effect which helps to demonstrate inability to avoid his fate.

and the world, yea, heaven itself – heaven, the seat
of God, the throne of the blessed, the kingdom of   25
joy – and must remain in hell for ever. Hell, ah,
hell for ever! Sweet friends, what shall become of
Faustus, being in hell for ever?

THIRD SCHOLAR Yet, Faustus, call on God.

FAUSTUS On God, whom Faustus hath abjured? On God,   30
whom Faustus hath blasphemed? Ah, my God, I
would weep, but the devil draws in my tears. Gush
forth blood instead of tears, yea, life and soul. O, he
stays my tongue! I would lift up my hands, but see,
they hold them, they hold them.   35

ALL Who, Faustus?

FAUSTUS Lucifer and Mephistopheles. Ah, gentlemen! I gave
them my soul for my cunning.

ALL God forbid!

FAUSTUS God forbade it indeed, but Faustus hath done it. For 40
vain pleasure of four-and-twenty years hath Faustus
lost eternal joy and felicity. I writ them a bill with
mine own blood. The date is expired, the time will
come, and he will fetch me.

FIRST SCHOLAR Why did not Faustus tell us of this before, that   45
divines might have prayed for thee?

FAUSTUS Oft have I thought to have done so, but the devil
threatened to tear me in pieces if I named God, to
fetch both body and soul if I once gave ear to
divinity. And now 'tis too late. Gentlemen, away,   50
lest you perish with me.

SECOND SCHOLAR O, what shall we do to save Faustus?

FAUSTUS Talk not of me, but save yourselves and depart.

THIRD SCHOLAR God will strengthen me. I will stay with Faustus.

5.2 *Left alone, Faustus embarks upon his final hour. He hears the clock strike eleven and is tormented by the reality that repentance is impossible and damnation inevitable*

55 **Tempt not God** Do not test God

69 **spheres** *see page 136*

71 **nature's eye** the sun

75 ***O lente...equi!*** *Latin:* O, run slowly, slowly, you horses of the night! *(see note below)*

76 **still** continually; incessantly

78 **O, I'll leap up...down** *'The image of this line may have been suggested by a familiar Renaissance emblem showing a man with one arm winged and raised towards heaven, the other weighted down towards hell' (David Bevington and Eric Rasmussen). Compare 5.2.34–35.*

80 **One drop...soul** *According to Christian doctrine, the blood of the crucified Jesus has the power to save the souls of repentant sinners; see line 101.*

81 **rend not** do not tear apart *(see 2.3.83, 5.1.69 and 5.2.47–48)*

83 **Where...gone** *'The movement towards repentance ended with the cry, "O, spare me, Lucifer!" [line 82] Because he has thus called on Lucifer, Faustus now loses the vision of Christ's blood' (J D Jump).*

84 **ireful** angry

85–86 **Mountains...wrath of God!** *These lines echo passages from the Bible; see Revelation 6.16, Luke 23.30 and Hosea 10.8.*

Language and structure: Faustus's final soliloquy

(See also pages 145–147 for comments on particular lines and the effect of the metre.)

67 Faustus's second line, with its string of monosyllables, famously echoes the striking of the clock. 'The agonised and eloquent clock-watching matches perfectly the legalism which has dominated Faustus from the beginning of the play' (Cleanth Brooks).

68 'the *perpetually* that falls with finality at the end of the first sentence returns in the mocking oxymoron [apparent contradiction] *perpetual day*' (J P Brockbank).

69 'the spiritual conflict is transformed into something that happens before our eyes' (Wolfgang Clemen).

71 The movement of the verse in *rise, rise again* serves to encourage precisely the regular daily motion that Faustus is desperate to stop.

75 There is a double irony in this line (*O lente...*). Firstly, the headlong rhythm of the verse runs completely counter to the slowness that Faustus is pleading for. Secondly, in the original poem from which this line is taken (the *Amores* by Ovid (43 BC–AD 17), which Marlowe had translated), the speaker wants the night to pass slowly, not to postpone damnation, but in order to relish the time spent with his lover. The sexual and sensual are never far from Faustus's mind, even at the point of death.

76–77 Note the accelerating cadence: only two disyllables (*devil and Faustus*) disrupt the heavy beat of monosyllabic words.

79 Streaming blood in this play is emblematic of eternal life. We should recall Faustus's earlier cry when his blood congeals: *Why streams it not* (2.1.66) and the moment when, in a futile attempt to repent, he begs his eyes to *Gush forth blood instead of tears* (5.2.32–33). Below, Faustus's plea to be hidden from *the heavy wrath of God* (86) echoes the Good Angel's warning right at the outset of Faustus's planned conjuring (1.1.74).

79–84 In the first half of the speech 'Religious concepts take on physical existence: Christ's blood does stream in the firmament; God does stretch out his arm' (William Tydeman).

| FIRST SCHOLAR | (*To the* THIRD SCHOLAR) Tempt not God, sweet friend, but let us into the next room and there pray for him. | 55 |

| FAUSTUS | Ay, pray for me, pray for me! And what noise soever ye hear, come not unto me, for nothing can rescue me. | 60 |

| SECOND SCHOLAR | Pray thou, and we will pray that God may have mercy upon thee. | |

| FAUSTUS | Gentlemen, farewell. If I live till morning, I'll visit you; if not, Faustus is gone to hell. | |

| ALL | Faustus, farewell. | 65 |

Exeunt SCHOLARS.

The clock strikes eleven.

| FAUSTUS | Ah, Faustus, | |

Now hast thou but one bare hour to live,
And then thou must be damned perpetually.
Stand still, you ever-moving spheres of heaven,
That time may cease and midnight never come!   70
Fair nature's eye, rise, rise again, and make
Perpetual day; or let this hour be but
A year, a month, a week, a natural day,
That Faustus may repent and save his soul!
O lente, lente currite noctis equi!   75
The stars move still; time runs; the clock will strike;
The devil will come, and Faustus must be damned.
O, I'll leap up to my God! Who pulls me down?
See, see where Christ's blood streams in the
      firmament!
One drop would save my soul, half a drop. Ah, my   80
      Christ!
Ah, rend not my heart for naming of my Christ!
Yet will I call on him. O, spare me, Lucifer!
Where is it now? 'Tis gone; and see where God
Stretcheth out his arm and bends his ireful brows!
Mountains and hills, come, come and fall on me,   85
And hide me from the heavy wrath of God!
No, no!

5.2 *Now the half hour strikes, and almost immediately afterwards, the hour of twelve. Faustus curses himself, then Lucifer, for having deprived him of the joys of heaven*

92–96 **Now draw...heaven** *The clouds are thought of as a human system which can digest Faustus's physical body and vomit it out in thunder, leaving the soul to ascend to heaven.*

93 **entrails** innards

labouring tempestuous

s.d. ***watch*** clock

98 **anon** very soon

101 **whose blood...me** *see line 80 above*

105 **limited** appointed; officially fixed

106 **wanting** lacking a

108 **Pythagoras'** *metempsychosis The Greek philosopher and mathematician Pythagoras (sixth century BC) put forward the idea that human souls transmigrate after death into the body of an animal, in a constant process of reincarnation and purification (see Shakespeare's* Twelfth Night *4.2, where Feste taunts Malvolio about Pythagoras' view).*

110 **Unto** into

113 **still** forever

114 **engendered me** brought me into being

118 **quick** alive

Ideas and interpretations

90–91 These lines refer to the astrological belief that a person's destiny is decided by the positions of the planets at the time of their birth. Is Faustus attempting to shift responsibility for his actions on to an inescapable Fate?

Language and structure: Faustus's final soliloquy

106–120 'Faustus...realises by now that he can only express [his vision of salvation] in purely hypothetical grammatical forms (*Why wert thou not..., Or why is this..., O soul, be changed...*)' (Hilary Gatti).

Then will I headlong run into the earth.
Earth, gape! O, no, it will not harbour me.
You stars that reigned at my nativity, 90
Whose influence hath allotted death and hell,
Now draw up Faustus like a foggy mist
Into the entrails of yon labouring cloud,
That when you vomit forth into the air,
My limbs may issue from your smoky mouths, 95
So that my soul may but ascend to heaven.

The watch strikes.

Ah, half the hour is past!
'Twill all be past anon.
O God,
If thou wilt not have mercy on my soul, 100
Yet for Christ's sake, whose blood hath ransomed
    me,
Impose some end to my incessant pain.
Let Faustus live in hell a thousand years,
A hundred thousand, and at last be saved.
O, no end is limited to damnèd souls. 105
Why wert thou not a creature wanting soul?
Or why is this immortal that thou hast?
Ah, Pythagoras' *metempsychosis*, were that true,
This soul should fly from me and I be changed
Unto some brutish beast. 110
All beasts are happy, for, when they die,
Their souls are soon dissolved in elements;
But mine must live still to be plagued in hell.
Curst be the parents that engendered me!
No, Faustus, curse thyself. Curse Lucifer, 115
That hath deprived thee of the joys of heaven.

The clock striketh twelve.

O, it strikes, it strikes! Now, body, turn to air,
Or Lucifer will bear thee quick to hell.

Thunder and lightning.

O soul, be changed into little waterdrops,
And fall into the ocean, ne'er be found! 120
My God, my God, look not so fierce on me!

5.2   *With a final desperate cry of 'Ah, Mephistopheles!', Faustus is dragged down to hell*

124   **I'll burn my books** *As Shakespeare's Prospero demonstrates in* The Tempest *(5.1.57), destroying books is a conventional way in which to abjure magic; for Faustus, of course, it is too late.*

Performance

121–124 These final lines are a cue to the actor. Faustus experiences a series of terrifying visions which embody a movement away from lost bliss into everlasting torment: firstly, of an angry God (121), then of devils in monstrous form that have come to take him (122), finally of hell-mouth itself (123). But what emotion lies behind his final cry – *Ah, Mephistopheles!*? One critic describes it as 'perhaps a curse, perhaps a sudden and final vain hope that his devilish companion may save him' (Stevie Simkin); in one production, Mephistopheles 'mysteriously extend[ed] his arm to the disappearing Faustus; whether an attempt to pull him back from the brink of hell or to push him on, the production did not say' (Peter J Smith).

The stage direction *exeunt with him* (they go out…) suggests that Faustus is dragged offstage by either Lucifer and Beelzebub, or a pack of attendant devils. Recent productions have portrayed his departure in widely differing ways. In the 1967 film, Helen herself reappeared to drag him into a smoke-filled hell-mouth, with Mephistopheles looking sombrely on; in 1970 Faustus was not dragged out at all, but simply dropped his cloak (the one he had donned when first conjuring), thereby symbolising the parting of the soul from his body. (See page 176 for further stage interpretations.)

Act 5 Scene 2

Enter LUCIFER, MEPHISTOPHELES and other DEVILS.

> Adders and serpents, let me breathe a while!
> Ugly hell, gape not. Come not, Lucifer!
> I'll burn my books. Ah, Mephistopheles!

The DEVILS exeunt with him.

Gerard Murphy as Faustus (RSC, 1989)

The Chorus reminds us of Faustus's wasted potential, and urges us to take his fate as a warning not to 'practise more than heavenly power permits'

2 **Apollo's laurel bough** *Apollo was the Greek and Roman god of music, poetry and the arts, among many other functions. He is often portrayed wearing a garland of laurel (bay), which was awarded to victors in competitions. This garland, the 'bays', has come to be associated with excellence in poetry.*

3 **sometime** once; formerly

4 **Regard** observe; take notice of

5 **exhort** give warning to

6 **Only to wonder at** to be satisfied with merely wondering at

7 **forward wits** presumptuous intellectuals

Terminat hora...opus Latin: The hour ends the day; the author ends his work *(a motto that might have been added by the original printer; in some productions, this line has been delivered by Wagner)*

Ideas and interpretations

Hilary Gatti observes that 'the Chorus...closes the tragedy, as it had begun, on a note of unequivocal orthodoxy'. However, depending on how the lines are performed, the Chorus need not be simply offering an orthodox denunciation of overreachers and exhortations to avoid meddling with unlawful arts; there can be genuine and heartfelt regret for what Faustus the scholar might have achieved and even admiration for the scientist who dared to *practise more than heavenly power permits*.

Epilogue

Enter CHORUS.

CHORUS   Cut is the branch that might have grown full
        straight,
     And burnèd is Apollo's laurel bough
     That sometime grew within this learnèd man.
     Faustus is gone. Regard his hellish fall,
     Whose fiendful fortune may exhort the wise   5
     Only to wonder at unlawful things,
     Whose deepness doth entice such forward wits
     To practise more than heavenly power permits.

Exit.

Terminat hora diem; terminat author opus.

Faustus with the Good and Evil Angels (RSC, 1989)

Exam practice

Extracts

1. Reread 5.1 from line 82 ('One thing...'). Writing about the appearance of Helen, William Tydeman observes, 'her entry is a crucial incident: winning her love represents both Faustus's finest hour and his most disastrous act, and any production must make it clear that both views are possible'. Discuss this view by close examination of the scene. (It will help to read the notes on pages 100–102 and the section on Marlowe's language – pages 144–148 – first.) In your answer you should:
   - discuss the language of Faustus's speech to Helen, demonstrating how its romantic and heroic qualities are constantly in conflict with images of destructiveness
   - comment on the presence of the Old Man
   - consider the implications of Faustus taking Helen as a paramour as it might have been viewed by Marlowe's audience.

2. Reread 5.2.65–123: Faustus's final soliloquy. D J Palmer wrote:

   > The effects Marlowe is striving for here are those of spontaneity; the conception is much more inward, and dramatises the fleeting thoughts as though they were actually passing through Faustus's mind at the time. Instead of the predictable controlled development of the first soliloquy [in 1.1], are confusion and contradiction, the very process of the struggle to come to terms with the situation...In the final speech, Marlowe created what was virtually a new vehicle for articulating with immediacy the flux and uncertainty of a mind under pressure.

   Write about the effects that Marlowe achieves in Faustus's final soliloquy, comparing it with his first soliloquy (1.1.1–65) and using the quotation from D J Palmer as a basis for your comments. (It will help to read the notes on pages 108–110 and the critical extract by Hilary Gatti – pages 170–172 – first.) In your answer you should:
   - show how the language here is much more spontaneous than in Faustus's first soliloquy and 'dramatises the fleeting thoughts as though they were actually passing through Faustus's mind at the time'
   - comment on the ways in which the language conveys 'confusion and contradiction, the very process of the struggle to come to terms with the situation'
   - show an understanding of Marlowe's use of blank verse.

3. The 1616 B-text ends differently from the 1604 A-text. Following Faustus's

final words, and preceding the Epilogue, there is a scene in which the three Scholars visit Faustus's room the following morning:

Enter the SCHOLARS.

FIRST SCHOLAR	Come, gentlemen, let us go visit Faustus,
	For such a dreadful night was never seen
	Since first the world's creation did begin.
	Such fearful shrieks and cries were never heard.
	Pray heaven the doctor have escaped the danger. 5

SECOND SCHOLAR	O, help us, heaven! See, here are Faustus' limbs,
	All torn asunder by the hand of death.

THIRD SCHOLAR	The devils whom Faustus served have torn him thus.
	For, 'twixt the hours of twelve and one, methought
	I heard him shriek and call aloud for help, 10
	At which self time the house seemed all on fire
	With dreadful horror of these damnèd fiends.

SECOND SCHOLAR	Well, gentlemen, though Faustus' end be such
	As every Christian heart laments to think on,
	Yet, for he was a scholar, once admired 15
	For wondrous knowledge in our German schools,
	We'll give his mangled limbs due burial;
	And all the students, clothed in mourning black,
	Shall wait upon his heavy funeral.

Exeunt.

If you were staging a performance of the play, would you include this scene or not? In your answer:

- express your own thoughts and feelings about this scene as part of the conclusion to the play, as well as suggesting how other audiences might respond to it
- judge what purpose this scene serves, and what effect it has, given that it does not appear in the A-text and may not be by Marlowe
- take into account the following views:
  (a) 'For [the three Scholars] Faustus's story is not to be concluded on a purely negative note. Although they recognise that in religious terms his experience must be accepted as a negative lesson, they express an understanding of the intellectual dilemma which the Faustian story represents' (Hilary Gatti).
  (b) 'In the last scene, as in Shakespeare's tragedies, normal life must resume as best it can. Marlowe…strikes an apt balance between horror, dismay and due reverence' (J P Brockbank).

Extended writing

4. Referring to the Epilogue, Hilary Gatti has expressed the view that the Chorus 'closes the tragedy, as it had begun, on a note of unequivocal orthodoxy'. The Prologue and Epilogue both offer a highly moralistic view of Faustus's life and death. What is the religious orthodoxy that they represent? What moral do they seem to be expressing and how far, in your opinion, does it represent your feelings about the 'intellectual dilemma' that you have been invited to contemplate in the rest of the play? (It will help to read the extract by Roger Sales on pages 173–174.)

Performance

5. In the 1967 film, Helen was played by Elizabeth Taylor (see pages 104 and 175); in the 1989 RSC production, Helen was played by a male actor (it was an all-male cast), which intensified a homoerotic strand which had been present throughout. In groups, discuss the advantages and disadvantages of an all-male *Doctor Faustus*.

6. The Old Man, like the Good and Evil Angels, is a figure from the morality plays (see pages 139–140) and in performance it is difficult to know how he ought to be presented: he is a new character and arrives without introduction. In groups, discuss the various ways in which the Old Man can be performed (for example, see page 98). What effect would you want to create with him, and how could it most effectively be achieved?

Marlowe's life and career

One of the many curious things about Christopher Marlowe is that biographies almost invariably begin with an account of his death. This is partly because his final few days – and hours – were documented in some detail; partly because they seem to form a suitable epitaph to the turbulent life of a government spy with a reputation for atheism and homosexuality; and partly because they were so dramatic that they instantly became the stuff of legend.

The precise facts of Marlowe's death will never be known, but the details which were offered at his inquest are substantially as follows. Marlowe had spent most of Wednesday 30 May 1593 in a house owned by a widow called Eleanor Bull, in Deptford, on the south bank of the Thames just east of the City of London. Three other men were present: Ingram Frizer, a shady businessman and 'fixer'; his associate, another dubious character called Nicholas Skeres who is known to have had criminal connections and had been involved in government intelligence work; and Robert Poley, an agent in the secret service. According to the inquest, a dispute arose after supper over who should pay the 'recknynge' (reckoning, or bill); Marlowe got angry, snatched Frizer's dagger and struck him with it, then Frizer grabbed the dagger and pierced Marlowe's face, through the top of his eye socket. The coroner's report unambiguously picks out Marlowe as having been the aggressor, declaring Frizer to have been acting in self-defence.

In the months and years which followed, this already dramatic story was embellished even further, especially by the puritan Thomas Beard (who had been at Cambridge with Marlowe, and would later become Oliver Cromwell's schoolmaster). Beard maintained that the atheist Marlowe 'even cursed and blasphemed to his last gasp' (medically impossible, given the manner of his death) and saw the playwright's fate as a 'manifest sign of God's judgement'. Marlowe's death, went the story, was clearly richly deserved after such an unashamedly sinful life.

Christopher Marlowe had been born in Canterbury in 1564, the same year as William Shakespeare. His father was a shoemaker and churchwarden. When Marlowe was fifteen, he gained a scholarship to the King's School, Canterbury. Here he would have received a thorough grounding in Latin and Greek grammar as well as encountering classical literature. In December 1580 he went on to Corpus Christi College, Cambridge and took his Bachelor of Arts degree four years later. While he was at Cambridge he wrote *Dido Queen of Carthage,* possibly in collaboration with fellow playwright Thomas Nashe, as well as some poetry, including a translation of the *Amores* by the poet Ovid. But he was initially refused permission to proceed from his BA to his Master of Arts degree because of a series of mysterious absences; and the College's decision was overturned only after intervention from Queen Elizabeth's Privy Council, who wrote to explain that 'Christopher Morley' (a variant spelling of Marlowe's name – he also appears as *Merlin, Marlin, Marly* and *Marlow*) had been 'employed…in matters touching the benefit of his country'. In other words, the young Marlowe had been working for Sir Francis Walsingham's

Marlowe's life and career

secret service, an organisation set up principally to counter the Roman Catholic threat to Queen Elizabeth and England.

Marlowe left Cambridge in 1587 and is next heard of two years later in London, lodging in Shoreditch, the suburb in which the Curtain and Theatre playhouses were situated. It was probably at the Theatre that Marlowe's first great play, *Tamburlaine*, was performed, a piece that was to enjoy continued popularity for many years. *Doctor Faustus* is believed to have been completed by 1589, and in the same year Marlowe had a spell in Newgate prison for his involvement in a street fight in which a man was killed. It was also probably around this time that he wrote *The Jew of Malta*, another tremendous box-office success.

In 1592 Marlowe was in trouble with the authorities yet again, this time in the Netherlands on a charge of counterfeiting currency and of intending to defect to join the English Catholic exiles, an accusation brought by a fellow-agent Richard Baines. But he seems to have escaped with a light sentence and went on that year to write his last two plays, *Edward II* and *The Massacre at Paris*.

On 11 or 12 May 1593 the dramatist Thomas Kyd, with whom Marlowe had once shared rooms, was arrested under suspicion of having written a public libel against Dutch immigrants living in London. Under torture Kyd claimed that some heretical writings which the authorities had found in his lodgings belonged to Marlowe. This was not the first time that Marlowe had been linked with 'atheism'. The playwright was ordered to give an account of himself to the Privy Council, which he did on 20 May. Marlowe was released on bail, but ordered to report back daily to the Council. Ten days later he was dead. He was twenty-nine years old.

On either 27 May or 2 June – just before or just after Marlowe's death – Richard Baines (the agent involved in the playwright's alleged counterfeiting) accused him of heresy in a report entitled 'A note containing the opinion of one Christopher Marly, concerning his damnable judgment of religion and scorn of God's word' (see page 158), a charge which helped to reinforce Kyd's claim that Marlowe had repeatedly expressed 'monstrous opinions'. Within four weeks, on 28 June, Frizer had received an official pardon from the Queen for Marlowe's death.

It is always dangerous to interpret a writer's work in the light of biographical details – and especially so when those details have come down to us via rival playwrights, paid informers and torture victims like Kyd. But it is impossible not to notice that both *Tamburlaine* and *Doctor Faustus* are about men who rise from base stock to celebrity; that *Edward II* explores the idea of homosexuality; that *The Jew of Malta* advertises the hypocrisy of Christians.

Whatever mysteries continue to surround his life and premature death, today Marlowe's reputation is secure as the man who did most to establish blank verse – the iambic pentameter that fellow playwright Ben Jonson called 'Marlowe's mighty line' – as the medium of Elizabethan and Jacobean drama. As the Victorian poet and critic Algernon Swinburne said, 'He is the greatest discoverer, the most daring and inspired pioneer, in all our poetic literature. Before him there was neither genuine blank verse nor a genuine tragedy in our language. After his arrival the way was prepared, the paths were made straight, for Shakespeare.'

Key dates in Marlowe's life and *Doctor Faustus*

(It is not known for certain when Marlowe's plays were written. The dates given below are those which are most widely accepted given our current knowledge.)

1564   born in Canterbury, possibly on 6 February
1566   Edward Alleyn born
1576   the Theatre opens
1577   the Curtain opens
1578   Marlowe at King's School, Canterbury, on a scholarship
1580   starts at Corpus Christi College, Cambridge
1584   receives his BA degree
1584–87   long periods of absence from Cambridge, probably working for the government secret service
1586   *Dido Queen of Carthage*
1587   receives his MA degree; *Tamburlaine*; the Rose playhouse opens on Bankside
1588   *Doctor Faustus*
1589   imprisoned briefly over the death of a man in a street fight
1589–91   *The Jew of Malta*
1591   sharing rooms with Thomas Kyd
1592   arrested in the Netherlands; *Edward II* and *The Massacre at Paris*
1593   *Hero and Leander*; plague closes playhouses for most of the year
       11 or 12 May: Thomas Kyd arrested; heretical papers found
       18 May: warrant issued for Marlowe's arrest
       20 May: appears before the Privy Council
       30 May: Marlowe killed in Deptford
       1 June: coroner's inquest; Marlowe buried
1599   Globe playhouse opens on Bankside near the Rose
1600   The Admiral's Men move to the Fortune playhouse
1603   The Admiral's Men become Prince Henry's Men
1604   *Doctor Faustus* A-text published
1616   *Doctor Faustus* B-text published

The text of *Doctor Faustus*

There are two versions of *Doctor Faustus*, neither of which was published in Marlowe's lifetime. The first quarto edition, published in 1604, is known as the A-text; the second, from 1616, the B-text. The B-text is about one-third longer than A, mainly because of material in the middle of the play which extends the Pope scene with the rescue of the rival Pope Bruno, and the scenes at the Emperor's court with the attempted revenge of the Knight. The 1616 B-text also contains passages which have clearly been copied from A.

Recent critics have tended to take the view that A (somewhat short for an Elizabethan play) focuses more on Faustus's inner thoughts and experiences, while B – which has more characters – makes fuller use of the Elizabethan stage (as, for example, when 'hell is discovered' – a stage direction – in the last Act). With its increased use of supernatural and allegorical characters, the B-text seems more obviously influenced by the morality tradition (see below, page 139). It also contains a final scene in which Faustus's dismembered body is discovered by his fellow scholars. These factors led some commentators to the theory that the A-text represents a slimmed-down version used when the company toured the play through the provinces, performing in innyards and other adaptable venues, while the B-text is the fuller script used in the London playhouses with their facility for more sophisticated theatrical effects.

However, the debate is complicated by the fact that in 1602 Philip Henslowe, owner of the Rose, is known to have paid William Birde and Samuel Rowley £4 for their 'adicyones [additions] in doctor fostes'. This has led some people to conclude that the additions described must be the passages only found in the B-text, and that A is therefore more authoritatively Marlovian.

One thing is now agreed upon, however: there is no possibility of reconstructing the script that Marlowe handed over to his first actors. Some editors prefer to use the A-text (as this book does), some the B; while the edition by David Bevington and Eric Rasmussen (1993) includes both complete texts. These editors are also among many who believe that Marlowe planned the whole work, but gave certain scenes – notably from the comic middle of the play – to another dramatist.

There are no Act-divisions in the actual A-text, but they are included here on the conviction that the A-text separates clearly into five distinct phases corresponding to the classical scheme. The choruses have been placed, not at the ends of Acts 2 and 3 as in some editions, but at the beginnings of Acts 3 and 4, thereby introducing the Acts as they would in a play such as Shakespeare's *Henry V*.

Marlowe's world

The Renaissance

The age during which Marlowe lived and worked is traditionally known as the Renaissance, though some people these days prefer to call it the 'early modern' period. It was a moment in European cultural history when extraordinary changes were taking place, especially in the fields of religion, politics, science, language and the arts.

Religion and politics

- In the century following the Reformation in 1534, people in Marlowe's England began to view the world and their own place in it very differently.
- Queen Elizabeth felt that she had to stand alone against a strongly Catholic Europe and maintain the Protestant religion in England established by her father Henry VIII.

- People began to think about the relationship between themselves as individuals and the authority of the state, while not everybody any longer accepted the idea that queens or kings ruled by 'divine right' (on God's authority).
- There were divisions in the Protestant Church, with extremist groups such as the Puritans disapproving of much that they saw in society and the Church.
- During this time people began to question the traditional beliefs in rank and social order – the ideas that some people should be considered superior simply because they were born into wealthy families; or that those in power should always be obeyed without question.
- England had become a proud and independent nation, and a leading military and trading power, especially after the defeat of the Spanish Armada in 1588.
- As trade became increasingly important, it was not only the nobility who could become wealthy. People could move around the country more easily and a competitive capitalist economy developed.
- James I succeeded Elizabeth in 1603. He was a Scot, interested in witchcraft, and a supporter of the theatre, who fought off the treasonous attempt of the Gunpowder Plot in 1605.

Science and discovery

- Scientists began to question traditional authorities (the accepted ideas handed down from one generation to the next) and depended instead upon their own observation of the world, especially after the development of instruments such as the telescope. The Italian Galileo (1564–1642) came into conflict with the Church for claiming that the Earth was not the centre of the universe.
- Explorers brought back new produce, such as spices, silks and gold, and created great excitement in the popular imagination for stories of distant lands and their peoples.

Language

- The more traditional scholars still regarded Latin as the only adequate language for scholarly discussion and writing (and liked it because it also prevented many 'uncultured' people from understanding philosophy, medicine, etc).
- But a new interest in the English language came with England's growing importance and sense of identity.
- The Protestants favoured a personal relationship with God, which meant being able to read the Bible themselves (rather than letting priests interpret it for them). This led to the need for a good version in English and The Authorised Version of the Bible (the 'King James Bible') was published in 1611.
- Grammar schools sprang up after the Reformation which increased literacy (but mostly among males in the middle and upper classes, and mainly in London).
- The invention of the printing press in the 1450s had led to more people having access to information and new ideas – not just the scholars.
- The English language began to be standardised in this period (into Standard English), but it was still very flexible and there was less insistence on following rules than there is nowadays.

- There was an enormous expansion in vocabulary, which affected every area of daily life: crafts, sciences, technology, trade, philosophy, food...
- English vocabulary was enriched by numerous borrowings from other languages. Between 1500 and 1650, over 10,000 new words entered the language (though many later fell out of use). Some 'purists' (who disliked change) opposed the introduction of new words.
- Marlowe therefore lived through a time when the English vocabulary was expanding amazingly and the grammar was still flexible, a time when people were intensely excited by language.

Marlowe's fellow playwright, Ben Jonson, had strong views about language:

Many writers perplex their readers and hearers with mere nonsense. Their writings need sunshine. Pure and neat language I love, yet plain and customary. A barbarous phrase hath often made me out of love with a good sense; and doubtful writing hath wrackt me beyond my patience.

Ben Jonson, 1637

Renaissance humanism

Marlowe would have been introduced to Renaissance humanism both at school in Canterbury and during his time at Cambridge. Humanism was based upon a study of the ancient Greek and Latin authors as models of eloquence and virtue, but importantly it also laid great stress upon the development of the subjective reader, an educated person who could use their understanding of the classics to investigate all other areas of human knowledge, thought and experience. Thus, while humanism did not lead to a sense of individualism as we might understand the term today, it did encourage distinctive thought and expression and the development of new ways in which to explore the validity of accepted truths.

Central to a humanist education was the *dispute* – the formal debate in which the speaker would be expected to defend or attack a given premise, according to whichever role had been assigned by the teacher. As critic Thomas Healy observes, 'Although sixteenth-century schools and universities were hardly arenas of intellectual freedom, Marlowe's education would have done more to facilitate than oppose his opportunities to think against the grain of received opinion, to question the assumed and to assert the unusual.'

Key dates

1558   Elizabeth I becomes Queen.
1564   Marlowe and Shakespeare born.
1565   The explorer John Hawkins introduces sweet potatoes and tobacco into England.

1567 Mary Queen of Scots abdicates in favour of her year-old son, James VI.
1568 Mary escapes to England and is imprisoned by Elizabeth.
1572 Francis Drake attacks Spanish ports in the Americas.
1576 James Burbage opens the first successful playhouse (The Theatre) in London.
1580 Francis Drake returns from a circumnavigation of the world.
1582 Pope Gregory reforms the Christian calendar.
1587 Mary Queen of Scots executed for a treasonous plot against Elizabeth; Drake partly destroys the Spanish fleet at Cádiz and war breaks out with Spain; the Rose playhouse opens on Bankside.
1588 Philip II of Spain's Armada is defeated by the English fleet.
1592–1593 Plague kills over 10,000 Londoners.
1593 Christopher Marlowe killed.
1595 Earl of Tyrone leads a new rebellion in Ireland.
1596 Tomatoes introduced into England; John Harington invents the water-closet (the ancestor of the modern lavatory).
1599 Earl of Essex concludes a truce with Tyrone, returns home and is arrested.
1601 Essex is tried and executed for treasonous plots against Elizabeth.
1603 Elizabeth I dies and is succeeded by James VI of Scotland as James I of England; Sir Walter Raleigh is jailed for plotting against James.
1604 James is proclaimed 'King of Great Britain, France and Ireland'; new Church rules cause 300 Puritan clergy to resign.
1605 Gunpowder Plot uncovered.
1607 First permanent English settlement in America at Jamestown, Virginia.
1610 Galileo looks at the stars through a telescope; tea is introduced into Europe.
1611 Authorised Version of the Bible.
1616 William Shakespeare dies.
1618 Raleigh executed for treason; physician William Harvey announces discovery of blood circulation.
1620 Pilgrim Fathers sail from Plymouth to colonise America.
1623 The First Folio of Shakespeare's plays published.
1625 James I dies and is succeeded by Charles I.

The playhouses, players and publishing

The playhouses

- The professional theatre was based in London, which had around 200,000 inhabitants in 1600.
- It was repeatedly under attack from the Puritan-dominated Guildhall, which wanted to abolish the playhouses totally because, in their opinion, they encouraged sinful behaviour.
- Acting companies performed in the courtyards of coaching inns, in the halls of great houses, in churches, and until the sixteenth century at markets and in the streets. The first purpose-built playhouse in London was the Red Lion, built around 1567; but the first really successful playhouse was the Theatre,

Shoreditch, opened in 1576 by James Burbage (when Marlowe was twelve). Most of Marlowe's plays were performed at the Rose and it is possible that *Dido Queen of Carthage, Tamburlaine, The Jew of Malta* and *Doctor Faustus* enjoyed earlier performances at the Theatre. Many of Shakespeare's early plays (up to 1599) were performed mainly at the Theatre or the nearby Curtain.

- In 1600, there were six public outdoor theatres: the Rose, the Curtain, the Swan, the Fortune, the Boar's Head and the Globe. The Theatre was dismantled to help build the Globe. The Rose was pulled down c. 1606.
- Some outdoor theatres held audiences of up to 3,000.
- Standing room was one penny; the gallery two pence; the 'Lords' Room' three pence; and it was more expensive still to sit on the stage. This was at a time when a joiner (skilled carpenter) might earn six to eight shillings (72 to 96 pence) per week. By 1614, it may have been six pence for the newly opened Hope Theatre (built by Philip Henslowe near where the Rose had stood).
- Outdoor theatre performances usually started about 2 pm or 3 pm (there was no artificial light).
- The season started around September, through to the beginning of Lent; then from after Easter to early summer. (Theatres were generally closed in summer because of the increased risk of plague: thousands died of the plague in summer 1593 and the theatres remained almost completely closed until 1594.) Some companies went on summer tours, playing in inns, and similar places.
- Nearly all theatres were closed during the Civil War, which began in 1642 (and most were demolished by 1656).
- There were some indoor theatres (called 'private' or 'hall' theatres) such as the Blackfriars, which was used up to 1609 almost exclusively by child actors (the minimum entrance fee of six pence indicates a wealthier audience). Plays developed which were more suited to the more intimate atmosphere, with the stage illuminated by artificial lighting.
- The star actor Richard Burbage and his brother Cuthbert had the licence of the Blackfriars and, by the end of Shakespeare's writing career, the King's Men had the use of both the Blackfriars and the Globe.
- The Rose was owned and managed by Philip Henslowe, who is of great importance to theatre historians, not only because he built the Rose (in 1587), the first playhouse on Bankside (and in 1600 the Fortune, north of the Thames), but because between 1592 and 1604 he kept a famous diary, or rather an account book. In this he made a record of all the theatre's business, including the companies who performed at his theatre, the titles of the plays, the takings, how much he paid for new work, and which props and costumes were in store. (There are references to Henslowe's 'Diary' in the notes to the text.) Henslowe's stepdaughter married the famous actor Edward Alleyn.

The players

- In 1572 parliament passed an Act 'for the punishment of Vagabonds'. As actors risked being classed as little better than wandering beggars, this Act required them to be attached to a theatre company and have the patronage (protection) of someone powerful. This meant that companies had to keep on the right side of patrons and make sure they didn't offend the Master of the Revels, who was responsible for censorship.

- Major companies in Marlowe's time included the Admiral's Men (who performed Marlowe's plays at the Rose) and the Queen's Men. The Chamberlain's Men (the group that Shakespeare joined, later known as the King's Men when James came to the throne) was formed in 1594 and was run by shareholders (called 'the housekeepers').

- It is now believed that the star actors in Marlowe's day were more famous than the playwrights. Actors like Edward Alleyn (1566–1626), who played most of Marlowe's major roles for the Admiral's Men, became great celebrities and had the opportunity to become comparatively wealthy. Indeed, in 1594, Alleyn acquired a financial interest in the Beargarden (replaced in 1614 by the Hope playhouse), later became part owner of the Fortune, and owned property in London and Sussex. By the time of his death, he had also built Dulwich College. Alleyn is known to have played Faustus, Tamburlaine and Barabas (in *The Jew of Malta*) and there are numerous references to his skill as an actor.

Under the Act for the punishment of Vagabonds of 1572, 'Common Players in Interludes' would be classed along with 'Jugglers, Pedlars, Tinkers' as 'Rogues, Vagabonds and Sturdy Beggars' unless they could get themselves licensed by two justices of the peace. From 1598 only great nobles had the authority to issue such licences.

Acting

- There was little rehearsal time, with several plays 'in repertory' (being performed) in any given period.
- We don't know about the style of acting, but modern, naturalistic, low-key acting was probably not possible on the stage of the Rose or the Globe. At the same time, Shakespeare appears to be mocking over-the-top delivery in at least two of his plays (*Hamlet* 3.2: Hamlet's first three speeches to the First Player; and *A Midsummer Night's Dream,* especially Act 5). Some commentators have suggested that Shakespeare is here parodying a traditional, declamatory style which might have been associated with Edward Alleyn.
- Actors certainly needed to be aware of their relationship with the audience: there must have been plenty of direct contact. In a daylight theatre there can be no pretence that the audience is not there.

Writing and publishing

- Plays were not really regarded as 'literature' in Marlowe's lifetime, and so most playwrights were not interested in publishing their plays in book form.

- Some playwrights' plays were, however, originally printed in cheap 'quarto' (pocket-size) editions. Some were sold officially (under an agreement made between the theatre company and the author), and some pirated (frequently by the actors themselves who had learned most of the script by heart).
- The only plays by Marlowe to have been printed during his lifetime were the two parts of *Tamburlaine* which appeared in 1590. But even these are curious as publications: not only do they fail to bear the author's name, but they also carry an explanation from the printer that he has cut out some comic scenes because he considers them 'fond [foolish] and frivolous'. Plainly the *Tamburlaine* acted in 1590 was quite different from the one performed and studied today.
- Collaboration was common in Marlowe's day. Shakespeare, for example, worked with John Fletcher on at least two plays, while Marlowe probably collaborated with Thomas Nashe on *Dido Queen of Carthage* and perhaps Nashe or Henry Porter on *Doctor Faustus*. It is also known that acting companies were not averse to changing scripts if they thought they could make them more attractive to potential audiences. In 1602, two playwrights were paid £4 by Henslowe to make additions to *Doctor Faustus*.
- In 1623, seven years after Shakespeare's death, two of his close friends, John Heming (or Heminges) and Henry Condell, collected together the most reliable versions of the plays and published them in a larger size volume known as the First Folio. But there was no such folio edition of Marlowe's work. Instead, all we have, as described by Richard Proudfoot, are 'six very different kinds of play, having in common their exciting innovative subject-matter, their sceptical engagement with orthodoxies, and their capacity to keep audiences guessing'.

Playwrights

It will be obvious, if only from the mere existence of William Shakespeare, that Marlowe was not writing in a dramatic vacuum; during his working life, and for a period beyond it up to the closure of the playhouses, there was a veritable industry of playwriting which produced several playwrights whose work has enjoyed enduring popularity.

- **William Shakespeare** (1564–1616) was only two months younger than Marlowe, but by the time of the latter's death was still only exploring the possibilities of his art, with plays such as the three parts of *Henry VI* and *Richard III*. But, within a few years, he had produced his first great tragedy, *Romeo and Juliet*, a brilliant comedy, *A Midsummer Night's Dream*, and an innovative history play, *Richard II*. By the time of his death, his friend and fellow playwright Ben Jonson was able to describe him as being 'not of an age, but for all time', a fact testified to by the continuing capacity of his plays for reinterpretation in the minds and theatrical performances of succeeding generations.
- **Ben Jonson** (1572/3–1637), like his friend Shakespeare (whom he loved and admired 'on this side idolatry'), began his theatre career as an actor. A fiery character, he killed a fellow actor in a duel and also spent time in prison for offending the authorities in his plays. Shakespeare himself acted in Jonson's first

success, *Every Man in his Humour* (1598), a satire mocking current affectations. Jonson is best known for his two great comedies *Volpone* (1605) and *The Alchemist* (1610), both biting satires on human greed and foolishness.

- **John Webster** (born c.1580, died c. 1632) is also thought to have started life as an actor, but little is really known about him. He is famous for two dark and violent tragedies of love, horror and political intrigue set in Renaissance Italy, *The White Devil* (1612) and *The Duchess of Malfi* (1614), both of which have determined women as their central characters.
- Among other popular dramatists were two who collaborated widely with other writers. **Thomas Middleton** (1580–1627) had a hand in numerous plays, but is best known for his major part in *The Changeling* (1622) and his probable authorship of *The Revenger's Tragedy* (1607). **John Fletcher** (1579–1625), a phenomenally prolific playwright, enjoyed a very successful collaboration with **Francis Beaumont** (1584–1616) and wrote at least three plays with Shakespeare: *Henry VIII* (1613), *The Two Noble Kinsmen* (c. 1613) and a lost play, *Cardenio* (acted at court in 1613).

Marlowe and Shakespeare

The romanticising of Marlowe's life, combined with alleged blanks in our knowledge of Shakespeare's, has encouraged the growth of some imaginative myths. In one of the most widely circulated, Marlowe does not die, but is spirited away to the continent by his secret-service friends. There he continues to write plays which are smuggled back across the Channel and attributed to a hack playwright called William Shakespeare…!

Shakespeare's only obvious allusion to any contemporary writer is to Marlowe. For example, in *As You Like It* (c. 1599) the shepherdess Phebe quotes a line from Marlowe's poem *Hero and Leander* (published 1598) – in Act 3 scene 5 she recalls one of the 'saws' (or sayings) of a 'Dead shepherd':

Dead shepherd, now I find thy saw of might,
'Whoever loved, that loved not at first sight?'

This second line is a direct quotation from Marlowe's poem.

Elsewhere in *As You Like It*, some critics have also seen an allusion to Marlowe's death when Touchstone says: 'it strikes a man more dead than a great reckoning in a little room' (3.3). Other commentators have pointed out that the term 'reckoning' was fairly commonplace and would not have been automatically linked to the story of Marlowe's death, and that the exact words of the coroner's report would not in any case have been familiar to the theatre-going public.

The Swan playhouse, c. 1596

The Rose playhouse

In about 1596 a Dutch visitor to London called Johannes de Witt saw a play in the Swan playhouse (on the south bank of the Thames just west of the Rose and the Globe) and made a sketch of the interior. De Witt's drawing – or rather a copy made by a friend (see page 130) – has ever since formed our mental picture of an Elizabethan playhouse interior.

The drawing raises as many questions as it seems to answer – not least about the dimensions of the stage and the uses of the gallery above it. Furthermore, we do not know how different the Globe or Rose might have been from the Swan (let alone how far we can depend upon the recollections of a tourist after a single visit, or his friend's artistic skill).

But thanks to an archaeological dig before the building of an office block in 1989, our knowledge about the Rose, and playhouses like it, has grown considerably. The archaeological excavations which followed the discovery of the Rose's foundations in Southwark were able to show for the first time the physical context in which the plays of Marlowe and his contemporaries were performed. We now understand a great deal about the layout of the Rose building and, most importantly, some of the dimensions of the stage once walked upon by Ned Alleyn and the Admiral's Men (see pages vi and 132).

According to Julian Bowsher, one of the archaeologists in charge of the dig:

> The building was a slightly irregular polygon whose frame comprised two parallel rings of walls that formed the galleries, surrounding an open yard. There was an entrance at the southern end and a stage projecting into the yard at the northern end...[the back wall of which] was clearly the same inner wall whose angles mirrored the external wall of the frame, thus providing, it seems, five planes. It had a broad but tapered frontage and covered an area of about 490 square feet....and it seems to have been open to the elements. [In the back wall of the stage] there would have been at least two doors...perhaps a larger one in the centre. The 'tiring house', where the actors would get 'attired', was clearly that area of the frame of the building behind the stage, which would have been useless for an audience.

In 1592 Henslowe paid to have the stage end of the Rose remodelled (see page vi). This second phase in the playhouse's life provided a covering to the stage – which was also thrust out slightly further into the yard, providing greater contact with the groundlings. The rebuilding also created a back wall to the stage which had three planes (rather than the original five), probably implying three openings for entrances and exits. The stage remained quite small compared with other playhouses, however, which might have ruled out the use of large-scale onstage props.

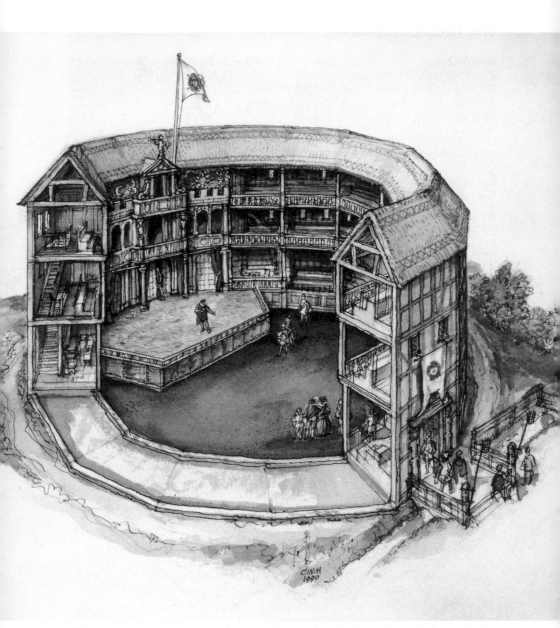

This is an artist's impression of what archaeologists think the Rose playhouse looked like between1587 and 1592. The illustration on page vi shows how they think it was remodelled, and where the first recorded performance of Doctor Faustus took place on 30 September 1594 (© C Walter Hodges)

The Globe playhouse

Shakespeare's Globe, built in 1599, was only a short distance from Henslowe's Rose. Using all the evidence available, a reconstruction of the Globe has been built in London, not far from the site of the original building.

The liberties

The Rose and the Globe were in an area of London known as a 'liberty', as were the Swan and, north of the river, playhouses such as the Theatre, the Curtain and the Blackfriars. The liberties were outside the jurisdiction of the City authorities. As Thomas Healy explains:

> Locating the playhouses in the liberties gave the theatre a type of cultural licence. It could enact and represent aspects of Elizabethan culture which were not permitted to be displayed within the City's walls. Audiences could resort to them, as to the brothels, taverns and bear-baiting pits, to partake of something different from the everyday, the expectation of entertainment which offered escape from the ordinary.

The independence of the liberties, according to Andrew Gurr, 'was a continued irritation to the Lord Mayor of the City, and the City Charter of 1608 finally abolished all the liberties and brought them under City government. By that time, of course, the playhouses were not only long established, but were under royal protection.'

Social, historical and literary context

Religion

The Reformation

Christopher Marlowe lived in the century of the Reformation: the religious and political movement to reform the Roman Catholic Church, which led to the establishment of Protestantism. Protestantism emphasised the prime importance of faith, and promoted a much more direct relationship between the individual and God, unmediated by the priests of the Church. With origins in earlier centuries, the Reformation became effective in the sixteenth when absolute monarchies gave it support by challenging the political power of the papacy and confiscating Church wealth. In England, the Reformation had been much more 'top-down' than in other Europeans countries, given that its impetus was Henry VIII's desire to rid himself of his first wife, the staunchly Catholic Catherine of Aragon; and the Anglican Church under Henry and Elizabeth retained much of the institutionalism that it had inherited from Roman Catholicism.

There are two towering figures of the Reformation, an awareness of whose teachings is central to an understanding of *Doctor Faustus*:

Martin Luther (1483–1546, like Faustus, a scholar at the University of Wittenberg) might be said to have initiated the Reformation in Europe by his protest in 1517 against the sale of indulgences (pardons of sins) by the Roman Catholic Church, an action which was to lead to the emergence of a new Protestant faith in 1530. (Lutheranism remains the principal form of Protestantism in Germany, and is the national faith of Norway, Sweden, Denmark, Iceland and Finland.) Luther's God has been described as both terrible and majestic, 'incomprehensible, inscrutable, infallible, immense, awesome and, above all, hidden' (Paul Sellic). Humans can have no understanding of him or his intentions through his works, and must be aware that sin is inevitable, but that we have the will to reject it by receiving God. Luther refused to address the key question of whether God, given his omnipotence, is ultimately the author of Satan's evil; or why God does not influence reprobates (hardened sinners) to become virtuous.

Jean Calvin (1509–64) was a French-born Swiss Protestant Church reformer. Calvin's position was very similar to Luther's, especially in the emphasis laid upon the central doctrine of predestination: a belief that certain souls are preordained by God, through the sacrifice of Jesus, to salvation, and the rest condemned to damnation. But Calvinism takes the concept further by insisting that God actually hardens the heart of the reprobate and that this condemnation of individuals to their doom is a vital part of his divine plan. He published *Institutes of Christian Religion* in 1536, which was translated into English in 1561.

Good and evil

Alongside Calvinism, there are earlier theologies present in *Doctor Faustus* which

134

relate to concepts of the soul. At times the play seems to represent the Manichaean view (put forward by the third-century prophet Manes in Persia) of a soul which is actually divided into two. Manichaeism's concept of dualism held that the material world was evil, being an invasion of the spiritual world by the powers of darkness, and it saw a reflection of this cosmic conflict in the soul of man. Followers believed that man has two souls: the good soul is divine and, left to itself, can do no evil; but, driven by the evil soul of the flesh and the devil, it is led to do things that it would normally shun. Faustus seems to adopt a Manichaean position when he says, 'The god thou servest is thine own appetite, / Wherein is fixed the love of Beelzebub' (2.1.11–12).

In opposition to this belief was the concept proposed by St Augustine (354–430), of a unitary soul which fluctuates between two contrary wills – good and evil. For Augustine, evil was attributable to the abuse of freedom, and the site of conflict was the will, rather than the soul itself. The will is not inherently evil, but it becomes so when it chooses to reject good. Both the fall of man and the fall of the angels came about through a perverse choice made by the free will. Augustine's position is important, for it implies that the soul itself is incorruptible; and, even for Calvinists such as William Perkins (1558–1602, a popular preacher in Cambridge), this had to be so: 'sin is not a corruption of man's substance, but only of his faculties. Otherwise neither could men's souls be immortal, nor Christ take upon him man's nature.'

Repentance and damnation

Central to this definition of the soul, was the concept of conscience. Towards the end of the play, Faustus displays both fear and despair. Elizabethan accounts of conscience show that fear was ordained by God, and that, while a person was capable of experiencing it, there was still hope for their salvation. But to deny hope was to give way to despair – for many Renaissance theologians the greatest of all sins, as it effectively gave the lie to God's promise that the door to heaven was always open to a truly repentant sinner.

It is difficult for us today to comprehend just how immediate and concrete concepts such as the soul, heaven and hell, salvation and damnation were to the average member of Marlowe's audience. Where we tend to see the Good and Evil Angels in *Doctor Faustus* as being merely allegorical abstractions, the average Elizabethan would recognise them as 'real' in a way that we cannot possibly imagine. And, while we should always remember that labels such as 'the average Elizabethan' can be extremely misleading when we are describing an age which encompassed such a wide variety of religious beliefs, it is nonetheless true to say that *Doctor Faustus* was written in the context of a society in which a deviation from orthodox belief was enough to brand a person an atheist. Despite that orthodoxy, a concept such as 'hell' is clearly capable of more than one interpretation even within a single play. For Mephistopheles, hell is a state of mind, the mental torment occasioned by the absence of God (1.3.76–82); elsewhere in the play, it is clearly a geographical location (e.g. 2.3.171–174). In *Doctor Faustus*, hell is both physical and spiritual: the torment of eternal deprivation and severance from God.

Magic and witchcraft

In Marlowe's time, superstitions surrounded every aspect of day-to-day life, especially at the key moments of birth, baptism, marriage and death. As Stevie Simkin says, 'In a culture that witnessed the death of at least 3000 people (predominantly women) convicted of witchcraft between 1542 and 1746...the fear and fascination engendered by the occult were evidently very near the surface...Astrology, lent authority by its classical roots, was also deeply embedded in the beliefs of the people.'

Astronomy

At the heart of *Doctor Faustus* are the hero's enquiries and speculations about the universe. It is clear from Faustus's discussions with Mephistopheles (in 2.3) that the Ptolemaic view, which had prevailed for many centuries, was struggling to provide all the answers. Ptolemy was a second-century Greek astronomer, mathematician and geographer who worked in Alexandria. His theory, described in the *Almagest,* placed the Earth at the centre of the universe, with the sun, moon and stars revolving around it, all set in a series of concentric spheres. By the mid sixteenth century, different interpretations of the Ptolemaic system had evolved (especially concerning how many spheres there were) and these were hotly debated, not least at Cambridge, Marlowe's university. In the 1616 B-text, when Mephistopheles gives his authoritative response to Faustus's questions (2.3.36–65), he rejects the view held by the traditionalists, that there were spheres of fire and crystal.

The alternative system to Ptolemy's was put forward in 1543 by the Polish astronomer Nicolaus Copernicus. Defying Church doctrine, Copernicus proposed that the sun was at the centre of the universe, thereby establishing a fundamental truth of modern astronomy soon to be built on by the Italian astronomer and physicist Galileo (properly Galileo Galilei; born in 1564, the same year as Marlowe and Shakespeare; died 1642). Marlowe does not overtly refer in the play to Copernicus's sun-centred theory, even though he must have been familiar with it. But there is possibly enough in Faustus's enigmatic reply 'Well, I am answered' (2.3.68) to suggest that at least part of Marlowe's audience would have been far from satisfied with Mephistopheles's explanations. In view of all the post-Copernican writings on astronomy that were circulating when Marlowe was creating this play, his audience might well have felt that they had been invited to question the orthodox cosmography of the age.

Violence and cruelty

It is important to bear in mind, when contemplating a story such as *Doctor Faustus,* that our modern standards of cruelty and our responses to acts of violence are likely to be different to those of Marlowe and his contemporaries. A Rose audience might have walked to the playhouse across London Bridge, passing beneath the rotting heads of traitors impaled on spikes as a warning against treachery; and they might have followed up their afternoon's theatrical entertainment with a visit to the next-door bearbaiting ring where they could watch a bear or bull baited by dogs, having laid bets on the outcome.

They might also have watched the punishment in 1579 of John Stubbs and his printer William Page, who had made the mistake of publishing a criticism of Queen Elizabeth's proposed marriage to the French Catholic Duke of Alençon: 'Not long after upon a stage set up in the market-place at Westminster, Stubbes and Page had their right hands cut off by the blow of a butcher's knife, with a mallet struck through their wrists' (reported by the historian William Camden, 1551–1623). Tyburn (near modern Marble Arch in London) was the main place of public executions. Roger Sales offers an explanation for this apparent display of cruelty when he writes:

> A Renaissance execution was meant to represent…a theatre of Hell. Agony had to be prolonged for as long as possible so that both the victims and the spectators were given a glimpse of the everlasting torments associated with Hell. The point that the execution represented not an end but, rather, merely the prelude to endless torture was reinforced by the way in which the spectacle continued after the eventual death of the victim. Dismemberment of the corpse, followed by the burning or display of its fragments, suggested that death offered no release from punishment.

Public spectacles such as these help us to understand the context in which Marlowe's audience would have experienced *Doctor Faustus*.

The sources of *Doctor Faustus*

The Damnable Life

In 1587 a book was published in Germany which was to become a best-seller across Europe. The *Faustbuch,* as it is now called, told the story of a man called Johann Faustus who sold his soul to the devil. It might have been based on the real-life activities of a Faustus who died around 1540, having allegedly practised the black arts. The earliest surviving English translation, *The History of the Damnable Life and Deserved Death of Doctor John Faustus* (referred to, for brevity, as the *Damnable Life*) was produced in 1592 by a translator known only by his initials, P F, but it was apparently not the first edition.

It is the *Damnable Life* that formed the key source for Marlowe's play, and provided him with the substance for virtually all the major scenes. There are a number of details which demonstrate how closely Marlowe followed its narrative. These include dramatic moments such as the appearance of the words '*Homo, fuge!*' and the use of warm coals to liquefy Faustus's congealed blood (in 2.1). Even the comic scenes have their origins in the *Damnable Life,* chapters of which bear titles such as 'How Faustus served the drunken clowns'.

The following extracts from the conclusion of *Damnable Life* give an idea, when compared with Faustus's final speech, of the ways in which Marlowe used his major source:

Damnable Life, lix. This sorrowful time drawing near so troubled Doctor Faustus that he began to write his mind…as followeth:

'Ah Faustus, thou sorrowful and woeful man, now must thou go to the damned company in unquenchable fire, whereas thou mightest have had the joyful immortality of the soul, the which thou now has lost.'

Damnable Life, lx. 'Oh, poor, woeful, and weary wretch! Oh, sorrowful soul of Faustus, now art thou in the number of the damned; for now must I wait for unmeasurable pains of death, yea, far more lamentable than ever yet any creature hath suffered…Ah, grievous pains that pierce my panting heart; whom is there now that can deliver me? Would God that I knew where to hide me or into what place to creep or fly! Ah, woe, woe is me; be where I will, yet am I taken.'

Damnable Life, lxi. 'Now thou, Faustus, damned wretch, how happy wert thou if as an unreasonable beast thou mightest die without soul, so shouldst thou not feel any more doubts! But now the devil will take thee away both body and soul and set thee in an unspeakable place of darkness…Ah, that I could carry the heavens on my shoulders, so that there were time at last to quit me of this everlasting damnation! Oh, who can deliver me out of these fearful tormenting flames, the which I see prepared for me? Oh, there is no help, nor any man that can deliver me, nor any wailing of sins can help me; neither is there rest to be found for me day nor night.'

The *Damnable Life,* however, was little more than an orthodox moral narrative; by exploring Faustus's inner conflicts and motivations, Marlowe turned the story into a powerful and ambiguous Renaissance tragedy, raising questions to do with sin, damnation and the bounds set upon human learning and experience.

Classical and biblical mythology

Other obvious sources for Marlowe's play are the Book of Genesis, which tells of humanity's first disobedience towards God and its subsequent awareness of good and evil, and the classical myths of Icarus and Prometheus. Icarus and his father Daedalus were imprisoned on Crete and longed to return home. Daedalus made wings for them both from feathers and wax, and warned his son not to fly too high. But, thrilled at flying, Icarus soared too near the sun. The wax melted and he plunged to his death in the sea. Icarus is the type of the overreacher, and therefore an ideal model to be evoked by the Prologue; while the story of Prometheus, who defied Jupiter's prohibition and gave fire to humans, though not overtly alluded to in the play, foreshadows Faustus's struggle to break through the limits placed upon human knowledge and offers a warning of the punishment that inevitably follows. (Prometheus was punished by being chained to a rock where a vulture gnawed his liver, which was constantly renewed.)

Historical figures

In addition to these literary and mythological sources, there were several historical figures, perhaps best described as philosopher–magicians, who can be seen as

Faustus's antecedents. Three of these are actually referred to in the play by Faustus himself: Henry Cornelius Agrippa von Nettesheim (1486–1535; 1.1.119), a German humanist scholar who wrote a book on the defence of magic; Roger Bacon (c. 1212–92; 1.1.156), an English experimental scientist interested in alchemy, astronomy and mathematics, who had to work secretly; and Pietro d'Abano (c. 1250–1316; 1.1.156), an Italian physician with a reputation as a conjurer and sorcerer.

Morality plays

Doctor Faustus has much in common with the morality plays which were popular in England throughout the late Middle Ages. Moralities typically told stories about the progress of the soul and humanity's relationship with virtue and temptation. In the most famous morality play, for example, *Everyman* (written in the early 1500s), the hero is told that he must make a journey – which we, the audience, recognise as the journey towards death. He goes round all his friends, who include allegorical figures such as Worldly Wealth and Kinship, asking if they will accompany him. All of them refuse – except Good Deeds, whom Everyman has hitherto neglected, but who is uniquely permitted to go with him on his final journey. The moral is clear: however materially successful our earthly life, it is only our virtue that will help us reach heaven.

In typical morality plays, personified human qualities such as Goodness, or the Seven Deadly Sins, would not only appear, but take part in disputes. One of the earliest (early fifteenth century), *The Castle of Perseverance,* contains features that clearly have a major influence on the structure and content of *Doctor Faustus:* a battle between vices and virtues; a mixture of allegorical figures (such as Backbiter) and diabolical agents (the devil Belyal); and the enactment of Death and Judgement. *A Pleasant Satire of the Three Estates* (c. 1552), by Sir David Lindsay, a Scottish poet and courtier, shows the temptation of Rex Humanitas ('King Humanity', another Everyman figure) by embodiments such as Sensuality, while Verity (truth) is put in the stocks and Chastity warned off. In both this play and *Faustus,* we also observe a kind of sub-plot involving 'low-life' characters and, interestingly, an attack on the Church.

The comic scenes in morality plays, frequently involving the devil, or Vice, were often characterised by knockabout physical comedy and carnival elements: a preoccupation with sex, food and drink, combined with a disruption of social ritual, order and hierarchy. In these moralities, Lucifer can be either a serious or a comic figure. The early *Fall of Lucifer,* for example, presents him before his rebellion as a figure who commands reverence; after his fall, however, he is reduced to a ludicrous no-hoper who resorts to trying to extinguish the flames of heaven with his own wind. In Bishop John Bale's *The Temptation of Our Lord* (1538), Satan attempts to corrupt Christ with the words:

Forsake the belief that ye have in God's word,
That ye are His son, for it is not worth a turd.

As J P Brockbank points out: 'Bale was not afraid of precipitous clashes between the high and low, reverent and blasphemous, spiritual and animal. Nor was Marlowe.'

Moralities were not only about the governance of the soul: some focus also on the behaviour of rulers and their responsibilities to the state. John Skelton's *Magnificence* (c. 1515), for example, shows a generous prince ruined by misguided generosity and bad counsellors, but saved by figures such as Good-hope and Perseverence. (Skelton was tutor to Prince Henry, later Henry VIII.) Some critics have seen in Lucifer's exercise of power over Faustus a parallel with the tyranny of a despotic Renaissance prince.

Plays with similar themes

For plays which seriously explore the progress of the soul in its journey towards death, and the fight between good and evil, we have to look back to the moralities mentioned above. From Marlowe's own time and the period following his death, most of the plays with similar themes give conjuring and magic a comic treatment.

Robert Greene's *Friar Bacon and Friar Bungay* (c. 1589), performed at the Rose, features the historical Roger Bacon who was reputed to have conjured a brazen talking head (see page 139). In the play, Bacon demonstrates his superiority over other magicians when the spirit of Hercules is quelled even by one of his frowns.

The Merry Devil of Edmonton (c. 1602), by an unknown author, has much in common with Marlowe's play, featuring as it does a magician, Peter Fabel, who has made a pact with the devil, signed in blood. Realising that he has sacrificed his soul for trivial powers, Fabel succeeds in trapping the devil into granting him a respite of seven years. All that is explained in the Prologue; in the remainder of the play, the magic element is confined to Fabel's kindly efforts in aiding the elopement of a pair of young lovers.

In Ben Jonson's *The Devil is an Ass* (1616), the exploits of a minor devil, Pug, form a sub-plot. Pug, who has been allowed one day on Earth, finds himself outdone in wickedness by the Londoners with whom he comes into contact. There are also elements of magic and conjuring – though this time performed by charlatans – in Jonson's more famous play *The Alchemist* (1610).

The Witch of Edmonton (1621) is a tragicomedy, probably co-written by John Ford, William Rowley and Thomas Dekker. One plot concerns an old woman, persecuted by her neighbours, who sells her soul to the devil. The play is interesting because of the sympathetic and humane presentation of the old woman.

Barnabe Barnes's *The Devil's Charter* (published 1607) has a number of echoes of *Doctor Faustus* (including a final dragging-away scene) and focuses on the evil life of the Borgia pope Alexander VI (Pope 1492–1503) and his children. Alexander has sold his soul to become Pope and the devil tricks him into thinking that the bargain will last longer than it does.

One serious play which centrally features magic and asks us to contemplate the nature of evil is, of course, Shakespeare's *Macbeth* (1606). Like Faustus, Macbeth becomes involved with the dark powers, and in the one comic moment, the castle porter imagines himself the door-keeper of hell, admitting damned souls.

The other great drama from a later century to be based on the Faust legend is the tragedy by the German playwright, Johann Wolfgang von Goethe (1749–1832). Goethe's *Faust,* published in two parts (1808 and 1832), is very different from Marlowe's, not least in its ending, when Faust's soul is saved from the clutches of hell by angels.

The characters

These notes provide references for discussion and essay writing. Nearly all the points are summaries of fuller notes in the text.

They can form the basis for quotation banks of:
• characters' key qualities
• moments of change, crisis or revelation
• issues for debate.

'*Doctor Faustus* represents a transition between dominant modes of drama, straddling as it does the medieval tradition and the emergent genre of Elizabethan tragedy' (Stevie Simkin). This means that figures such as the Good and Evil Angels and the Old Man have to be discussed in terms of the roles they perform and the abstractions that they represent, rather than as rounded 'characters' in the traditional sense.

But does this also apply to the major characters? Una Ellis-Fermor wrote, 'The character of Faustus, it cannot be too often repeated, is not that of one man, but of man himself, of Everyman. There are no details, no personal traits, no eccentricities or habits, nothing that is intimate or individual.' William Tydeman, on the other hand, felt that Faustus was 'invested with a psychological ambiguity which contributes greatly to the human interest of the work that bears his name, and has encouraged actors to attempt varied readings of the role on stage'.

Are Faustus and Mephistopheles merely expanded versions of the Everyman and Vice figures from the medieval moralities? Or do they display enough individual character traits to make us interested in them as human beings?

Faustus

In modern times Faustus's name has always been given a pronunciation which reflects the character's German origins (*Fau* rhyming with *how*). Many people believe, however, that in Marlowe's day the name might have been pronounced *fost-us* or *forst-us*. The evidence for this is found in documents from the Rose playhouse, where the play was widely performed: Philip Henslowe, the owner of the Rose, spells the name, among other variations, as: ffostose, ffostus, fastes and fosstes, and the list of properties refers to 'i dragon in fostes'.

The characters

1.1
Faustus's opening soliloquy:
1–4 'the very word end itself (carrying of course another doom-laden sense in this play) occurs five times between lines 4 and 18' (William Tydeman).

39–47 Faustus is very selective in his quotations. The omissions lead some commentators to say that 'Faustus's impatience is bred as much by arrogance and misunderstanding of the traditional disciplines as by an eagerness to go beyond their bounds' (David Bevington and Eric Rasmussen) and that 'this is an illustration of Faustus's foolishness, in spite of his supposed great learning' (Stevie Simkin). Does Faustus deliberately neglect to complete the quotations? Is he making a point about the lack of logic in the scriptures? Or is he displaying a closed mind? (The B-text has a speech by Mephostopheles: 'When thou took'st the book / To view the Scriptures, then I turned the leaves / And led thine eye' (5.2.99–101).)

47 'The whole soliloquy has been driving towards this moment when Faustus experiences the ultimate frustration of all earthly ambitions' (Roma Gill).

52 Faustus's description of necromantic books as heavenly.
'Faustus's first soliloquy is a second prologue, but the hero's to his own design, not Marlowe's to the play.' (J P Brockbank).

92 Are Faustus's ambitions here altruistic or mischievous? For example, dressing students in silk. 'Faustus's spirit of disinterested enquiry is undoubtedly adulterated by less worthy motives: the desire for personal kudos and wealth, for pomp and luxury, for sensual satisfaction' (William Tydeman).

1.3
87 By using the word 'manly', 'Faustus expresses the sense of human self-sufficiency which he enjoys at this stage in his career. For the reader or listener there is irony in his arrogant recommendation of manliness to a supernatural being' (J D Jump). 'The unhappy devil speaks with a bleak infinity of misery and experience to the uncomprehending doctor who is exuberant, overconfident, and so ignorant that he can offer to instruct his mentor: *Learn thou of Faustus'* (Roma Gill).

Ideologically the significance of 1.3 'lies in its demonstration that Faustus is in full possession of all the facts: he has been cautioned about the consequences that will ensue if he persists in his chosen action, and urged by Mephostopheles…to restrain his folly. He can now make no appeal on grounds of ignorance' (Roma Gill).

2.1
1 'Even before he abjures God, Faustus expresses a sense of being isolated and trapped' (Jonathan Dollimore).

132 How much of Marlowe is in Faustus? This line has 'the same note of bravado that we hear in the Baines note and the Kyd letters' (Paul Kocher). It demonstrates 'a type of adolescent refusal [in Faustus] to recognise the powers he has invoked' (Thomas Healy). 'After the bond is signed, the discussion is renewed, but while the devil loses nothing in dignity of serious discourse, we can already detect a change in Faustus; his sceptical levity takes on a more truculent and jeering tone' (W W Greg). Is Faustus displaying a kind of adolescent bravado here?

184 Is he expressing doubt that the books contain all that Mephistopheles promises? If so, why?

2.3
19 'Faustus is beginning to lose his confidence in the heroic consolations of evil and his moral distress is becoming genuine' (J P Brockbank).
27–31 W W Greg points out that there are two attractive qualities that can be claimed for Faustus throughout: one is 'a genuine tenderness towards his students'; the other, shown here, 'a love of beauty in nature and art'. But how strongly do these qualities come across?
31 'my Mephistopheles', 'sweet Mephistopheles', etc. How far do you see a homoerotic element in their relationship? Would it help to bring it out on stage?
170–173 'O, this feeds my soul!': 'his exultant disgust springs from his enjoyment of sharing the privilege of Lucifer's throne (like a royal guest) and being superior to the vices that overtake mankind' (J P Brockbank). Do you agree? Is Faustus guilty of all of these sins?

4.1
145 Is his 'distrust' a distrust of God (the sin of despair), or of Lucifer?

5.1
63–66 'Is it that Faustus cannot repent because he is without grace, and cannot have grace because he will not repent?' (J P Brockbank).
76–78 'Faustus…shows himself now, perhaps for the first time, to be truly a lost soul' (Cleanth Brooks).
78 Is it significant that, in confirming his allegiance, he now talks of 'our' hell?
82–88 'It is precisely this love of "vain pleasure", this need for constant stimulation and the avoidance of boredom, this inconsistent attitude to life's immense possibilities which connect the aspiring but easily distracted scholar with the boisterous prankster of the central scenes' (William Tydeman).
93–95 'Even at the brink of damnation, Faustus looks to mortal love, or satisfaction of his lusts, for salvation' (Stevie Simkin).

5.2
47–48 'Unlike the Old Man, Faustus is a physical coward' (William Tydeman).
75 The sexual and sensual are never far from Faustus's mind, even at the point of death.
124 What emotion lies behind his final cry?

Mephistopheles

There are many variations on the spelling of this character's name, all variants on the *Faustbuch*'s Mephostophiles. In the 1604 A-text of *Doctor Faustus,* he is variously Mephostophilis (a form commonly used by editors and critics today), Mephastophilis, Mephastophilus and Mephistophilis. In the 1616 B-text, he is mainly Mephostopheles, but also occasionally Mephastopheles. (Shakespeare, in *The*

Merry Wives of Windsor, mentions Mephostophilus.) This book uses a ninth –
Mephistopheles – the version in popular usage.

1.3
25 Faustus describes the form that Mephistopheles first takes as 'too ugly'.
47–52 Mephistopheles did not come in answer to Faustus's magic incantations, but
simply because he heard someone abuse the name of God. As he says, 'I came now
hither of mine own accord.'
65–74 Mephistopheles's replies are 'dignified, courteous, terse' (William Tydeman).
78–84 For Mephistopheles, hell is the absence of God.
In the 1967 film, Mephistopheles weeps as he utters 'Why this is hell…' and is
totally sincere in his attempt to dissuade Faustus from a course of action that will
damn him. In this speech, 'Mephistopheles promptly displaces Faustus as the
intellectual centre of the play. His eloquence sticks to the facts and sheds the airy
and fiery qualities which continue to characterise the fantasies of Faustus…he is not
a tempter' (J P Brockbank).

2.1
42 'As before, none of the devil's answers are reassuring…man is tempted only
because misery loves company' (J P Brockbank).
73 and 82 Mephistopheles's asides create a new actor–audience relationship,
turning Mephistopheles into a cunning plotter.
133 In a 1980 production, Mephistopheles 'became a passive and helpless
spectator of Faustus's ruin, an almost fatherly figure hopelessly watching his son
slide down the slippery slope as he had once slid himself' (William Tydeman). But
how does this interpretation accommodate lines such as 2.1.73 and 82?
148–149 Mephistopheles refuses to provide Faustus with a wife.

3.2
30–35 Mephistopheles's expression of annoyance at being summoned against his
will is at variance with his earlier comment that he does not come at command, but
only when he chooses. Do you agree?

Language and structure

Marlowe's verse

Metre

It is possible to describe where the heavy stress falls in any English word. For
example, these three words (from the Prologue) have their heavy stress on the first
syllable: **mar**ching, **for**tunes, **judge**ments; while in these the heavy stress is on the
second syllable: In**tends**, per**form**, Where**as**.

All Marlowe's verse has a pattern of light and heavy stresses running through it,

known as the metre. You can hear the metre if you read these lines out loud, over-emphasising the heavily stressed syllables:
- Nor **spor**-ting **in** the **dall**-i-**ance** of **love** (Prologue 3)
- In **courts** of **kings** where **state** is **o**-ver-**turned** (Prologue 4)
- Of **ri**-per **years** to **Wit**-ten-**berg** he **went** (Prologue 13).

No actor would ever perform the lines in that monotonous way, but they would certainly be aware that the metre was always there, helping to give the verse form and structure.

Sometimes, to point out that a syllable has to be sounded to make the metre work, it will be accented, like this:
- To practise magic and conceal**èd** arts (1.1.104).

Varying the metre

Most of the lines in *Doctor Faustus* are not as regular as the first three quoted above. In fact, most will have an irregular stress pattern, like this one:
- The **stars move still**; **time runs**; the **clock** will **strike** (5.2.76).

This line is part of a final soliloquy in which the disjointed rhythm can help the actor to convey Faustus's turmoil.

Occasionally a line will contain an extra syllable (11 rather than 10):
- And **then** │ thou **must** │ be **damned** │ per-**pet-** │ u-al-**ly** (5.2.68).

Here the infinity of damnation is emphasised by the adverb with its extra syllable, following a succession of monosyllables. There are also eleven syllables in the line:
- O, I'll **leap** │ **up** to │ my **God**! │Who **pulls** │ me **down**? (5.2.78).

Lisa Hopkins has remarked that 'at the very moment that he aspires most fervently to escape damnation, his language aspires to escape the formal structures of the verse'.

Some lines are very noticeable, because they are clearly short:
- And **hide** me **from** the **hea**vy **wrath** of **God**!
  No, no! (5.2.86–87).

The isolation of the negatives – 'No, no' – helps the actor to convey Faustus's desperation.

A collection of heavy stresses together can add emphasis:
- **Ah, Faust**us,
  Now hast thou but one bare hour to live (5.2.66–67).

These introductory words in Faustus's final speech – a succession of monosyllables, all stressed – starkly express the awfulness of the fate awaiting him, reinforcing the sense of tragic doom.

Dividing the line into feet

Just as music has a number of beats in a bar, so Marlowe's (and Shakespeare's) verse has five 'feet' in a complete line, made up of stressed and unstressed syllables. A five-feet line is called 'pentameter' (pent = five; meter = measure).

Iambic pentameter

A foot which contains an unstressed syllable followed by a stressed one (the standard 'beat': dee-**dum**) is called an 'iamb'. Verse which has five iambs per line as its standard rhythm is called 'iambic pentameter'. Iambic pentameter which does not rhyme is also sometimes known as 'blank verse'. This is the standard verse form for both Marlowe and Shakespeare.

Special effects can be gained by varying the iambic metre. But in this line the perfectly regular metre helps to express the Scholar's straightforward and unaffected admiration for Helen:

* Too **sim**- | ple **is** | my **wit** | to **tell** | her **praise** (5.1.26).

Alexandrines

An alexandrine is an iambic line of six feet, rather than five: in other words, iambic hexameter. When alexandrines are inserted into pentameter verse, they can have a variety of effects. For example, J D Jump has observed that, while exhorting himself to be 'resolute', Faustus's irresolution can be felt in the rhythm of:

* Now **go** | not **back**- | ward. **No,** | **Faus-tus,** | be **res**- | o-**lute**.

  Why **wave**- | rest **thou**? | O, **some**- | thing **sound**- | eth **in** | mine **ears** (2.1.6–7)

while Faustus's desperation and agony are tellingly expressed in:

* One **drop** | would **save** | my **soul,** | **half** a | drop. **Ah,** | my **Christ**! (5.2.80)

  with the juxtaposed heavy stresses (soul | half) in the third and fourth feet.

Caesuras

Many lines contain a noticeable pause or break in the middle; this is called a caesura (from a Latin verb meaning 'to cut'). The caesura not only helps to add variety to a block of verse, it can also emphasise particular words or phrases, or suggest a break in the speaker's thought. Perhaps the best-known example is in Faustus's famous speech on seeing Helen:

* Her **lips** | sucks **forth** | my **soul.** | | **See** where | it **flies**! (5.1.94).

The fourth foot is not iambic; this creates a heavy stress each side of the caesura (highlighted by the alliteration), which helps to express Faustus's great sense of wonder and yearning. Caesuras are particularly common in alexandrines, where the longer lines encourage a definite pause.

Run-on lines

When Marlowe started writing, blank verse was still relatively in its infancy and the tendency with many writers was to allow the caesura always to fall exactly in the middle of the line, or to have a natural pause at the end of the line. Marlowe avoids this monotony, creating pauses in a variety of different positions and often allowing the sense of the verse to run on from one line to the next. This is particularly noticeable in Faustus's last speech with blocks of verse such as:

- Fair **na-** | ture's **eye,** | **rise, rise** | again, | and **make**

  Per**pet-** | ual **day;** | or **let** | this **hour** | be **but**

  A **year,** | a **month,** | a **week,** | a **nat-** | ural **day** (5.2.71–73).

Here the run-on lines and regular iambic rhythm help the actor to convey the anguish of a man who recognises that he cannot halt his headlong fall into damnation.

The layout of the verse

A single foot can contain syllables from different words, and any one word can be broken up by the foot divisions. This line, for example, is made up of only four words:

1st	2nd	3rd	4th	5th	foot
• These **met-**	a**phys-**	ics **of**	ma**gi-**	ci**ans** (1.1.51).	

Marlowe's plays abound in exotic and romantic-sounding names, many of which are four or five syllables long: *Mephistopheles*, for example, accounts for half a line.

Rhyme

Although rare in *Doctor Faustus*, Marlowe does occasionally use rhyme. The most notable example is at the very end of the play where the rhyming couplet gives the moral message a proverbial ring while also signalling a conclusion to the drama:
- Whose deepness doth entice such forward wits
  To practise more than heavenly power permits. (Epilogue 7–8).

The small amount of rhyme in *Doctor Faustus* is used for a variety of different effects. In 2.1, Mephistopheles's jingling reply is almost comic and helps to deflect Faustus from thinking about the seriousness of his intended act – handing over the signed deed:

FAUSTUS   But may I raise up spirits when I please?
MEPHISTOPHELES   Ay, Faustus, and do greater things than these. (2.1.86–87)

while the rhymes in 3.1 aptly underline Faustus's mockery of the Pope:
- Anon you shall hear a hog grunt, a calf bleat, and an ass bray,
  Because it is Saint Peter's holy day. (3.1.86–87)

Verse and prose

It is never totally clear why writers such as Marlowe and Shakespeare choose to write some scenes, or passages, in verse, and others in prose.

Although there are many occasions in their plays where the more serious scenes, involving great passions, are in verse, while those about ordinary people and comedy are in prose, there are also significant examples where this is not the case. In *Doctor Faustus*, for example, the tense and portentous scene between Faustus and his fellow scholars immediately preceding his death (5.2.1–65) is in prose. As a rule in this play, however, the more serious moments are in verse and the comic sequences in prose. The Horse-courser scene, for example (4.1.113–195), is in prose, except for the moment when Faustus is left alone to meditate 'What art thou, Faustus...?' (143–148).

The prose in the play is used with great flexibility, ranging from the comic cleverness of Wagner in 1.2, possibly written by Marlowe's collaborator (and foreshadowing Feste, the 'corrupter of words', in Shakespeare's *Twelfth Night*), to the sombre pathos of Faustus's final conversation with his fellow scholars in 5.2.

Structure and style

The structure of *Doctor Faustus* has been the subject of a great deal of discussion. Many critics see little merit in the central comic scenes and accuse the play of being incoherent and broken-backed, 'a ruined cathedral' (Una Ellis-Fermor). In the view of Cleanth Brooks, for example, Faustus has little to do after signing the deed 'except to fill in the time before the mortgage falls due and the devil comes to collect the forfeited soul'. Others prefer to see in the structure a reflection of medieval morality play tradition, in which serious moral episodes are parodied and burlesqued in scenes of knockabout farce. Supporters of this view argue, moreover, that after the Seven Deadly Sins have entertained Faustus with 'a representation of the bonds which will fetter him until his destruction at the end of the play', the ensuing comic scenes constantly remind us of the 'consequences of following passion wherever it leads' (Nigel Alexander). In one particular episode – that of the Knight's horns (4.1) – there is a clear allusion to the myth of Actaeon (see page 155), commonly evoked in Marlowe's time to show that anyone who desires forbidden things will inevitably be punished.

There are also notable parallels between the serious scenes and the comic ones, most obviously when Faustus's necromancy is replayed in the inept conjuring of Robin and Rafe. In 1.4, for example, Robin's reply that he would accept only a well-roasted shoulder of mutton in return for his soul (lines 12–15), is a parody of the bargain that Faustus is about to make, highlighting its foolishness. Secondly, Wagner engages Robin as his servant for seven years (28–29), exactly as Faustus will enlist Mephistopheles for twenty-four: neither will be getting much value out of the agreement. Finally, Wagner's threat that Robin's lice will be turned into devils and tear him in pieces, backed up by the entrance of Balioll and Belcher, foreshadows the more serious threats uttered by the Evil Angel to Faustus, and supported by Lucifer's appearance (at 2.3.82–87); in both cases, the devils' purposes are to convince and terrify a subject who is attempting to repent. And in 2.2, when Robin declares that he can obtain wine 'at any tavern in Europe *for nothing*' (26–27), we are reminded of Faustus, who proposes to indulge himself in sensual and intellectual pleasures while seemingly dismissing the fact that a reckoning will ultimately have to be made.

Roger Sales sees a further possible parallel with the Faustus plot in 3.2. Comparing this Robin and Rafe scene with Faustus's antics in 3.1, he observes: 'The clown who created the part of Robin seems to have been an experienced juggler. Perhaps that is all that Faustus becomes as a result of his contract with Lucifer.' At the end of 3.2, Robin and Rafe are absurdly pleased with their transformations into dog and ape, which helps us to appreciate just how deluded Faustus is to be satisfied with his transformation into a spirit. Even the farcical moment of Faustus's leg-pulling in Act 4 prefigures later more serious events: it grotesquely foreshadows his eventual dismemberment by devils.

Inversion and parody

The comic scenes are part of a wider system of inversion and parody in which words are employed in heavily ironic reversals of their traditional meanings. Faustus is assured that nations will 'canonise' him for his exploits in magic (1.1.122), a term normally applied to the creation of saints; he boasts of the 'virtue' of his 'heavenly' words (1.3.28); he is urged to 'pray devoutly' to Lucifer (1.3.55); and he utters the final words of Jesus on the cross, '*Consummatum est*' (2.1.74), at the moment of signing away his soul. (As Jonathan Dollimore observes, 'Faustus is not liberating himself, he is ending himself: "it is finished".') Whether deliberately or not, Faustus pursues a career which has striking parallels with Christ's: he longs for the power to bring the dead to life again (1.1.25); enacts parodies of miracles; and prepares his fellow scholars for his imminent death in a blasphemous version of the Last Supper (5.1.1–8). Stage productions have sometimes brought out this unholy parallelism visually.

The chiastic structure

Roy T Eriksen has been foremost among critics in asserting that, far from being incoherent, the play's structure is intricately designed. Eriksen describes a symmetrical, or **chiastic**, structure – one in which a series of scenes in the first half is paralleled in reverse order by scenes in the second half. According to Eriksen, therefore, the play has an outer frame of morning scenes (1.1 and, in the B-text, 5.3 – see page 117), with an inner frame of midnight scenes (see 2.1.28 and 5.2.116 s.d.), while the twenty-four years in between suggest the twenty-four hours of a day. Individual events also contribute to this chiastic structure. For example, Faustus's reference to suicide at 2.3.22–26 balances an attempt at 5.1.52; while in 1.4 and 2.2 Robin's antics not only parody Faustus's conjuring, but also foreshadow (in his threatened cuckolding of his master: 2.2.17–19) the punishment that Faustus will later inflict on the Knight (4.1.64–100).

The chiastic structure is also reflected within individual exchanges and is clearly seen in:

FAUSTUS	How comes it then that thou art out of hell?
MEPHISTOPHELES	Why, this is hell, nor am I out of it. (1.3.77–78)

Language and structure

The style of this dialogue also reminds us that Marlowe would have honed his rhetorical skills in the *dispute*, the formal debate which was central to his education in Canterbury and Cambridge and which is reflected throughout *Doctor Faustus*. Everything one Angel says produces an equal and opposite reaction from the other; the influences of Valdes and Cornelius are balanced by those of the Scholars; Faustus's prayers to Christ are negated by his conjurations to the devil. Such 'antithesis of voices generates an anxiety that is both theological and artistic. Faustus's often flippant agnosticism is not simply his own pathway to hell; it is also, for Marlowe, a shifting point of view from which to explore uncertainties' (David Bevington and Eric Rasmussen).

Imagery

A number of critics have commented on the ways in which the imagery of the play relates to its themes.

Aspiration, ascent and overreaching

Caroline Spurgeon finds in the play an 'imaginative preoccupation with the dazzling heights and vast spaces of the universe…a magnificent surging upward thrust and aspiration', adding that Marlowe seems 'more familiar with the starry courts of heaven than with the green fields of earth'. The 'topless towers' from one of the play's most famous lines (5.1.92) are 'recurrent symbols [in Marlowe's plays] for illimitable aspiration, and Marlowe habitually juxtaposes them to the all-consuming element of fire'. That quotation is by Harry Levin whose famous book on Marlowe, *The Overreacher*, is about the Marlovian heroes who ambitiously strive to go beyond the limitations imposed upon normal human beings:

> Till, swoll'n with cunning of a self-conceit,
> His waxen wings did mount above his reach,
> And melting heavens conspired his overthrow. (Prologue 20–22)

Feeding and gluttony

Harry Levin observed the shift from such images of aspiration to images of gluttony: 'After the prologue speaks of overreaching, the emphasis shifts from the heavenly to the hellish…With this shift, the rising verse subsides toward a dying fall, and the ethereal image of flight gives way to grosser images of appetite.'

Faustus's hunger for knowledge and power is represented in imagery of feeding invoked in lines such as 'surfeits upon…necromancy' (Prologue 25); 'How am I glutted with conceit of this!' (1.1.80); and 'O, this feeds my soul!' (2.3.170). C L Barber notes that this imagery extends into the comic scenes, such as 2.2 (see 25–27): 'Grotesque and perverse versions of hunger appear in the comedy. Like much of Shakespeare's low comedy, the best clowning in *Doctor Faustus* spells out literally what is metaphorical in the poetry.' In this respect, the picture of the Pope and the Cardinal gluttonously feasting in 3.1, for example, is a visual embodiment of their corruption.

Life and blood

Streaming blood in this play is emblematic of eternal life. When Faustus exclaims, 'See, see where Christ's blood streams in the firmament!' (5.2.79), we should recall his earlier cry when his blood congeals: 'Why streams it not' (2.1.66) and the moment when, in a futile attempt to repent, he begs his eyes to 'Gush forth blood instead of tears' (5.2.32–33). In performance this imagery is visually enhanced by the drawing of blood to sign the deed (2.1.53–72) and, in some productions, by the sight of Faustus's dismembered limbs at the very end.

Diction

Much of the play's diction is characterised by duality of meaning. At 1.3.15, for example, 'the word "perform" ambivalently suggests both active accomplishment and illusory fabrication of dramatic spectacles' (David Bevington and Eric Rasmussen); and there is a similar effect with a word such as 'deed' (2.1.60 and 117), which ought to imply something active and liberating, but in reality applies to the limiting contract to which Faustus binds himself. There is a similar duality of meaning in the words 'resolve' and 'resolute'. T McAlindon has pointed out that these are key words in the play (see 1.1.82 and 135, for example), but that Faustus increasingly comes 'to occupy a world where to be resolved is to disintegrate or dissolve' (David Bevington and Eric Rasmussen).

William Tydeman has observed that Faustus's diction in reviewing his orthodox studies abounds in finite terms: '*Settle* thy studies'; '*sound* the depth'; '*level* at the end…' (1.1.1–4). But then, finding his present studies inadequate, 'Faustus reaches beyond to a world apparently brimming with limitless possibilities, and his imagery too is released from bondage. The "quiet poles" are invoked, winds are raised, clouds rent.'

Themes

The major themes in *Doctor Faustus* can be expressed in a series of questions, constantly addressed throughout the play: What is hell? When is Faustus damned? What does he gain? Why doesn't he repent?

What is hell?

Mephistopheles famously defines hell as a state of mind: 'Why, this is hell, nor am I out of it' (1.3.78), and later: 'Hell hath no limits, nor is circumscribed / In one self place, for where we are is hell, / And where hell is must we ever be' (2.1.126–128). Milton's Satan was to express a very similar view of hell: 'Which way I fly is hell;

myself am hell' (*Paradise Lost*, Book IV, line 75; published 1667). For Mephistopheles, hell is the absence of God (see 1.3.79–82).

Mephistopheles's definition raises interesting questions, such as: if hell is a state of mind, can it also be a geographical location which can be visited? Discussing Faustus's response to the Seven Deadly Sins – 'O, this feeds my soul!' (2.3.170) – J P Brockbank observes, 'his exultant disgust springs from his enjoyment of sharing the privilege of Lucifer's throne (like a royal guest) and being superior to the vices that overtake mankind. He asks to visit hell and return safely, but hell has already visited him and left him contaminated.'

When is Faustus damned?

One of the ambiguities of the play concerns the question of whether Faustus does indeed become 'a spirit in form and substance', as he stipulates in the deed (2.1.97–98); in the middle scenes he certainly seems to have the spirit's ability to be invisible or lose a leg without suffering harm (3.1 and 4.1); but why then does he succumb to the threat of being torn to pieces (2.3.82, 5.1.69 and 5.2.47–48); and why at the culmination of his twenty-four years are devils able to inflict such physical torment upon him (in the B-text)?

Some commentators maintain that Faustus is indeed transformed into a spirit (at 2.1.97–98) and claim that he is therefore damned from this point – given that 'spirit' in this play invariably means 'devil'. (W W Greg points out that the stage direction in the B-text for the first entry of the Good and Bad Angels is '*Enter the Angel and Spirit*.') Others maintain that the question is left open, pointing out that the words 'Be I a devil' (2.3.16) can mean either 'Even if I were a devil' or 'It doesn't matter that I am a devil'. If we take the view that Faustus is damned from the moment of signing the deed, we have to ask why Mephistopheles is willing to help Faustus commit the ultimate sin of despair (see 5.1.51 s.d.) – a refusal to believe God's word that any soul can be saved.

W W Greg famously argued (in 1946) that it is Faustus's sexual relationship with a devil in Helen's shape – the sin of demoniality – that damns him (5.1.110). If that is so, there is added irony in the thought that Helen's kiss could make Faustus 'immortal' and a chilling literalness in the fact that her lips 'sucks forth' his soul (94). T W Craik, however, points out that since Faustus does not realise that his 'paramour' is a devil in Helen's shape, he does not intend to commit demoniality and therefore cannot be damned for sinning inadvertently. Nicolas Kiessling makes the point that demoniality was not necessarily unforgivable during Marlowe's lifetime anyway.

What does Faustus gain?

The conventional view is that Faustus gains very little from his bargain, and that the central scenes – in which we see Faustus exercising the powers he has bought – are studiedly anticlimactic. J P Brockbank, for example, while offering the opinion that:

'The scenes [in Acts 3 and 4] remind us that great magicians...are at best reputable court entertainers and not masters of empire', goes on to observe that the Emperor's desire to see the wart on the neck of Alexander's paramour (4.1.70–72) is the sole example of 'calculated dramatic bathos' – deliberate anticlimax.

Christopher Ricks takes an unusual approach to the argument that Faustus strikes a poor bargain, getting very little in return for his soul. He points out that, at a time when the plague was rife, Faustus's request for twenty-four years of guaranteed life 'is the greatest and most fundamental thing he buys'.

Why doesn't Faustus repent?

In Act 2 Faustus bitterly accuses Mephistopheles of having damned his soul, and asks 'Is't not too late?' The Evil Angel replies 'Too late', but the Good Angel counters with 'Never too late, if Faustus can repent' (2.3.79–81). In the context of this question – *why doesn't Faustus repent?* – the word *can* in the Good Angel's 'can repent' carries huge significance. It suggests that repentance might well be beyond Faustus's control – a harsh and unforgiving view of humanity's relationship with God. Interestingly, the later (1616) B-text has the Good Angel say: 'Never too late, if Faustus *will* repent', implying that, if Faustus *is willing* to repent, he will find forgiveness and salvation.

Only a few lines later, Faustus calls on Christ: 'Ah, Christ, my Saviour, / Seek to save distressèd Faustus' soul!' (2.3.84–85). But Christ either does not hear, or chooses not to help; instead Lucifer appears. What are we to make of this? Max Bluestone considers God's non-appearance to be 'an inexplicable rebuff'. Robert West says that true repentance has to withstand hell's onslaughts and that Faustus's is therefore not wholehearted. David Bevington and Eric Rasmussen state:

> Does the absence of Christ at this critical juncture suggest a conspiracy in heaven? Not necessarily; the orthodox explanation might be that we all have to be left to face the devil alone, as was Christ in the wilderness, and that in any event the Good Angel continues to urge Faustus to repent. We are left none the less with the perception that God (Christ) is starkly absent from the play, and that in his separation from God Faustus finds repentance seemingly impossible.

How impressive is the Old Man (in 5.1) as a force for good, supporting Faustus in his attempts to repent? Roger Sales identifies a key weakness in his presentation and stature: 'One of the problems for spectators...is that Faustus has the most memorable lines. The Old Man might have the kind of choric authority that was granted to characters like Good Counsel in earlier drama and yet, rhetorically, he is eminently forgettable.' When Faustus rejects him and calls for his punishment 'Faustus...shows himself now, perhaps for the first time, to be truly a lost soul' (Cleanth Brooks).

Perhaps, the question of Faustus's failure to repent is unanswerable, and we can merely wonder, with J P Brockbank: 'Is it that Faustus cannot repent because he is without grace, and cannot have grace because he will not repent?'

Classical allusions

It is no surprise, given the education that Marlowe would have received, to find that the play abounds in classical allusions. Here is a summary of them; some have fuller notes on the relevant pages of the text.

Allusion	Reference	Explanation	Notes
Icarus	Prologue 21–22	Icarus flew too near the sun and plunged to his death in the sea (see page 138 and Ovid, *Metamorphoses*)	Faustus is also an overreacher
Jove	1.1.78; 1.3.91; 3 Chorus 3	Jupiter: king of the Roman gods	often used for the Christian God at this time ('Jupiter' is used for the Roman god at 5.1.106)
Musaeus	1.1.118	poet surrounded by a crowd of spirits in the underworld (see Virgil, *The Aeneid*)	scholars gather round Faustus in the same way
Queen of Love	1.1.131	the Roman goddess Venus (the Greeks' Aphrodite)	Valdes claims that the spirits they will conjure will be comparable to the ultimate in female beauty
golden fleece	1.1.133	the object of Jason's quest (see Ovid, *Metamorphoses*)	the fleece represents golden treasure brought back to Spain from the Americas
Elysium	1.3.61	the classical 'heaven'; Virgil placed it in Hades (the underworld) in *The Aeneid*	Faustus does not see a difference between hell and the pagan heaven
Penelope	2.1.161	the faithful wife of Odysseus in Homer's *The Odyssey*	she is the epitome of chastity and all the domestic virtues
blind Homer	2.3.27	the supposed author of *The Iliad* and *The Odyssey*	Faustus has conjured the greatest poet ever
Alexander …Oenone	2.3.28	Alexander was Homer's name for Paris in *The Iliad*; in later poems, Oenone was the nymph he deserted for Helen	Faustus has heard Homer sing of it

Allusion	Reference	Explanation	Notes
he that built… music	2.3.29–31	a reference to Amphion, ruler of Thebes, a great harpist (mentioned in Ovid, *Metamorphoses*)	Faustus has heard the greatest harpist
Olympus	3 Chorus 4	the highest mountain in Greece, home of the Greek gods	in classical myth, Olympus is the highest known peak
Maro's golden tomb	3.1.13	the great Roman epic poet Publius Vergilius Maro (70–19 BC), now known as Vergil or Virgil	there are many medieval stories about Virgil as a magician, such as this one
Styx, Acheron… Phleg-ethon	3.1.45–46	three of the rivers of Hades, the Greek underworld (Acheron is also mentioned in 1.3.16)	Faustus swears by them as representing the power of hell
Diana and Actaeon	4.1.63–64	Actaeon saw the goddess Diana (Artemis) bathing; he was turned into a stag and torn to pieces by his own hounds	the fate of Actaeon, commonly interpreted in Marlowe's time as a punishment for desiring forbidden things, echoes that of Faustus
thread of vital life	4.1.106	the Three Fates spun out the thread of a person's life, measured it, and cut it off at the allotted span	Faustus sees the end of his life approaching
Helen of Greece	5.1.12	Helen of Troy, wife of the Spartan king Menelaus (see 5.1.100), and reputedly the most beautiful woman in the world	Helen provides an apt culmination to Faustus's twenty-four years of dedicated sensuality; she destroyed Ilium (Troy; also called Dardania at line 24) and will play a part in Faustus's destruction too
Sir Paris	5.1.23	the son of Priam, King of Troy, whose abduction of Helen started the Trojan War	*Sir* 'assimilates Paris to the hero of a medieval romance' (J D Jump): is this how Faustus sees himself?

Allusion	Reference	Explanation	Notes
launched …ships	5.1.91	Helen's flight with Paris caused the vast Greek fleet to set sail in pursuit	Helen's destructive power is stressed throughout the speech
Achilles	5.1.102	in some versions of the Troy myth, Paris fires an arrow which fatally strikes the Greek hero Achilles in the heel – the only part of his body which is not invulnerable	Faustus continues to romanticise the episode (see 5.1.23 above), here fantasising that he is Paris, killing the greatest of all the Greek heroes
hapless Semele	5.1.107	Semele asked to see Jupiter in his full brilliance (instead of his customary mortal disguise) and was consumed by his lightning (see Ovid, Metamorphoses)	this, in essence, is to be Faustus's fate
Arethusa's azured arms	5.1.109	the nymph Arethusa awakened the lust of a god and was transformed into a fountain	more fantasising: Faustus speaks as though he were a god and she were one of his conquests
O lente… equi!	5.2.75	a line from Ovid's Amores: the speaker begs the goddess of dawn to delay as he lies in his mistress's arms	the sexual and sensual are never far from Faustus's mind, even at the point of death
Apollo's laurel bough	Epilogue 2	Apollo was the Greek and Roman god of music, poetry and the arts	all Faustus's learning and culture have counted for nothing

Criticism

'Doctor Faustus has occasioned more controversy than any other of Marlowe's plays, and indeed more than any other Elizabethan play with the exception of Hamlet' (William Tydeman and Vivien Thomas). In addition to continuing debates concerning the relative merits of the A- and B-texts, critics have tended to focus on six key areas:
• The figure of Faustus as a tragic hero: Is he a Promethean seeker after knowledge (see page 138) or, in the words of the critic Leo Kirschbaum, 'an unstable, foolish worldling'? And, if he is the latter, does this reduce him to a figure who excites little sympathy or interest?

- The world that Faustus inhabits and his conditioning by Renaissance and Reformation tensions: What is the nature of his sin and why is he damned?
- Genre: Is *Doctor Faustus* a heroic tragedy or a morality play – or something else altogether? How should we respond to the mixing of tragic and comic genres?
- Related to this is the question of structure. Is the play, in Una Ellis-Fermor's image, 'a ruined cathedral'? Do the comic scenes have any merit?
- Many critics have asked what can be learned by paying attention to the variety of language of Marlowe's play.
- Finally, recent approaches have demonstrated that *Doctor Faustus* cannot be restricted to a single, limiting meaning, and that the play is, to use Jonathan Dollimore's term, an 'interrogative text', one which brings together opposing arguments but ultimately denies us a single point of view.

An overview

Lisa Hopkins, 2000

[Palgrave Macmillan Publishers: an extract from *Christopher Marlowe: A Literary Life* by Lisa Hopkins (2000)]

In this introductory extract, Lisa Hopkins helpfully poses a central question about the play and its author when she asks, just before this extract: 'did Marlowe…, as many have assumed, share Faustus's unbelief?' ('New Critical' refers to the so-called New Critics in the first half of the twentieth century, such as William Empson and Cleanth Brooks, who focused on a close analysis of texts. For the Baines note see page 120. Francis Spira was an Italian Catholic lawyer who converted to Lutheranism in 1548 but then renounced his Protestant faith and was convinced he was destined for hell; his example was frequently cited in sermons against despair.)

> Some critics have been very reluctant to believe in an atheist Marlowe. Michael Keefer sums up an earlier stage of *Faustus* criticism by deploring the fact that 'the moralists insisted, with New Critical obstinacy, that even if both Faustus and his creator died swearing, no connection could be admitted between the meanings generated by the 'forme of *Faustus* fortunes' [Prologue 8]…and what other texts might suggest about the poet's opinions', and Leo Kirschbaum certainly exemplifies this stance when he demands, '[w]hat has biography to do with a play which we are presumably watching in the theatre? Whatever Marlowe was himself, there is no more obvious Christian document in all Elizabethan drama than *Doctor Faustus*.'
> Nicholas Brooke declares
>
> > [i]t seems to me clear that Marlowe was not strictly an atheist at all…The 'atheism' for which he should have stood his trial, and which he hints throughout his plays, was not atheism at all, but blasphemy, a repeated protest against the nature of God implied in His treatment of Man, a protest whose bitterness implies acceptance of the *existence* of God.

Criticism

And writing from a very different perspective, Lawrence Danson declares that '[o]bviously it is not an atheist's play in any sense beyond what an Elizabethan Privy Council might construe', and adds 'that Marlowe shares Faustus' desperate theology cannot be proven'.

As John Mebane remarks, however, 'an interpretation which comes to terms with the biographical record is more convincing than one which ignores it', and others have been more willing to allow of a correspondence. A.L. Rowse declares sweepingly 'Faustus *is* Marlowe', even suggesting that Marlowe himself dabbled in witchcraft, Una Ellis-Fermor referred unhesitatingly to 'Marlowe's Satanism', and Paul Kocher was sure that the Baines note did indeed represent an accurate transcript of Marlowe's opinions (and indeed of a specific articulation of them). Constance Brown Kuriyama interestingly points out that '[t]he only common oaths in Marlowe are the mild, omnipresent "marry" and "i'faith." Perhaps Marlowe, like some modern free thinkers, had decided that it would be inconsistent to swear by what he did not believe in', while Robert Ornstein wonders pertinently 'whether the legend of Marlowe's atheism could have flourished well into the seventeenth century, if *Dr. Faustus*, his one play that held the Jacobean stage and reading public, had seemed as obviously orthodox to viewers then as it does to scholars today'. Finally, George T. Buckley sees him as 'one of the best examples of what is well called Renaissance paganism. His atheism, if such it was, seems not to have been an organized philosophical system, but a temper of mind that expressed itself in life and action', influenced largely by Machiavellianism.

The religious opinions endorsed by the play itself – or, given its textual state, selves – are no clearer than those of its creator. For Lily Campbell, the crucial question is whether or not we believe in a continuing possibility of repentance – '[s]urely the suspense which every witness of the play has felt could not be maintained if there were not a continuous uncertainty as to the final outcome of the play' – but 'it is not the initial sin and its consequences that hold us in suspense as we read or behold Marlowe's *Doctor Faustus*. Rather it is the continuing struggle of conscience, the conflict between hope and despair', and she thinks that Marlowe may have been influenced in this respect by the case of Francis Spira, who fell prey to religious despair. Greg famously ascribed Faustus' damnation to demoniality, but T.W. Craik argues against that, while Empson went so far as to doubt whether Faustus was indeed damned at all. It is thus simply not clear whether Faustus might have been saved if he had espoused Catholicism, or had been a better Protestant, or had repented more genuinely, or whether he was, as Calvinists would believe, damned from the outset. It is not even absolutely clear that God exists, only that the Devil does.

In one way, though, it is profoundly appropriate that we should be left in so much doubt about *Doctor Faustus*, because this duplicates and enacts the hero's, and indeed arguably the entire culture's, own experience of choice between inscrutable spiritual alternatives. (In an irony which Marlowe cannot have planned but which does not work entirely to the play's disadvantage, we cannot even choose securely which text to read it in.) Michael Keefer points out that Faustus' 'habitual, his characteristic, mode of speech is second-person self-address', which may well increase the audience's sense of being part of a dialogue. The questions raised by Faustus are thus made frighteningly real and close to us, and all the more so because Marlowe presents them as both unanswered and, ultimately, unanswerable.

Faustus

William Hazlitt, 1820

Hazlitt is typical of most nineteenth-century critics, who saw Faustus as a Romantic liberator and seeker after knowledge.

> Faustus himself is a rude sketch, but it is a gigantic one. This character may be considered as a personification of the pride of will and eagerness of curiosity, sublimed beyond the reach of fear and remorse. He is hurried away, and, as it were, devoured by a tormenting desire to enlarge his knowledge to the utmost bounds of nature and art, and to extend his power with his knowledge. He would realise all the fictions of a lawless imagination, would solve the most subtle speculations of abstract reason; and for this purpose, sets at defiance all mortal consequences, and leagues himself with demoniacal power, with 'fate and metaphysical aid'. The idea of witchcraft and necromancy, once the dread of the vulgar and the darling of the visionary recluse, seems to have had its origin in the restless tendency of the human mind, to conceive of and aspire to more than it can achieve by natural means, and in the obscure apprehension that the gratification of this extravagant and unauthorised desire, can only be attained by the sacrifice of all our ordinary hopes, and better prospects to the infernal agents that lend themselves to its accomplishment. Such is the foundation of the present story. Faustus, in his impatience to fulfil at once and for a moment, for a few short years, all the desires and conceptions of his soul, is willing to give in exchange his soul and body to the great enemy of mankind. Whatever he fancies, becomes by this means present to his sense: whatever he commands, is done. He calls back time past, and anticipates the future: the visions of antiquity pass before him, Babylon in all its glory, Paris and Oenone: all the projects of philosophers, or creations of the poet pay tribute at his feet: all the delights of fortune, of ambition, of pleasure, and of learning are centered in his person; and from a short-lived dream of supreme felicity and drunken power, he sinks into an abyss of darkness and perdition. This is the alternative to which he submits; the bond which he signs with his blood!

Una Ellis-Fermor, 1927

Still in the tradition of Hazlitt, Una Ellis-Fermor presents a picture of Faustus as Everyman, and the embodiment of the Renaissance scholar.

> The character of Faustus, it cannot be too often repeated, is not that of one man, but of man himself, of Everyman. There are no details, no personal traits, no eccentricities or habits, nothing that is intimate or individual. Marlowe could not

have told us where, or in what way, Faustus differed from any other man. He was concerned only with that part of him which was common to all men, yet in virtue of which he exceeded all men, his mind.

William Empson, 1946

The poet and critic Sir William Empson represents those many scholars who have linked Faustus with his creator.

If Marlowe had not been murdered so soon, he would very probably have been burned alive. It was not hard for him to imagine hell fire. The tension of both realising and denying the religion was thrust upon him in its most practical form. Surely that is the nerve of the terrific flippancy when Faustus tells Mephistopheles himself that he still doesn't believe in hell.

William Tydeman, 1984

Tydeman looks at Faustus from the point of view of the actor (and quotes from *Hamlet*).

For the actor of Faustus, the basic problem obviously lies in reconciling the varying aspects of the character's complex nature: is his love of horseplay and practical joking a basic facet of his personality or something which only manifests itself once the bargain with Lucifer is struck? Should the player convey the impression of a noble mind o'erthrown, or of a man in whom noble aspiration and petty desires have been inextricably mixed from the start?... [We can simplify the role, yet] the complete text can be treated as providing us with a much more interesting if paradoxical case-history, of a man whose loftier intellectual ambitions are compromised by a fatal tendency to cut a dash, to bask in applause, to make fun of the less gifted, to indulge in his own need for sensual gratification.

Redemption and damnation

W W Greg, 1946

The scholar Sir Walter Wilson Greg was influential in arguing that Faustus irrevocably damns himself when he commits the sin of demoniality with the succuba that takes the form of Helen.

Consider, too, a point critics seem to have overlooked, the circumstances in which Helen is introduced the second time. Urged by the Old Man, Faustus has attempted a last revolt; as usual he has been cowed into submission, and has renewed the blood-bond. He has sunk so low as to beg revenge upon his would-be saviour –

Torment, sweet friend, that base and aged man,
That durst dissuade me from thy Lucifer,
With greatest torments that our hell affords. [B-text 5.1.79–81]

And it is in the first place as a safeguard against relapse that he seeks possession of Helen –

> One thing, good servant, let me crave of thee
> To glut the longing of my heart's desire;
> That I may have unto my paramour
> That heavenly Helen which I saw of late,
> Whose sweet embraces may extinguish clear
> Those thoughts that may dissuade me from my vow,
> And keep mine oath I made to Lucifer. [B-text 5.1.85–91]

Love and revenge are alike insurances against salvation. 'Helen' then is a 'spirit,' and in this play a spirit means a devil. In making her his paramour Faustus commits the sin of demoniality, that is, bodily intercourse with demons.

The implication of Faustus' action is made plain in the comments of the Old Man and the Angels. Immediately before the Helen episode the Old Man was still calling on Faustus to repent –

> Ah, Doctor Faustus, that I might prevail
> To guide thy steps into the way of life! [A-text 5.1.36–37]

(So 1604: 1616 proceeds:)

> Though thou hast now offended like a man,
> Do not persever in it like a devil:
> Yet, yet, thou hast an amiable soul,
> If sin by custom grow not into nature … [B-text 5.1.38–41]

But with Faustus' union with Helen the nice balance between possible salvation and imminent damnation is upset. The Old Man, who has witnessed the meeting (according to the 1604 version), recognizes the inevitable:

> Accursèd Faustus, miserable man,
> That from thy soul exclud'st the grace of heaven
> And fliest the throne of his tribunal-seat! [A-text 5.1.111–113]

The Good Angel does no less:

> O Faustus, if thou hadst given ear to me
> Innumerable joys had followed thee…
> Oh, thou hast lost celestial happiness… [B-text 5.2.104–105, 111]

And Faustus himself, still haunted in his final agony by the idea of a salvation beyond his reach –

> See, see, where Christ's blood streams in the firmament!
> One drop would save my soul – [A-text 5.2.79–80]

shows, in talk with his students, a terrible clarity of vision:

> A surfeit of deadly sin, that hath damned both body and soul…Faustus' offence can ne'er be pardoned: the Serpent that tempted Eve may be saved, but not Faustus [A-text 5.2.11–12, 15–17]

and Mephostophilis echoes him:

Ay, Faustus, now hast thou no hope of heaven! [B-text 5.2.92]

It would be idle to speculate how far the 'atheist' Marlowe, whom gossip accused of what we call 'unnatural' vice, may have dwelt in imagination on the direst sin of which human flesh is capable. But in presenting the fall and slow moral disintegration of an ardent if erring spirit, he did not shrink from depicting, beside Faustus' spiritual sin of bartering his soul to the powers of evil, what is in effect its physical complement and counterpart, however he may have disguised it in immortal verse.

J C Maxwell, 1947
[Palgrave Macmillan Publishers: an extract from *Doctor Faustus: A Casebook* (1969)]

Maxwell, on the other hand, argues that pride and curiosity damn Faustus. (He refers to articles by James Smith, Leo Kirschbaum and W W Greg.)

Pride, then, is at the heart of the picture, and sensuality merely one of its fruits. What other sins go to make up the whole scheme? There is one theme of the first importance that I find mentioned only by [James] Smith…: that of *curiosity*. Structurally, this is perhaps the most important aspect of Marlowe's treatment of sin in the play. Pride is the ultimate source of Faustus' fall, and sensuality is a pervasive element of his character after it. But it is curiosity that is most notably operative in the conduct of the action. Moreover, it is largely owing to a failure to apprehend the nature, as indeed the existence, of this sin that there have arisen the misrepresentations of Marlowe's purpose which have seen in Faustus a largely sympathetic picture of a typically Renaissance striving for 'knowledge infinite'.

Curiosity is a theme which links the intellectual and sensual aspects of Faustus' sin. It is 'the vice which has as its object the intellectual satisfaction to be derived from knowing all sensual pleasures. …It was, of course, considered a greater vice than the pursuit of these pleasures for their own sakes.' (See A. A. Parker, *The Allegorical Drama of Calderón* (1943) p. 196.) It is notable that it is what is really being described at certain points in the play where Kirschbaum sees only straightforward sensuality. When Mephistophilis offers the show of devils

to delight *thy mind*,
And let thee see what magic can perform
(my italics) [B-text 2.1.84–85]

it is his curiosity that he is ministering to, rather than his 'sensual satisfaction' (Kirschbaum…), though the purpose is rightly described by Kirschbaum as being 'to distract his mind from spiritual concern'. The show of the Seven Deadly Sins, again, is not just 'satisfaction of the senses' (Kirschbaum…). Smith here quotes Augustine to the effect that the curious man, as opposed to the voluptuous, seeks after the opposites of what is beautiful, etc., 'not that he may be vexed by them, but merely out of the lust to experience and to know' (…). That is certainly Faustus' attitude here: 'O, how this sight doth delight my soul' [B-text 2.3.163], and the fundamental unrealism of the curious man is grimly brought out in his 'O, might I see hell and return again safe, how happy were I then' [B-text 2.3. 165–166]. And the 'dramatic irony' noted by Kirschbaum (…) in the lines, 'That sight will be as pleasing unto me / As Paradise was to Adam, the first day / Of his creation', is more forcible if we contrast Faustus' misdirected lust for knowledge with the natural and properly directed desire to know all that it concerned him to know that Adam had in the state of innocence.

If we return to follow the action chronologically, we note that Faustus' first use of his power is to ask about hell, and when he expresses doubt whether this can be hell, 'sleeping, eating, walking and *disputing*' (my italics) [B-text 2.1.142], the 'curious' disposition is epitomized – it is none the less something that Marlowe treats on its own account because it is followed immediately by a plunge into sensuality: the two things, Marlowe indicates, go together. The 'curiously barren discussion on astronomy' (Greg…) of [2.3] also falls into place from this point of view. That it is abortive is the main point of it…In any case, there is a marked contrast suggested between the idle curiosity of an undisciplined mind that will not even apply itself to solving its questions for itself, and the proper use of the intellect which, even without the aid of revelation, can discover 'who made the world'.

It is not only Faustus who is obsessed by curiosity throughout the play. It is in varying degrees a characteristic vice of those who consult him, the Emperor [4.1], the Duke of Anholt [Vanholt; 4.2], even Faustus' friends the scholars [5.1]. That the source for all these displays of Faustus' power is in the *Faust Book* does not detract from their significance in Marlowe's play; nor does the fact that 'the intellectual satisfaction to be derived from knowing all sensuous pleasures' is obviously more suitable for presentation on the stage than direct sensual enjoyment. Those facts merely show Marlowe's skill in using his material to the best effect.

The points arising out of this examination that seem to me important for the understanding of the play are: (i) No insistence on the pervading, and increasing, sensualism of Faustus ought to obscure the fact that he falls, like Man, and like Lucifer himself [1.3.69–70], through the spiritual sin of pride. (ii) In some cases what has been taken to be straightforward sensuality has rather an intellectual quality that assimilates it to what the scholastics called 'curiosity'. (iii) That this curiosity has greater importance for the central acts than even Smith, to whom is due the credit for rediscovering this motif, has demonstrated. (iv) In the representation of Faustus' character, the presence of this vice of curiosity mediates the transition that has sometimes seemed unduly abrupt, between the essentially spiritual pride to which he succumbs, and the direct sensuality in which his earthly career culminates. The double appearance of the succuba who impersonates Helen symbolizes this transition; she appears first to satisfy the curiosity of the Scholars, and returns to glut Faustus' sensual desire.

Helen Gardner, 1948

[Palgrave Macmillan Publishers: an extract from *Doctor Faustus: A Casebook* (1969)]

Dame Helen Gardner agrees that pride, and its two faces – presumption and despair – damn Faustus. She refers to a sermon by the poet, John Donne (1572–1631), who

Criticism

became Dean of St Paul's (one of his daughters became Edward Alleyn's second wife).

We are unfortunate in possessing Marlowe's greatest play only in an obviously mutilated form; but in spite of possible distortion and some interpolation in the centre, the grandeur of the complete reversal stands out clearly. Apart from its opening and concluding choruses, which provide an archaic framework, and the short closing scene in the 1616 text, where the scholars find the mangled body of Faustus, the play begins and ends with the hero in his study. In the first scene Faustus runs through all the branches of human knowledge and finds them inadequate to his desires. Logic can only teach argument; medicine stops short where human desire is most thwarted, since it cannot defeat death; law is a mercenary pursuit; and divinity, which he comes to last, holds the greatest disappointment: it is grounded in the recognition of man's mortality and his fallibility. The two texts from Jerome's Bible insult his aspiration: *Stipendium peccati mors est*, and *Si peccasse negamus, fallimur, et nulla est in nobis veritas.* He turns instead to magic because it is:

> a world of profit and delight,
> Of power, of honour, and omnipotence.

He decides to 'tire his brains to get a deity'. The sin of Faustus here is presumption, the aspiring above his order, or the rebellion against the law of his creation.

But when he is last seen alone in his study it is the opposite sin which delivers him to damnation: the final sin of Faustus is despair. However much he may call in his fear on God or Christ, it is the power of Lucifer and the bond with Lucifer which he really believes in. It is to Lucifer he prays: 'O, spare me, Lucifer!' and 'Ah, rend not my heart for naming of my Christ!' [John] Donne gives presumption and despair as one of the couples which the Schoolmen have called sins against the Holy Ghost 'because naturally they shut out those meanes by which the Holy Ghost might work upon us...for presumption takes away the feare of God, and desperation the love of God'. They are the two faces of the sin of Pride. Faustus tormented by devils is obsessed by their power; but the Old Man is safe from them, because of his faith. The great reversal from the first scene of *Doctor Faustus* to the last can be defined in different ways: from presumption to despair; from doubt of the existence of hell to belief in the reality of nothing else; from a desire to be more than man to the recognition that he has excluded himself from the promise of redemption for all mankind in Christ; from haste to sign the bond to desire for delay when the moment comes to honour it; from aspiration to deity and omnipotence to longing for extinction. At the beginning Faustus wished to rise above his humanity; at the close he would sink below it, be transformed into a beast or into 'little water-drops'. At the beginning he attempts usurpation upon God; at the close he is an usurper upon the Devil.

Cleanth Brooks, 1966
[Palgrave Macmillan Publishers: an extract from *Doctor Faustus: A Casebook* (1969)]

Brooks is among many critics who have addressed the question of when Faustus can be said to be truly beyond redemption.

> On a purely legalistic basis, of course, Faustus's case *is* hopeless. He has made a contract and he has to abide by it. This is the point that the devils insist on relentlessly. Yet there are plenty of indications that Faustus was not the prisoner of one fatal act. Before Faustus signs the bond, the good angel twice appears to him, first to beg him to lay his 'Damned book aside' and later to implore him to beware of the 'execrable art' of magic. But even after Faustus has signed the bond, the good angel appears. In [2.3] he adjures Faustus to repent, saying: 'Repent yet, God will pity thee.' The bad angel, it is true, appears along with him to insist that 'God cannot pity thee.' But then the bad angel had appeared along with the good in all the early appearances too.
>
> There are other indications that Faustus is not yet beyond the possibility of redemption. The devils, in spite of the contract, are evidently not at all sure of the soul of Faustus. They find it again and again necessary to argue with him, to bully him, and to threaten him. Mephistopheles evidently believes that it is very important to try to distract Faustus from his doleful thoughts. The assumption of the play is surely that the devils are anxious, and Mephistopheles in particular goes to a great deal of trouble to keep Faustus under control. There is never any assumption that the bond itself, signed with Faustus's blood, is quite sufficient to preserve him safe for hell. At least once, Lucifer himself has to be called in to ensure that Faustus will not escape. Lucifer appeals to Faustus's sense of logic by telling him that 'Christ cannot save thy soul, for he is just, / There's none but I have interest in the same.' But Lucifer employs an even more potent weapon: he terrifies Faustus, and as we shall see in [5.1], a crucial scene that occurs late in the play, Faustus has little defence against terror.
>
> In [5.1], a new character appears, one simply called 'an Old Man'. He comes just in the nick of time, for Faustus, in his despair, is on the point of committing suicide, and Mephistopheles, apparently happy to make sure of Faustus's damnation, hands him a dagger. But the Old Man persuades Faustus to desist, telling him: 'I see an angel hovers o'er thy head, / And with a vial full of precious grace, / Offers to pour the same into thy soul: / Then call for mercy, and avoid despair.'
>
> The Old Man has faith that Faustus can still be saved, and testifies to the presence of his good angel, waiting to pour out the necessary grace. But Faustus has indeed despaired. It may be significant that Faustus apparently does not see the angel now. At this crisis when, as Faustus says, 'hell strives with grace for conquest in my breast', Mephistopheles accuses him of disobedience, and threatens to tear his flesh piecemeal. The threat is sufficient. A moment before, Faustus had addressed the Old Man as 'my sweet friend'. Now, in a sudden reversal, he calls Mephistopheles sweet – 'Sweet Mephistopheles, intreat thy lord / To pardon my unjust presumption, / And with my blood again I will confirm / My former vow I made to Lucifer.' The answer of Mephistopheles is interesting and even shocking. He tells Faustus: 'Do it then quickly, with unfeigned heart, /

Lest greater danger do attend thy drift.' There is honour among thieves, among devils the appeal to loyalty and sincerity. 'Unfeigned heart' carries ironically the very accent of Christian piety.

Faustus, for his part, shows himself now, perhaps for the first time, to be truly a lost soul. For he suddenly rounds upon the Old Man and beseeches Mephistopheles to inflict on him the 'greatest torments that our hell affords'. The pronoun is significant. Faustus now thinks of hell as 'our hell', and the acceptance of it as part of himself and his desire to see the Old Man suffer mark surely a new stage in his development or deterioration.

Christian morality or tragedy?

Leo Kirschbaum, 1943
[Palgrave Macmillan Publishers: an extract from *Doctor Faustus: A Casebook* (1969)]

Kirschbaum disliked Romantic simplifications of the play and sees it more as a Christian morality than a tragedy, with Faustus an 'unstable, foolish worldling', 'a wretched creature who for lower values gives up higher values'. ('Eschatology' means the study of, or a person's views of, death and judgement, heaven and hell.)

Outside the theatre, we may mightily agree or disagree with the eschatology inherent in *Doctor Faustus*. But *in* the theatre, as we watch the play, we understand and accept (if only for the nonce) that man's most precious possession is his immortal soul and that he gains Heaven or Hell by his professions and actions on earth. *In* the theatre, we accept Marlowe's premises. That these premises were inherent in his first audience is of incidental interest to us as students and appreciators of the drama. The premises are instinct in every word, line, passage, speech, action of the play. The Christian view of the world informs *Doctor Faustus* throughout – not the pagan view. If we do not accept that Faustus's selling his soul to the devil for earthly power and pleasure is a serious business, we simply are not hearing what Marlowe wrote.

Critics confound Marlowe the man and Marlowe the playwright. They consider that the man was an atheist and so interpret *Doctor Faustus*. What if the play were anonymous? What has biography to do with a play which we are presumably watching in the theatre? Whatever Marlowe was himself, there is no more obvious Christian document in all Elizabethan drama than *Doctor Faustus*. Or critics will consider the protagonist as a representative of the Renaissance superman. Whatever their feelings and thoughts on the revival of learning and the Reformation are, let them open-mindedly look at the play unfolding on the stage before them. For earthly learning, earthly power, earthly satisfaction, Faustus goes down to horrible and everlasting perdition. It does not matter what *you* think of Hell or what Marlowe privately thought of Hell. What does matter is that in terms of the play, Faustus is a wretched creature who for lower values gives up higher values – that the devil and Hell are omnipresent, potent, and terrifying realities. These are the values which govern the play. You must temporarily accept them while you watch the play. You need not ultimately accept them. But you should not interpret the play in the light of *your* philosophy or religion or absence of religion. You cannot do so if you hear it properly – as a play, as an entity, as a progressive action, as a quasi-morality in which is clearly set forth the hierarchy of moral values which enforces and encloses the play, which the characters in the play accept, which the playwright advances and accepts in his prologue and epilogue, which – hence – the audience must understand and accept.

Nicholas Brooke, 1952

[Palgrave Macmillan Publishers: an extract from *Doctor Faustus: A Casebook* (1969)]

Brooke takes a very different view; for him the play does not have a Christian conclusion. (He refers first to the final scene in the B-text.)

> In the end Faustus does despair, the devil he has constantly feared tears him to pieces, and the scholars draw back the curtain to reveal the gory mess that was 'admirèd man'. But, as with *Tamburlaine*, inevitable death does not make a tragedy. *Tamburlaine* is not tragic, *Faustus* is; and the difference lies in Faustus's tortured awareness that it should have been otherwise. Had his Will been what he felt it to be, he would have been triumphant, independent of angels and devils; he would have realized his supreme urge to self-originated power, and Heaven and Hell remained mere fables. But as Faustus fails, greatness as Man imagines it can only remain outside human power, must reside in superhuman God and Devil; and so in the end, it is extinction not mercy that Faustus craves:
>
> > O soul, be changed to little water-drops
> > And fall into the ocean, ne'er be found. [5.2.119–120]
>
> That is not a Christian conclusion; at its tragic end as throughout its length, Marlowe's Morality is inverted; there are still two Hells, Lucifer's and Faustus's. But in the end, it would seem, Faustus has become fully conscious of Heaven as well. If so, he still cannot or will not accept it: it stands for a way of life he has rejected as unworthy of him; but it happens to be the one God insists upon. Faustus becomes aware, not only that he is wrong, but that the power of God is to have made man desiring a greatness he cannot achieve: that is the constant bitter irony that I have noted throughout the play – man's nature is in direct opposition to his fate.

Structure

J P Brockbank, 1962

In opposition to traditional voices such as William Hazlitt's in 1820 that 'The intermediate comic parts, in which Faustus is not directly concerned, are mean and grovelling to the last degree', Brockbank observes purpose and design in the comedy. (The Pope's words he refers to are in the B-text 3.1.132–135.)

> Just as the tragedy is precisely focused on the presumption of man, so too is the comedy. Tragedy, remembering that man is mortal, makes death confound his pride of life; comedy, remembering that human life goes on, humiliates the man

who affects to be superior to his fellows. The Pope's words will serve as motto to both sides of the play:

> He grows too proud in his authority,
> Lifting his lofty head above the clouds,
> And like a steeple overpeers the church;
> But we'll pull down his haughty insolence.

Marlowe clowns to a purpose.

Stevie Simkin, 2000
[Pearson Education Limited: an extract from *A Preface to Christopher Marlowe* by Stevie Simkin (2000)]

Simkin points out that the 'carnivalesque' features of the comedy can be seen as integral to the play. ('Aristotelian' refers to the Greek philosopher Aristotle's views on tragedy in his *Poetics*.)

Readings illuminated by the work of the Russian thinker Mikhail Bakhtin (1895–1975) have concentrated on the so-called carnivalesque aspects of *Faustus* (particularly in its B-text version). Bakhtin's most significant work is his book *Rabelais and his World*, which he wrote in the 1940s, but which was not published until 1965 (in the Soviet Union); it was first translated into English in 1968. Ostensibly a study of Rabelais' *Gargantua and Pantagruel* (1532), its scope is actually much wider, comprising as it does an investigation of the festive life of early modern Europe. It has been enormously influential in studies of early modern culture, including English culture, and of the drama in this period in particular. Briefly, Bakhtin's work focuses on what he describes as the 'second life' or 'second culture' that existed in this society, sustained by the common people. The celebrations and holidays associated with carnival are interpreted as challenges to the dominant class and culture in a society constructed on a strictly hierarchical basis. The significance of carnival, Bakhtin insists, extends beyond the period of festivity that traditionally preceded the period of Lent in the Christian calendar. Under the conditions of carnival, official ideology (which seeks to consolidate the status quo) is challenged, order is disrupted and hierarchies are reversed. Crucial elements of carnival include a focus on the materiality of the body – the emphasis is on those functions and aspects of the body and associated processes that Bakhtin defines as grotesque (the mouth, the anus, the buttocks, the genitals) and degrading (defecation, urination and copulation). All things that are traditionally seen as spiritual and exalted (and therefore to be endorsed by the dominant ideology) are debased. Liberating laughter that subverts, parodies and ridicules official culture is also a crucial element of the carnivalesque. Bakhtin identifies what he calls the concept of grotesque realism as the heritage of the culture of folk humour. 'The essential principle of grotesque realism', he writes, 'is degradation, that is, the lowering of all that is high, spiritual, ideal, abstract; it is a transfer to the material level, to the sphere of earth and body' (Bakhtin, 1984, p. 19). In the light of this kind of understanding, we may choose to challenge the common interpretation of the comic interludes as distortions of Marlowe's 'original' play, and instead see them as carnivalesque elements which are integral to the text.

While the play ostensibly deals with a 'tragical history' that involves complex theological issues, it may be that alongside the serious strand runs a seam that can be exploited to throw the dominant, Aristotelian trajectory of the plot off course.

Language

D J Palmer, 1964
[Palgrave Macmillan Publishers: an extract from *Doctor Faustus: A Casebook* (1969)]

Palmer focuses on the language to stress the confidence of Faustus in the opening soliloquy, expressed through the 'deliberate, preconceived movement' of the speech, contrasted with the desperation of the final soliloquy. (He mentions *The Spanish Tragedy*, the play by Marlowe's one-time room-mate Thomas Kyd, c. 1587. 'Senecan rhetoric' refers to the Roman dramatist and philosopher Seneca (c. 4 BC–AD 65); he had a considerable influence on Elizabethan and Jacobean playwrights.)

> In sheer virtuosity there was nothing in Elizabethan drama to match Faustus' last speech for several years to come. The kind of advance in the technique of the soliloquy which it represents can be measured by comparing it with the soliloquy at the opening of the play. There Faustus' rejection of legitimate studies is displayed in a schematised logical progression which summarises and crystallises the steps which led him to necromancy. The speech is evidently contrived, and within its conventions it does not require us to suppose that it represents any particular moment in Faustus' psychological history. The conception of the final soliloquy is radically different: it does move in the plane of time, as the stark simplicity of the first monosyllables announces:

> Ah, Faustus,
> Now hast thou but one bare hour to live.

> The effects Marlowe is striving for here are those of spontaneity; the conception is much more inward, and dramatises the fleeting thoughts as though they were actually passing through Faustus' mind at the time. Instead of the predictable controlled development of the opening soliloquy, here are confusion and contradiction, the very process of the struggle to come to terms with the situation. Of course, the deliberate preconceived movement of the earlier speech befits our impression of the confident Faustus which the beginning of the play requires, and the action must open on a comparatively low emotional pitch, while at the catastrophe the situation demands a frantic and desperate Faustus, and high tension. But the soliloquies are not accounted for in terms of their contexts alone: there is an essential difference in their dramatic representation of inner processes. In the final speech, Marlowe created what was virtually a new vehicle for articulating with immediacy the flux and uncertainty of a mind under pressure.

It is only the exaggeration of this vital difference to say that previous soliloquies demanded an orator, while this calls for an actor. As an attempt to turn the speech of distraction into poetry, Faustus' last soliloquy is comparable with Kyd's development of Senecan rhetoric, particularly with the way Kyd deploys stage madness as an occasion for wild and whirling words.

The licence Marlowe boldly permits himself with metre here is the fundamental means of creating an impression of bursts of rapid speech punctuated by irregular pauses. Figures of repetition, like 'Fair nature's eye, rise, rise again', 'See, see, where Christ's blood ...', 'Mountains and hills, come, come', and climactic constructions, such as

> The stars move still, time runs, the clock will strike,
> The devil will come, and Faustus must be damn'd,

allow the poetry to take wing, until the flight is sharply arrested often by means of a heavy caesura. A static delivery is impossible, and the strenuous vehemence carried by the disjointed verse insists upon the physical movements implied by the sense. It is impossible to give full weight to 'O, I'll leap up to my God! Who pulls me down?' with the same gesture as in

> Then will I headlong run into the earth.
> Earth, gape! O, no, it will not harbour me.

The chimes of the clock are a further cue for action, and this device illustrates how Marlowe succeeds in organically relating the speech to the stage, compared with the static and perhaps literally sedate character of the opening soliloquy. This final scene has returned to Faustus' study, where the play began; yet however localised, the swift transitions which the soliloquy makes in its verbal imagery, from the heavens and planets, to the earth with her mountains and thence to the ugly gaping of hell-mouth, seem to conjure the whole creation to witness the catastrophe. It is a magnificent recollection of the medieval stage which transforms Faustus' study into a microcosm.

Hilary Gatti, 1989

[Routledge and Professor Hilary Gatti: an extract from *The Renaissance Drama of Knowledge: Giordano Bruno in England* by Professor Gatti (1989)]

A further perspective on the final soliloquy is offered by Hilary Gatti ('metaphysic' means a particular way of understanding the immaterial world, the nature of time and being, etc).

Marlowe creates in these final verses of Faustus's monologue a subtle contrast between two forms of purification on death. On one side we have the painless purification of water imagery in the vision of the ocean silently absorbing, as one of its cosmic rights, its component 'little water drops'; on the other the roaring, hissing, punishing purification by thunder, serpents, damnation, and hell-fire. Faustus's mind clearly tends with ardent desire towards the first of these visions, although he realizes by now that he can only express such a vision in hypothetical grammatical forms ('Why wert thou not', 'Or why is this', 'O soul be chang'd'). The alternative form of purification, which is warded off for as long as possible by Faustus's ever weaker negative verbs ('Ugly hell gape not; come not *Lucifer*') is only irrevocably accepted in the final line, and in a spirit of despairing, exhausted recognition of a fact and its consequences. Rather than repenting, Faustus recognizes in his final words the force of a reigning metaphysic too strong and entrenched to resist. As in his opening monologue, although with a far deeper anguish which Marlowe's poetry evokes powerfully in the broken irregularity of his pentameters, Faustus's mind is working according to a logical pattern of thought centred on the theme of a choice of alternative books. With his alternative metaphysic, or art 'wherein all naturs treasury is contain'd', relegated to the status of a dangerous heresy by the realities of the situation in that particular Wittemberg [sic]…Faustus brings his speech and his life to a close with lucid if exhausted logical precision on the inevitable consequences of his intellectual adventure: 'I'll burn my books; ah *Mephostophilis*'.

The pessimism of Marlowe's final tragic vision is only partially qualified by the brief comments of the two scholars who discover Faustus's dead body. For them Faustus's story is not to be concluded on a purely negative note. Although they recognize that in religious terms his experience must be accepted as a negative lesson, they express an understanding of the intellectual dilemma which the Faustian story represents:

> tho *Faustus* end be such
> As every Christian heart laments to think on:
> Yet for he was a Scholar, once admired
> For wondrous knowledge in our Germane schools,
> We'll give his mangled limbs due burial:
> And all the Students clothed in mourning black,
> Shall wait upon his heavy funeral. [B-text 5.3.13–19]

Such ambivalence is at once suffocated by the Chorus, who close [sic] the tragedy, as it had begun, on a note of unequivocal orthodoxy, bringing the intellectual experience represented by Faustus under a moral and theological sign of rigorous negativity. As in the opening of the tragedy, the Chorus uses a pagan symbol to express the Faustian intelligence, recognized as having made an attempt to re-establish the values of '*Apollo*'s laurel bough'. But the bough has been duly burnt, and the lesson must be learned by the audience who are recalled by the Chorus to the values (which are also linguistic and dramatic forms and formulas) of the medieval morality play:

> regard his hellish fall,
> Whose fiendful fortune may exhort the wise
> Only to wonder at unlawful things,
> Whose deepness doth intice such forward wits,
> To practise more than heavenly power permits. [Epilogue 4–8]

The question here is not whether Marlowe's schematically conceived, theologically dominated Middle Ages fully represent the complex characteristics of that period. He is writing in a recognizable Renaissance convention which underlined its own achievements as a reawakening of lost forms of thought and knowledge, and marked out the centuries intervening between the illuminated cultures of classical antiquity and the modern rebirth as a period of shadows and darkness. But Marlowe was also writing in the agitated, blood-filled final years of the sixteenth century, in a Europe torn by the struggle between Reformation and Counter-Reformation, with even the comparatively peaceful Elizabethan England overshadowed by increasing religious tensions and oppressive legislation, aggravated by growing political uncertainty due to the ageing of the Virgin Queen. In such a situation, Marlowe brings his final tragedy to a close on a note of fierce intellectual pessimism which consciously projects his audience backward into a past age. The intellectual impulses forward seem to be irrevocably blocked by the Chorus's assumption of its own intellectual authority and dominion. It has taken possession in its own terms of the classical images which define the Faustian attempts to break new intellectual territory. Icarus has fallen as the Chorus predicted, and Apollo's laurel bough has burnt. Both a new science and a new poetry or drama appear irrevocably compromised; and Marlowe's final moment of tragic vision seems to lead with both a logical and biographical inevitability towards his shadowy and premature death.

An interrogative text

Jonathan Dollimore, 1984
[Pearson Education Limited: an extract from *Christopher Marlowe: Longman Critical Readers* ed. Richard Wilson (1999)]

Dollimore says that critics have tended to see the play as *either* vindicating Faustus as a Renaissance man striving after knowledge, *or* as vindicating Christian orthodoxy thanks to its morality play structure. He, however, sees the play as doing neither of these. Instead the play interrogates, questions and challenges power within an orthodox framework: 'the inscribing of a subversive discourse within an orthodox one', and leading the way for later playwrights to question and challenge other forms of power.

> The final chorus of the play tells us that Dr Faustus involved himself with 'unlawful things' and thereby practised 'more than heavenly power permits' [Epilogue 6, 8]. It is a transgression which has revealed the limiting structure of Faustus's universe for what it is, namely, 'heavenly *power*'. Faustus has to be destroyed since in a very real sense the credibility of that heavenly power depends upon it. And yet the punitive intervention which validates divine power also compromises it: far from justice, law and authority being what legitimates power, it appears, by the end of the play, to be the other way around: power establishes the limits of all those things.
>
> It might be objected that the distinction between justice and power is a modern one and, in Elizabethan England, even if entertained, would be easily absorbed in one or another of the paradoxes which constituted the Christian faith. And yet: if there is one thing that can be said with certainty about this period it is that God in the form of 'mere arbitrary will omnipotent' could not 'keep men in

awe'. We can infer as much from many texts, one of which was Lawne's *Abridgement* of Calvin's *Institutes*, translated in 1587 – around the time of the writing of *Dr Faustus*. The book presents and tries to answer, in dialogue form, objections to Calvin's theology. On the question of predestination the 'Objector' contends that 'to adjudge to destruction whom he will, is more agreeable to the lust of a tyrant, than to the lawful sentence of a judge'. The 'Reply' to this is as arbitrary and tyrannical as the God which the Objector envisages as unsatisfactory: 'it is a point of bold wickedness even so much as to inquire the causes of God's will' (...). It is an exchange which addresses directly the question of whether a tyrannical God is or is not grounds for discontent. Even more important perhaps is its unintentional foregrounding of the fact that, as embodiment of naked power alone, God could so easily be collapsed into those tyrants who, we are repeatedly told by writers in this period, exploited Him as ideological mystification of their own power. Not surprisingly, the concept of 'heavenly power' interrogated in *Dr Faustus* was soon to lose credibility, and it did so in part precisely because of such interrogation.

Dr Faustus is important for subsequent tragedy for these reasons and at least one other: in transgressing and demystifying the limiting structure of his world without there ever existing the possibility of his escaping it, Faustus can be seen as an important precursor of the malcontented protagonist of Jacobean tragedy. Only for the latter, the limiting structure comes to be primarily a socio-political one.

Lastly, if it is correct that censorship resulted in *Dr Faustus* being one of the last plays of its kind – it being forbidden thereafter to interrogate religious issues so directly – we might expect the transgressive impulse in the later plays to take on different forms. This is in fact exactly what we do find; and one such form involves a strategy already referred to – the inscribing of a subversive discourse within an orthodox one, a vindication of the letter of an orthodoxy while subverting its spirit.

Roger Sales, 1991

[Palgrave Macmillan Publishers: an extract from *Christopher Marlowe* by Roger Sales (1991)]

Roger Sales questions the opinion of the Renaissance scholar Dame Frances Yates that the Epilogue expresses the 'moral' of a story which condemns Faustus's actions unreservedly. Sales sees the Epilogue rather as continuing the debates which have run throughout the play.

Frances Yates suggests in *The Occult Philosophy in the Elizabethan Age* (1983) that this concluding homily [the Epilogue] contains the 'moral' (p. 119) of the play. This allows her to claim that *Doctor Faustus* is part of the late sixteenth-century movement against Renaissance ideas. She also situates *The Jew of Malta* within the same context. Marlowe's resolutions should not, however, be read so literally. They may offer an answer to conflicts and yet this is no guarantee that they themselves will not be open to conflicting interpretations. Orthodox voices are certainly heard throughout *Doctor Faustus*. Both the Good Angel and the Old Man put the Christian case against Faustus's actions. There are also disconcerting moments when Mephostophilis, who has seen the 'face of God', joins the chorus of disapproval. The comic scenes in the earlier part of the play raise a series of potentially damning questions about Faustus's contract with Lucifer, even though they can be seen as representing a blasphemous critique of blasphemy. The increasing emptiness of Faustus's theatricality also casts a dark shadow over the contract. The play does not, however, confine itself to a straightforward homily on Faustus's 'hellish fall'. He has the most memorable lines. His theatricality, particularly during the scenes in Rome, is capable of filling empty spaces. He provides the spectators on this occasion with highly orthodox pleasures. Here and elsewhere, the categories that are taken as read by the resolution are unsettled. It is, for instance, difficult to maintain the sharp distinction between the lawful and the 'unlawful' if Lucifer is seen as a Renaissance prince who legally binds his subjects to him to prevent them from rebelling. Lucifer and his followers gloat over Faustus's execution. So too does the Chorus who delivers the resolution. Heaven and Hell appear to be on the same side. The Chorus, like the Old Man and the Good Angel, has no solution to the problem of how to describe the pleasures of Heaven. He just maintains that there are 'things' which are not permitted by 'heavenly power'. Lucifer and Mephostophilis control their kingdom along the same lines. They actively prevent Faustus from acquiring any knowledge that might threaten their power. The resolution needs to be seen as continuing rather than settling the debates and disputes that run throughout the play.

Thomas Healy, 1994

Healy sees Faustus's encounter with Helen as embodying the conflict between the audience's sympathies and their adherence to conventional morality.

> Despite what conventional morality might indicate about this scene, the reader's or audience's sympathies are aesthetically drawn to Faustus's fantasy. Hellish illusion becomes more attractive and desirable than Christian certainties. This is not to propose that Marlowe is here 'of the devil's party'. What he is doing is dramatically forcing the suspension of certain norms which governed an Elizabethan construction of the satanic and Christian, the hellish and heavenly (which in Marlowe's age were understood as realities with firm definitions in ways no longer imagined in Britain). Faustus's creation of a heroic theatre in which he casts himself in a major role is sufficiently alluring for it to linger imaginatively with readers or spectators, regardless whether the play is concluded as a conventional morality or as radically questioning the nature of heaven and hell. The making of the event in poetry undermines attempts to understand it prosaically, and the poetry challenges the assumptions of prosaic understanding.

Performance

Although *Doctor Faustus* may have been performed as early as 1588, the first recorded performance was on 30 September 1594 by the Admiral's Men at the

Rose. Edward Alleyn played Faustus, and Henslowe's 'Diary' shows that the play was a huge success, enjoying regular performances in the years that followed. Stories of extra devils appearing on stage show that the play had achieved some kind of notoriety (as did Shakespeare's *Macbeth* a few years later, for similar reasons), and also suggest that performances of the play in Marlowe's time employed a variety of spectacular stage effects. Having witnessed later performances in Henslowe's other playhouse, the Fortune, John Melton wrote in 1620:

> There indeed a man may behold shag-haired devils run roaring over the stage with squibs in their mouths, while drummers make thunder in the tiring-house and the twelve-penny hirelings make artificial lightning in their heavens.

In company with many of Shakespeare's plays, the versions of *Doctor Faustus* performed in the late seventeenth and eighteenth centuries were often debased and trivialised, turning Marlowe's work into a comedy of devils and magic tricks. When a serious version did finally appear in 1885 (with the great Henry Irving as Mephistopheles) it showed the epic influence of two major nineteenth-century works based on the Faust legend: Goethe's *Faust* (see page 141) and the 1859 opera by the French composer Charles François Gounod (1818–93).

It was down to William Poel and the Elizabethan Stage Society to perform the play simply and without the encumbrances of unwieldy sets. Their 1896 production with its simple staging was to influence a production at Cambridge University which led to the foundation of the Marlowe Dramatic Society in 1908. The twentieth century saw a renewal of interest in the play and some memorable productions. Nevill Coghill's 1966 interpretation at Oxford (filmed a year later) featured Richard Burton as Faustus, with his wife Elizabeth Taylor playing Helen. Burton's studiedly unheroic and unromantic performance was widely considered to have been disappointing, the high point of the production being Andreas Teuber's passionate Mephistopheles.

John Barton's 1974 production for the RSC is one of many that have made major cuts to the text – with, in this case, additions based on the *Faustbuch*. Barton's justification for cutting most of the comic scenes was that 'Though in theory the sub-plots provide a complementary comment on the main action by showing the abuse of necromantic powers in trivial pranks, in practice they tend to trivialise the tone of the play itself.' Ian McKellen played Faustus as a man in mental torment, with glove puppets representing the Good and Evil Angels, underlying the notion that hell is a state of mind.

There have been a number of all-male productions. Almost inevitably these bring out an underlying homoeroticism, perhaps exploiting the audience's beliefs about Marlowe's sexuality. In Barry Kyle's 1989 RSC interpretation, 'A recurrent motif was that of defiled sanctity' (David Bevington and Eric Rasmussen), one striking example of which was Mephistopheles's first appearance as a bleeding Christ, wearing a crown of thorns.

The ambiguity of the ending (the B-text includes a scene in which the Scholars discover Faustus's remains, for example – see page 117) has given scope for a wide variety of conclusions, represented here by two accounts, the first of Clifford Williams's 1968 production at Stratford, described by Nigel Alexander; the second, of a 1977 production by the Medieval Players, recalled by Lois Potter.

> Faustus finished his final speech grovelling in abject terror on the ground. The clock finished striking. Nothing happened. After a long moment Faustus raised his head and looked round the totally empty stage. He started to laugh. As he reached the hysteria of relief, the back wall of the stage gave way and fell forward in sections revealing an ominous red glow and a set of spikes…The denizens of hell emerged with a kind of slow continuous shuffle until Faustus was surrounded by a circle of these skeletal figures – including the Seven Deadly Sins. He was then seized and carried shrieking through the teeth of hell mouth which closed leaving the wall of Faustus's study again intact.

> There was no diabolical reaction at the end of [Faustus's] speech. He nodded grimly, realising what the silence meant ('*this* is hell'), went inside the inner stage, and drew the curtains. A few moments later, the scholars opened them, to reveal him hanging from a noose.

Doctor Faustus on video

The only available performance on video is the 1967 film (Columbia Pictures).

The plot of *Doctor Faustus*

Prologue

The Chorus announces that we are about to see a different kind of play, and introduces the figure of Faustus, describing how, from humble beginnings, he became a great scholar but brought about his own destruction after practising necromancy.

Act 1

1.1: Faustus is in his study, attempting to decide how best to extend his already considerable learning. He rejects the disciplines in which he has so far excelled – logic, philosophy, medicine, law and theology – declaring them all unrewarding compared with necromancy and the potential power it offers. Having made up his mind to practise necromancy, Faustus sends his servant Wagner with an invitation to Valdes and Cornelius, who are already skilled in the black arts. Despite warnings from the Good Angel that he is courting damnation, Faustus listens to the Evil Angel's temptations and enthusiastically daydreams about the powers that magic will give him. When Valdes and Cornelius arrive, they tempt him with further instances of the benefits of conjuring and offer to give him some basic instruction in the black art.

1.2: Some of Faustus's fellow-scholars have noted his absence. When they question Wagner, only to be informed that he is dining with the infamous Valdes and Cornelius, they are immediately alarmed for the safety of his soul.

1.3: That night, Faustus begins his incantations. He succeeds in raising a devil, Mephistopheles, one of Lucifer's ministers, who is told to change his ugly appearance to that of a Franciscan friar. Faustus is delighted that his conjurations have had such power, but Mephistopheles informs him that he came only because he heard someone abjuring the scriptures, as devils always do in the hope of securing a man's soul and swelling the population of the damned. In answer to Faustus's questions, Mephistopheles explains that he is one of the rebellious spirits forever damned with Lucifer. Laughing off the devil's warnings, Faustus offers to surrender his soul to Lucifer in return for twenty-four years of pleasure and power.

1.4: Faustus's servant Wagner threatens Robin (the Clown) with painful torments unless he agrees to bind himself to Wagner in servitude for seven years, and raises up two devils to enforce his threats.

Act 2

2.1: At midnight in his study, Faustus wavers irresolutely between God and Lucifer as the Good and Evil Angels contend for his soul. Swayed by the temptations of wealth and power, Faustus calls up Mephistopheles who informs him that, in order to secure the bargain, he will be required to sign a deed in his own blood.

Faustus agrees, but, as he attempts to sign, his blood congeals, as though unwilling for him to go through with the agreement. Mephistopheles fetches some hot coals to liquefy the blood, and Faustus seals the bargain. No sooner has he done so, however, than words appear on his arm saying *'Homo, fuge!'* – 'Fly, O man!' – and, to distract Faustus, Mephistopheles conjures devils to present him with crowns and rich clothes. The deed specifies 'that Faustus may be a spirit in form and substance', and that Mephistopheles will be at his command, doing whatever Faustus desires, remaining invisible in his house, appearing whenever and in whatever shape Faustus chooses. In return, Lucifer is allowed to carry Faustus off, 'body and soul, flesh, blood, or goods' at the end of twenty-four years.

Faustus begins his twenty-four years by asking Mephistopheles a series of questions about hell, scoffing at the concept of eternal torment. Mephistopheles provides Faustus with a 'wife' in the form of a devil dressed like a woman, with fireworks, whom Faustus rejects. Mephistopheles promises him courtesans instead, and gives him a book of necromantic spells, astronomy/astrology and plants.

2.2: Robin has stolen one of Faustus's books of magic and tells his fellow-stableboy Rafe what delights he will be able to accomplish.

2.3: Though filled with misgivings about his pact with Lucifer, and having listened to the promptings of the Good and Evil Angels, Faustus is unable to repent. He consoles himself with reminders of the pleasures he has experienced thanks to his new-won powers and then questions Mephistopheles about the universe. But the devil angrily departs when Faustus pushes him to state who made the world, returning with Lucifer and another of his chief ministers, Beelzebub. Lucifer reminds Faustus of his pact and distracts him with a show of the Seven Deadly Sins: Pride, Covetousness, Wrath, Envy, Gluttony, Sloth and Lechery.

Act 3

Chorus: Wagner gives an account of Faustus's travels to view the universe and informs us that he has arrived in Rome.

3.1: Faustus reminds Mephistopheles of the travels they have enjoyed and Mephistopheles confirms that, in accordance with Faustus's request, they are now in the Vatican where they can witness – and mischievously participate in – the celebration of 'holy Peter's feast'. At the banquet which follows, the invisible Faustus disrupts the feast by snatching food and wine. Believing that they are being haunted by a ghost from purgatory, the friars ineffectually attempt an exorcism by using the ceremony of excommunication.

3.2: Robin, accompanied by Rafe, has stolen a goblet from a tavern and attempts to hide it from the furious inn-keeper by conjuring. His incantations succeed in raising Mephistopheles, who angrily turns Robin into an ape and Rafe into a dog.

Act 4

Chorus: The Chorus reports that, having completed his travels, Faustus has returned to Germany where he is welcomed by admiring friends. Faustus is now a famous man and has been invited to court by the Emperor, Charles V.

4.1: At court, the Emperor asks Faustus to conjure the shapes of Alexander and his paramour, which he does, much to the Emperor's amazement and admiration. But Faustus has been angered by a Knight's insulting interruptions and punishes him by causing horns to sprout from his head. Having sufficiently humiliated the Knight, Faustus instructs Mephistopheles to remove the horns, and the Emperor promises to reward Faustus for the demonstration of his art.

Pestered by a horse-dealer, Faustus agrees to sell his horse for forty dollars, but warns the man not to ride the animal into water. After the horse-courser has departed, gloating over his bargain purchase, Faustus descends into a fit of despair, which he tries to allay with sleep. No sooner has he shut his eyes, than the horse-courser returns, complaining bitterly that, having ridden the horse into water, he found himself left with nothing under him but a bundle of hay. Attempting to rouse Faustus, he pulls at his leg – which immediately comes off. The terrified horse-courser readily agrees to pay Faustus another forty dollars. Wagner then enters to tell the once more two-legged Faustus that the Duke of Vanholt has asked to see him.

4.2: At the court of the Duke of Vanholt, Faustus instructs Mephistopheles to fetch grapes to satisfy the longing of the pregnant Duchess.

Act 5

5.1: Nearing the end of his twenty-four years, Faustus has made a will, bequeathing his possessions to Wagner, and is now sharing a last supper with his fellow scholars. When they enter, the scholars ask Faustus to let them see Helen of Troy, the most beautiful woman who has ever lived. He agrees and the scholars depart, expressing their inability to bestow upon her the praise she deserves. An Old Man appears and begs Faustus to give up necromancy and repent. Faustus despairs, and the Old Man has to step in to prevent him from ending his life with the dagger offered by Mephistopheles. Faustus is now torn between repentance and despair, but is once again swayed by Mephistopheles's threats and, to atone for his defection, promises to reaffirm in blood the pact made with Lucifer twenty-four years before, asking the devil to torment the Old Man who had pleaded with him to repent.

To console and distract himself, Faustus asks Mephistopheles to raise Helen once again. When she appears, Faustus is enthralled by her beauty and, to the dismay of the Old Man, takes Helen as his paramour.

5.2: Faustus tells the appalled scholars of his pact with Lucifer and they promise to stay in an adjoining room until morning and pray for him. Left alone, Faustus embarks upon his final hour. He hears the clock strike eleven and is tormented by the reality that repentance is impossible and damnation inevitable. Now the half hour strikes and, almost immediately afterwards, the hour of twelve. With a final desperate cry of 'Ah, Mephistopheles!', Faustus is dragged down to hell.

Epilogue

The Chorus tells us of the wasted potential that was Faustus, and urges us to take his fate as a warning not to 'practise more than heavenly power permits'.

Study skills

Referring to titles

When you are writing an essay, you will often need to refer to the title of the play. There are two main ways of doing this:

- If you are handwriting your essay, the title of the play should be underlined:
  <u>Doctor Faustus</u>

- If you are word-processing your essay, the play title should be in italics: *Doctor Faustus*.

The same rules apply to titles of all plays and other long works including very long poems, novels, films and non-fiction, such as: *Animal Farm* and *The Diary of Anne Frank*. The titles of shorter poems and short stories are placed inside single inverted commas; for example: 'Timothy Winters' and 'A Sound of Thunder'.

Note that the first word in a title and all the main words will have capital (or 'upper case') letters, while the less important words (such as conjunctions, prepositions and articles) will usually begin with lower case letters; for example: *The Taming of the Shrew* or *Antony and Cleopatra*.

Using quotations

Quotations show that you know the play in detail and are able to produce evidence from the script to back up your ideas and opinions. It is usually a good idea to keep quotations as short as you can (and this especially applies to exams, where it is a waste of time copying chunks out of the script).

Using longer quotations

There are a number of things you should do if you want to use a quotation of more than a few words:

1. Make your point. ———— *In answer to Faustus's probing questions, Mephistopheles describes hell as a state of mind:* ———— 2. A colon introduces the quotation.

3. Leave a line (optional). ————
4. Indent the quotation. ———— *Hell hath no limits, nor is circumscribed*
6. Keep the same line-divisions as in the script. *In one self place, but where we are is hell, And where hell is must we ever be.* ———— 5. No quotation marks.

7. Continue with a ———— *This idea reinforces his earlier…* follow-up point, perhaps commenting on the quotation itself.

Using brief quotations

Brief quotations are usually easier to use, take less time to write out and are much more effective in showing how familiar you are with the play. Weave them into the sentence like this:

- In admitting that he is 'deprived of everlasting bliss', Mephistopheles is…
- If, as the deed specifies, Faustus becomes 'a spirit in form and substance', he…
- As the Good Angel tells him, it is 'Never too late, if Faustus can repent', the key word here being…

If you are asked to state where the quotation comes from, use this simple form of reference to indicate the *Act, scene* and *line*:

* Sweet Helen, make me immortal with a kiss (5.1.93)…

In some editions this is written partly in Roman numerals – upper case for the Act and lower case for the scene; for example: (5.i.93), or (V.1.93), or (V.i.93).

Further reading

The texts

The website http://www.perseus.tufts.edu/Texts/Marlowe.html allows you to look at the A- and B-texts side by side and also includes Marlowe's source: the *Damnable Life*.

There is a very full introduction and detailed notes in the edition of *Doctor Faustus* by David Bevington and Eric Rasmussen (The Revels Plays, Manchester University Press, 1993). This edition contains both the A- and B-texts.

Useful introductory criticism

The best introduction to Marlowe's plays and the context in which they were written is Stevie Simkin, *A Preface to Marlowe* (Preface Books, Longman, 2000).

Two very helpful introductions to *Doctor Faustus* are:

Michael Mangan, *Doctor Faustus* (Penguin Critical Studies, 1989);

J P Brockbank, *Marlowe: Dr Faustus* (Edward Arnold, 1962).

Lisa Hopkins, *Christopher Marlowe: A Literary Life* (Literary Lives, Palgrave, 2000) follows Marlowe's career, play by play, and includes a very clear and helpful chapter on *Doctor Faustus*, '1589–1592: Daring God out of Heaven'.

The classic 'new historicist' approach to the literature from this period is Stephen Greenblatt, *Renaissance Self-fashioning: From More to Shakespeare* (University of Chicago Press, 1980). Greenblatt's book places dramatists such as Marlowe in the context of an emerging sense of self in sixteenth-century England, and contains a chapter on Marlowe's doomed defiance: 'Marlowe and the Will to Absolute Play'.

Criticism since 1980

Richard Wilson, ed., *Christopher Marlowe* (Longman Critical Readers, 1999) contains some excellent essays, including: Jonathan Dollimore, '*Doctor Faustus*: Subversion through Transgression' (1984); and Hilary Gatti, 'Bruno and Marlowe: *Doctor Faustus*' (1989).

Further reading

Roger Sales, *Christopher Marlowe* (Macmillan Dramatists series, 1991) is full of quotations from contemporary documents. It sees Marlowe's work in the context of the stage-play world of Elizabethan society and has a chapter devoted to *Doctor Faustus* (pp 133–160).

Thomas Healy, *Christopher Marlowe* (Writers and their Work series, Northcote House, 1994) is a brief (86 pages) but detailed survey of Marlowe's plays, demonstrating their place within the Protestant culture that they interrogated.

Simon Shepherd, *Marlowe and the Politics of Elizabethan Theatre* (Harvester Wheatsheaf, 1986) is interesting on Marlowe's relationship to other drama of the time.

J A Downie and J T Parnell, eds, *Constructing Christopher Marlowe* (Cambridge University Press, 2000) includes a number of absorbing new essays including: Lois Potter, 'Marlowe Onstage'; Julian Bowsher, 'Marlowe and the Rose'; and Richard Proudfoot, 'Marlowe and the Editors'.

Other recent critical approaches are to be found in:

Clare Harraway, *Re-citing Marlowe: Approaches to the Drama* (Ashgate, 2000);

Stevie Simkin, *Marlowe: The Plays* (Palgrave, 2001);

Sara Munson Deats, *Sex, Gender and Desire in the Plays of Christopher Marlowe* (Associated University Presses, 1997), which looks at gender issues.

Earlier criticism

Harry Levin, *The Overreacher* (Harvard University Press, 1952) was ground-breaking in its argument that Marlowe's characters strive to go beyond permitted norms. There is an extract from it in the Casebook (see below).

John Jump, ed., *Marlowe: Doctor Faustus: A Casebook* (Macmillan, 1st edition, 1969) contains a wide variety of critical essays, but only up to 1966, including:

> W W Greg, 'The Damnation of Faustus' (1946)
> J C Maxwell, 'The Sin of Faustus' (1947)
> Helen Gardner, 'The Theme of Damnation in *Doctor Faustus*' (1948)
> Nicholas Brooke, 'The Moral Tragedy of Doctor Faustus' (1952)
> Harry Levin, 'Science without Conscience' (1952)
> D J Palmer 'Magic and Poetry in *Doctor Faustus*' (1964)
> Cleanth Brooks, 'The Unity of Marlowe's *Doctor Faustus*' (1966)

Performance

William Tydeman, *Doctor Faustus: Text and Performance* (Macmillan, 1984) surveys a number of performances to make interesting observations on the different interpretations and approaches to design.

Marlowe's life

Charles Nicholl, *The Reckoning: The Murder of Christopher Marlowe* (Jonathan Cape, 1992) is a work of historical detection on Marlowe's death and makes fascinating speculations about the writer's connections with the Elizabethan underworld.

Marlowe's life is also the subject of an exciting novel by Anthony Burgess, *A Dead Man in Deptford* (Hutchinson, 1993).

William Urry, *Christopher Marlowe and Canterbury* (Faber and Faber, 1988) is an impressive reconstruction of the writer's early years and contains some surprising discoveries.

The standard academic biography of Marlowe remains J Bakeless, *The Tragical History of Christopher Marlowe* (Harvard University Press, 1942).

The theatre of Marlowe and Shakespeare

Andrew Gurr, *The Shakespearean Stage: 1574–1642* (Cambridge University Press, 3rd edition, 1992) is both encyclopedic and extremely readable.

Julian Bowsher, *The Rose Theatre: An Archaeological Discovery* (with a Foreword by Ian McKellen; Museum of London, 1998) and 'Marlowe and the Rose' (in *Constructing Christopher Marlowe*; see above) contain fascinating facts, unearthed during the archaeological dig of 1989, about the playhouse with which Marlowe was most closely connected.

David Scott Kastan and Peter Stallybrass, eds, *Staging the Renaissance* (Routledge, 1991) includes Jonathan Dollimore's essay on *Doctor Faustus*.

Michael Hattaway, *Elizabethan Popular Theatre: Plays in Performance* (London, 1980) contains an interesting view of *Doctor Faustus* as part of the commercial theatre in Marlowe's day.

Exam practice and discussion

1. In the context of all Marlowe's plays, it has been suggested that the heroes are 'tragic, but only in a weak sort of way'. Explore the presentation of Faustus in the light of this suggestion.

2. *Either:*
   'Faustus is sympathetic and credible enough for us to believe that his downfall results from a human failure…; he is an unhappy figure who acts against his own better nature, and whose agonised death is a matter for regret rather than applause. This is what gives him his tragic stature for all his personal weaknesses and defects' (William Tydeman). How far does this analysis satisfy you?

Exam practice and discussion

Or:
What impression have you formed of Faustus himself? What does he represent for you? He has been variously described as:
- a self-centred hedonist (someone who lives only for pleasure) whose sole aim is self-gratification
- a spiritual pioneer, seeking to break through the barriers that a repressive God has set up to prevent mankind's progress
- an adolescent dreamer indulging in pointless fantasies of immortality and omniscience
- a representative of a wholly praiseworthy impulse in humanity: the endeavour to overcome our human limitations through acts of necessary if reckless courage.

Consider these descriptions before offering your own response to Faustus the man and what he represents.

3. 'In many productions the performance of the demon has often been deemed to outshine that of the protagonist, the main reason being that a consistent portrait is more easily achieved' (William Tydeman). What is there in the creation of Mephistopheles which might cause him to outshine Faustus in performance? In what ways might his portrait be described as 'more consistent' than that of Faustus?

4. 'But even in human terms Faustus is culpable – he is obstinately indifferent to an intellect and experience manifestly superior to his own' (J P Brockbank). How far would you agree with this comparative assessment of Faustus and Mephistopheles? What evidence is there to show that Mephistopheles's intellect is superior to Faustus's?

5. *Either:*
What is the importance of the comic scenes in the context of the whole play?
Or:
- 'Though in theory the sub-plots provide a complementary comment on the main action by showing the abuse of necromantic powers in trivial pranks, in practice they tend to trivialise the tone of the play itself' (John Barton).
- The comic scenes are there 'to treat Faustus's heinous sins satirically by exposing them to grotesque exaggeration and caricature' (David Bevington).

Discuss these two contrasting views on the comic scenes and offer your own opinion. Do they trivialise the tone of the play, or serve to offer a critical perspective on a character we may otherwise sympathise with too much?

6. Richard Proudfoot wrote, 'The play…depends on the alternation of tones and moods'. Illustrate his statement by close reference to both the overall structure and particular sections.

7. 'Dramatic figures in [Marlowe's] plays are vehicles for actions, they are not psychologically complex…[Their] identities are linked to determined roles' (Thomas Healy). How far would you agree that our interest in Faustus rests not in his being like a 'real' person, but in what he represents – the way in which he challenges previous structures of knowledge and belief – and in the fate that he endures?

8. Do you consider *Doctor Faustus* to be a tragedy? You might like to examine the significance of the ideas of tragedy current at the time the play was written.

9. *Either:*
   'An impressive opening, a marvellous ending, an indifferent middle.' Does this twentieth-century comment represent to you a fair summary of *Doctor Faustus*? Support your views by detailed illustration from the text.
   Or:
   Many critics have considered *Doctor Faustus* disjointed and incoherent, a great play with massive flaws, like 'a broken-backed cathedral'. Is *Doctor Faustus* a unified whole, in your opinion, or merely a series of miscellaneous incidents linked by the figure of Faustus himself?

10. • The critic Leo Kirschbaum wrote: 'Whatever Marlowe was himself, there is no more obvious Christian document in all Elizabethan drama than *Doctor Faustus*'
    • conversely, Irving Ribner believed that 'The play is not a mirror of Christian certainty but of agnostic intellectual confusion'
    • while Paul Kocher, even more forcefully, wrote: *Doctor Faustus* is a drama 'of decisively anti-Christian colouring written by a man of violently anti-Christian beliefs'.
    Compare these different standpoints and express your own opinion. From what you know of Christian beliefs in Marlowe's time, is *Doctor Faustus* 'a Christian document' or not? (It will help to read the sections about religion on pages 134–135.)

11. How far would you agree with critics such as Harry Levin, who believed that the essence of Faustus's tragedy lies in his Promethean daring and his doomed but heroic attempt to gain for humanity some access to the secrets of the universe and some mastery over our fate? (The Titan Prometheus defied Jupiter's law and gave fire to humans.)

12. How helpful do you find Jonathan Dollimore's interpretation that 'From Faustus's point of view…God and Lucifer seem equally responsible in his final destruction, two supreme agents of power deeply antagonistic to each other yet temporarily co-operating in his demise' (i.e. enemies who collaborate to bring about his destruction)?

13. The A-text of *Doctor Faustus* (see pages 121–122) is divided into scenes but not acts. What argument is there for imposing a regular five-act structure on the play?

14. *Either:*
    It has been suggested that Marlowe's audience would have seen *Doctor Faustus* as 'a simple morality play'. Consider this view of the play, using Act 2 scene 1 as your starting point.
    Or:
    The critic Robert Potter takes the view that, at its most primary structural level, *Doctor Faustus* is a medieval morality play, but it is also a heroic play, and at its highest level 'a new kind of psychological tragedy'. Which of these elements – morality, heroic play, psychological tragedy – seems to you to be most strongly represented in *Doctor Faustus*? Consider all three in your response.

15. *Either:*
    Remind yourself of 1.3.36–103 (from 'Now, Faustus, what…' to 'I will, Faustus') and 2.1.120–144 (from 'Now, Faustus, ask…' to '…Walking, disputing, etc.').

What does Marlowe's presentation of Mephistopheles in these sections tell the reader about sixteenth-century attitudes to hell and damnation?
Or:
Evaluate the importance of those aspects of religion in Elizabethan society which have most influenced your understanding of *Doctor Faustus*. You might like to examine the significance of belief in the devil and notions of damnation and salvation that were current in Elizabethan society.

16. Stevie Simkin wrote: 'A soul that is destined to be damned is simply a pitiable spectacle, containing very little one could call tragic or even dramatic. Only when we understand Faustus as one who chooses his alliance with the devil, realizes the consequences of his actions, and then chooses to believe that God is incapable of extending forgiveness to him, do we have potential for real dramatic engagement.' What kinds of 'real dramatic engagement' might an audience feel with *Doctor Faustus*, and how far does it derive from the elements that Simkin describes?

17. How far would you agree with the view that *Doctor Faustus* is 'intended to question a theology that portrays a human soul tormented and obliterated by a divinity that offers only the illusion of a way out' (Stevie Simkin)?

18. • 'However distinguished his mind, Faustus's moral frailties are such as to secure him our sympathy even as we deplore his false sense of values.' (William Tydeman)
    • 'The central problem with most orthodox interpretations of *Doctor Faustus* is that they often verge on lack of sympathy, even open hostility. To the extent that Faustus is a negative object lesson, we are distanced from him.' (David Bevington and Eric Rasmussen)
    Do you feel sympathy for Faustus, or does the fact that he is 'a negative object lesson' distance you from him?

Performance

1. What is the most effective staging for *Doctor Faustus*? Describe your ideal staging (entrances, levels, shape of the stage, colour, overall design…) and explain your decisions by reference to key moments in the text.

2. If you were directing a performance of the play, how would you make notions of hell and damnation meaningful to a modern audience? Think about the presentation of Mephistopheles, Lucifer and Beelzebub and figures such as the Good and Evil Angels and the Seven Deadly Sins, as well as the staging of moments such as the scene in which Faustus is carried off to hell.

3. 'In John Barton's 1974 version [of *Doctor Faustus*], Ian McKellen [who played Faustus] ventriloquised the lines of two puppets representing the good and evil angels, and, in the original plan, was to have played Mephistopheles as well' (Lois Potter). What effects could be achieved if the actor playing Faustus also performed the parts of the Good and Evil Angels and Mephistopheles? Discuss the advantages and disadvantages, and the interpretations of the play that might be suggested by this kind of performance.

4. In the 1989 RSC production, David Bradley's Mephistopheles was 'saturnine,

reptilian, cadaverous, insinuating, glacial, moving stiffly in his cassock' (David Bevington and Eric Rasmussen) as if 'carrying Hell with him in his bones, [watching Faustus] like a ferret' (Michael Schmidt). If you were cast in a production of the play as Mephistopheles how would you perform the role? Discuss the qualities that your ideal Mephistopheles would possess and explore ways in which they might be conveyed to the audience.

5. The following stage effects are from the B-text version of 5.2 (the final four are also in the A-text). How might they (a) have been achieved on the stage of the Rose; (b) be achieved today on a modern stage?
    *   *Enter Lucifer, Beelzebub and Mephistopheles* [*above*].
    *   *Enter the Good Angel and the Bad Angel at several doors.*
    *   *Music while the throne descends.*
    *   *Hell is discovered.*
    *   *The clock strikes eleven* (65 s.d.)...*The watch strikes* (96 s.d.)...*The clock striketh twelve* (116 s.d.).
    *   *Thunder and lightning* (118 s.d.).
    *   *Enter Devils* (121 s.d.).
    *   [*The Devils*] *exeunt with him* (124 s.d.).

For group discussion

1. '*Doctor Faustus* is both the consummation of the English morality tradition and the last and finest of Marlowe's heroic plays. As a morality it vindicates humility, faith and obedience to the law of God; as an heroic play it celebrates power, beauty, riches and knowledge' (J P Brockbank). Discuss how helpful you find Brockbank's description as an assessment of the elements of morality play and heroic tragedy in *Doctor Faustus*.
2. William Tydeman asks: 'But should we rather read *Faustus* as a prophetic parable anticipating the selfish amorality of scientific materialism, prepared to sacrifice life itself in the ruthless pursuit of power through knowledge? Or is it an allegory of our mortal condition, the dissection of a species doomed to dream of reaching summits of achievement its fallible constitution must always deny it?' In what ways does the play help you to clarify your thoughts about the modern world and humanity's place in it?
3. Does *Doctor Faustus* have a central argument, thesis or 'message', in your opinion? Does the play show, for example:
    *   how blind humanity is to the reality of heaven, hell and the immortality of the soul
    *   that we should do all we can to avoid the human waste and suffering that we witness in Faustus (and which is expressed in the Epilogue's first line)
    *   that, with Faustus, we all share a fundamental inability to accept our human limitations?
    Or is there a quite different argument being proposed, in your view?
4. 'Failed Superman or foolish sinner?' Which of these comes closer to describing Faustus, and what do both descriptions leave out of your own picture of the man?

Exam practice and discussion

5. Does the Calvinist theology of predestination (see pages 134–135) turn Faustus into the martyr of a spiteful deity, the victim of a harsh and vengeful God?
6. If you were directing a performance of the play, what discussion would you have with the actor playing Faustus about how to say his final line 'Ah, Mephistopheles!'? What emotion lies behind that cry?
7. 'The most successful productions have been those which were not afraid of the comedy and which also gratified the desire for spectacle' (Lois Potter). What opportunities exist for 'spectacle' in *Doctor Faustus* and how far should a director make a production exciting to look at?

Some quotations for discussion

These quotations are a selection of critics' views and assumptions about the play. You are invited to question them, using evidence from the text and from performances that you have seen.

1. '*Doctor Faustus* is a play about knowledge…about knowledge of means and its relation to knowledge of ends. It is a play, thus, that reflects the interest of the Renaissance' (Cleanth Brooks).
2. 'Marlowe invites us to see the splendour of man, but to contemplate the species at its most abject too' (William Tydeman).
3. 'Marlowe created a revolution in English drama by refusing to pass overt judgement on his leading figure's conduct' (William Tydeman).
4. Marlowe makes 'his protagonist a figure of potential dignity and nobility of purpose…yet the cocky mountebank and illusionist are never far below the surface' (William Tydeman).
5. *Doctor Faustus* depicts a Christian religious cosmos in extensive detail, but does so without offering any sense of goodness or justice in that system. The play is instead a protest against a system that imposes 'a limitation upon the aspirations of man, holding him in subjection and bondage, denying him at last even the comfort of Christ's blood, and dooming him to the most terrible destruction' (Irving Ribner).
6. The play's unity of vision lies in its perception that man's nature 'is in direct opposition to his fate' (Nicholas Brooke).
7. 'It is not the initial sin and its consequences that hold us in suspense as we read or behold Marlowe's *Doctor Faustus*. Rather it is the continuing struggle of conscience, the conflict between hope and despair' (Lily Campbell).
8. 'Faustus's pact with the devil, because an act of transgression without hope of liberation, is at once rebellious, masochistic and despairing' (Jonathan Dollimore).
9. 'The frivolity has an uneasy edge to it; the illusions effected by the conjurer and his assistant disguise but at the same time manifest the illusion and self-deception in which Faustus exists' (D J Palmer).
10. 'The obvious banality and futility of what Faustus accomplishes…forms a deliberately ironic variation on the perennial theme of the Vanity of Human Wishes' (William Tydeman).
11. 'The comic scenes form an integral part of the play because they question Faustus's actions. They may contain blasphemy, for instance when Wagner

mocks the blessing [see 1.2], and yet they still manage to suggest orthodox responses to Faustus's contract with Lucifer' (Roger Sales).

12. 'A production which sees *Faustus* as romantic and tragic will be embarrassed by the comic scenes, but one which treats him simply as a fool risks boring and alienating the audience' (Lois Potter).

13. 'Farce and tragedy are inextricably related in the play's structure.' The middle scenes are 'an extraordinary phantasmagoria, grotesquely satirical, sometimes sinister, sometimes absurd, an illusionistic impression of twenty-four wasted years' (Malcolm Kelsall).

Discussing critical opinions

These questions refer to the extracts from critical essays on pages 156–174.

1. Reread the extracts by Hazlitt and Ellis-Fermor (pages 159–160). How far do you see Faustus as 'Everyman' and how far as an individualised dramatic character?

2. Use William Tydeman's comments (page 160) as a basis for your own ideas about how the part of Faustus should be played on the stage or on film.

3. Reread the extracts by Greg, Maxwell, Gardner and Brooks (pages 160–166). When, in your opinion, is Faustus damned? From the outset? When he first conjures Mephistopheles? From the moment he signs the pact? After his encounter with Helen? Only in his final moments? Or is it impossible to say with any certainty? Evaluate the critics' arguments in coming to your own conclusion. (It will also help to reread the sections on religion, pages 134–135.)

4. Reread the extracts by Kirschbaum and Brooke (pages 166–167). Is *Doctor Faustus* a Christian tragedy, in your opinion?

5. Reread the extracts by Brockbank and Simkin (pages 167–169) and explain what purposes the comic scenes serve as part of the structure of *Doctor Faustus*.

6. Reread the extracts by Palmer and Gatti (pages 169–172). Write a detailed critical account of Faustus's final soliloquy, paying close attention to the language.

7. Reread the extracts by Dollimore, Sales and Healy (pages 172–174). Does *Doctor Faustus* offer an orthodox moral, in your opinion, or is it a play which questions orthodox standpoints? In your answer make sure that you address the question of how far we sympathise with Faustus and what effect that degree of sympathy has on our attitude to his damnation.

Personal responses

1. Has the play given you any new perspectives on humanity? Have you learned anything about yourself?

2. Robert G Hunter has observed that *Doctor Faustus* can be interpreted differently by people with different religious (and presumably non-religious) views. How do your religious or non-religious views affect your interpretation of the play?

3. 'As with *Hamlet*, the definitive "meaning" of *Doctor Faustus* can never be pinned down once and for all' (William Tydeman). What is its 'meaning' for you?

4. What has your engagement with the play taught you about the relative merits of 'Marlowe in the study' (learning about the play by studying the text) and 'Marlowe in performance' (learning by watching the play acted out, or performing it yourself)?
5. The critic William Empson suggested that, in an original version of Marlowe's play (later censored), Faustus escapes damnation and punishment of any kind. Would this make a more satisfying ending in your view?

Analysing the verse

This section is designed to reinforce what you learned about Marlowe's verse on pages 144–148 – how the underlying iambic pentameter works, and what effects can be achieved by varying it. Find each of the lines referred to and look at their context before completing activities 1 to 4:

1. As a way of becoming used to stress patterns, read the following lines out loud and then write them down, marking the heavy stresses:
    (a) 'Not marching now in fields of Trasimene' (Prologue 1)
    (b) 'And this the man that in his study sits' (Prologue 28)
    (c) 'Yet level at the end of every art,
        And live and die in Aristotle's works.' (1.1.4–5)
2. Write about the effect of:
    (a) the extra syllable in the line:
        'See, see where Christ's blood streams in the firmament!' (5.2.79)
    (b) the repetition in:
        'Fair nature's eye, rise, rise again, and make
        Perpetual day' (5.2.71–72)
    (c) the use of rhyme in:
        'Whose deepness doth entice such forward wits,
        To practise more than heavenly power permits.' (Epilogue 7–9)
    (d) the repeated heavy stresses in:
        'Now hast thou but one bare hour to live' (5.2.67)
    (e) the repetition in:
        'I do repent, and yet I do despair.' (5.1.64)
    (f) the use of monosyllables in:
        FAUSTUS   How comes it then that thou art out of hell?
        MEPHISTOPHELES   Why, this is hell, nor am I out of it. (1.3.77–78)
3. To practise identifying the metre, write down the following lines and then divide them into feet and mark the heavy stresses:
    (a) 'In courts of kings where state is overturned' (Prologue 4)
    (b) 'Then read no more; thou hast attained that end.' (1.1.10)
    (c) 'These metaphysics of magicians' (1.1.51)
4. Explain how the rhythm enhances the meaning in the following lines:
    (a) 'O, what a world of profit and delight,
        Of power, of honour, of omnipotence,
        Is promised to the studious artisan!' (1.1.55–57)

(b) 'Her lips sucks forth my soul. See where it flies!' (5.1.94)
(c) 'Fair nature's eye, rise, rise again, and make
     Perpetual day (5.2.71–72)

Analysing the imagery

Trace the imagery of feeding and satiety (for example at 1.1.80). Show how this extends into the dialogue of the comic scenes, and explore the ways in which it relates to the theme of Faustus's ambitions and damnation.

Gerard Murphy as Faustus and David Bradley as Mephistopheles (RSC, 1989)